MAPPING RACIAL LITERACIES

MAPPING RACIAL LITERACIES

*College Students Write about
Race and Segregation*

SOPHIE R. BELL

UTAH STATE UNIVERSITY PRESS
Logan

Published by Utah State University Press
An imprint of University Press of Colorado
245 Century Circle, Suite 202
Louisville, Colorado 80027

 The University Press of Colorado is a proud member of
the Association of University Presses.

The University Press of Colorado is a cooperative publishing enterprise supported,
in part, by Adams State University, Colorado State University, Fort Lewis College,
Metropolitan State University of Denver, Regis University, University of Colorado,
University of Northern Colorado, University of Wyoming, Utah State University, and
Western Colorado University.

∞ This paper meets the requirements of the ANSI/NISO Z39.48–1992 (Permanence of
Paper)

ISBN: 978-1-64642-109-1 (paperback)
ISBN: 978-1-64642-110-7 (ebook)
https://doi.org/10.7330/9781646421107

Library of Congress Cataloging-in-Publication Data

Names: Bell, Sophie R., author.
Title: Mapping racial literacies : college students write about race and segregation /
    Sophie R. Bell.
Description: Logan : Utah State University Press, [2020] | Includes bibliographical refer-
    ences and index.
Identifiers: LCCN 2020051114 (print) | LCCN 2020051115 (ebook) | ISBN
    9781646421091 (paperback) | ISBN 9781646421107 (ebook)
Subjects: LCSH: English language—Rhetoric—Study and teaching (Higher)—
    Social aspects—United States. | College students' writings. | Culturally relevant
    pedagogy—United States. | Anti-racism—Study and teaching (Higher)—United States. |
    Racial justice in education—United States. | Racism in language.
Classification: LCC PE1405.U6 B45 2020 (print) | LCC PE1405.U6 (ebook) | DDC
    808/.042071173—dc23
LC record available at https://lccn.loc.gov/2020051114
LC ebook record available at https://lccn.loc.gov/2020051115

Cover photograph by Nick Starichenko/Shutterstock

To my students

For sharing this work with me and—wherever you could—making it your own. Thank you for your patience, insight, humor, and risk-taking. Thank you for making every possible use of the opportunities offered in our classroom, in particular when you have been able to push my thinking, and that of other students, in new and productive ways.

To my mother, Claudia Swett Gwardyak

For her unequivocal support of every attempt I've made to write, since the days when she sat at the typewriter and transcribed my youthful ideas. For her own work against racism and sexism. For her unshakable faith in education as a tool of liberation, and the work she does to put that faith into action.

To my late father, Michael Davitt Bell

For his love of teaching and writing and his commitment to racial and gender justice. For his excitement about passing that love and commitment on to the next generations of our family.

In essence, meaningful opportunities for cross-racial contact are dimin-
ishing, especially in schools. What effect is that having on students,
both White and of color, and their teachers? What are the implications
for classroom performance and academic achievement? Interpersonal
relations? Our evolving democracy? What can we *as educators and*
citizens do to ensure that the arc of the moral universe continues to bend
toward justice in our society?

   Beverly Daniel Tatum, *Can We Talk about Race? And Other*
   Conversations in an Era of Resegregation xi

Racism is a structural phenomenon that fabricates interdependent
yet paradoxical relationships between race, class, and geography.
[Countering it] requires a new racial literacy, meaning the capacity to
decipher the durable racial grammar that structures racialized hierar-
chies and frames the narrative of our republic.

   Lani Guinier, "From Racial Liberalism to Racial Literacy: *Brown*
   v. Board of Education and the Interest-Divergence Dilemma,"
   Journal of American History 117

CONTENTS

ACKNOWLEDGMENTS

The premise of this book is that teachers can and must continually learn alongside their students. I am extremely grateful to my students for teaching me so much over the years. In particular, as a white teacher exploring the role of racial literacy and racial geography in my students' lives, and my own, there have been many things I have struggled to understand and process in the conversations and writing that take place in my classes. I have appreciated the opportunity to learn with and from my students during this process. However, expecting to learn exclusively from my students in these areas would be irresponsible. I have also benefited enormously from the insights and generosity of other people who listened to these stories, encouraged me to theorize and write about them, and helped me move this account of my teaching out of my classroom and into this form. This process has been exciting, nerve-wracking, and error ridden, and I am grateful for many forms of support and correction along the way.

This book was written during a semester's leave and three semesters of course release. In the teaching-intensive field of composition, supporting classroom research is crucial to fostering pedagogies conducive to student learning and teacher growth. I thank St. John's College of Liberal Arts and Sciences for providing this for me, and Dean Jeffrey Fagen in particular.

When I brought my initial idea to Utah State University Press, Michael Spooner agreed it would make a valuable contribution and helped me buckle down and clear the decks for writing. When Michael retired, Rachael Levay stepped in with creativity, conviction, and strategic thinking that anchored my progress. The anonymous readers for the press offered a generous combination of compassion and critique. While affirming that this portrait of learning had value for other teachers, teachers-in-training, and teacher-leaders, they pointed out my areas of confusion and wrongheadedness. In short, they modeled exactly what I strive for as a teacher and needed as a writer. Finally, Daniel Pratt's cover design captured the spirit of this project in a delightfully unexpected way.

The editorial collective of *Radical Teacher* has provided a decades-long home base for critical analysis of educational politics, attention to the complexities of classrooms, and warm fellowship for embattled teachers. Dick Ohmann in particular has encouraged and supported my writing about schools since I taught high school in the 1990s.

The idea of writing about the racial politics of my classroom was fostered by colleagues at St. John's and beyond. Members of the St. John's Teaching and Race Working Group from 2015 to 2017 introduced me to the racial history of composition studies and explored how to bring that history into our classrooms: I am profoundly grateful for the insights and wisdom of Collin Craig, Ashwak Fardoush, Ikuko Fujiwara, Sharon Marshall, Amanda Moulder, and Alison Perry. I deeply appreciate the members of the New York Metropolitan American Studies Association Americanist writing group—Jeff Allred, Sarah Chinn, Anna Mae Duane, Joseph Entin, Hildegard Hoeller, Meg Toth, Jennifer Travis—who never batted an eye when I started writing about my students' writing as well as nineteenth-century American literature. These colleagues' keen insights and crucial questions shaped many early chapter drafts. Late in the project, Amanda Moulder and Liz Kimball formed an indomitable small writing group. Their keen eyes and generosity with field-related expertise and creative solutions to rhetorical and pedagogical problems were especially crucial as I wrote chapter 3 and the introduction. Stephanie Wade offered a generous ear to the dilemmas of this project and advice for centering oneself when the way is unclear. Gabriel Brownstein helped me apply for crucial support. Anne Geller offered advice and encouragement through the process of finding a publisher. Sharon Marshall and Tamara Issak modeled how to honor dual commitments to teaching and writing, offering me daily inspiration. Dohra Ahmad helped me see vernacular language's connection to racial literacy, inspiring and encouraging chapter 3.

My sister Cathleen Bell offered countless daily encouragements to keep writing and incisive help describing my research methodology. Elisabeth Kanner listened to many of these teaching stories on repeat and responded with a relentless focus on student learning. She routinely used humor to deflate roadblocks, as well as pretension, in my teaching and writing. Hannah Weyer told me to write down these stories. Meg Toth offered accountability and companionship while launching this project on a shared semester's leave. Betsy Klimasmith offered crucial help with the book proposal. Nadya Bech-Conger listened while I talked through the entire concept at enormous length, which was invaluable as I wrote the introduction. Gayle Kirshenbaum unpacked problems and offered inspiration with her powerful writing, listening, and activism. Kathy Belden offered compassionate fellowship, mentoring, and expertise on creating books that promote racial awareness, while remaining vigilant about one's own misperceptions. Lena Entin affirmed that this work mattered beyond academics. Claudia Bell, Walter Gwardyak, Audrey Entin, David Entin, Dorothy Riehm, Leslie Holt, and Amy Smoucha offered me time and space to write, fed me while I was writing, and offered generous interpretations of my daily progress.

Writing about institutional change is good, but changing institutions is better. While I developed this curriculum and wrote this book, people on the campus where I teach began to undertake the difficult task of improving the university's culture and practices of equity and inclusion for students, faculty, and other community members from marginalized and minoritized groups. Student activists—in particular, the members of Spectrum, Students of Consciousness, the Black Student Union, and the NAACP—displayed courage, clarity, and leadership in imagining and demanding concrete, positive changes. Many administrators and faculty members put themselves on the line when students called for institutional change, doing deep work on many levels to create conditions to make it happen. In 2020, several faculty have founded the Critical Race and Ethnic Studies Program. At the university level, Nada Llewellyn, Manouchkathe Cassagnol, and Monique Jernigan have stepped forward to offer creative, transformative, engaged leadership. I acknowledge their inspiring work and also acknowledge others who are changing my institution in ways I don't know about. I hope the classroom work I describe in this book contributes to building capacity for such institutional change. However, the entrenched inequalities my students report will remain unchanged without the leadership of courageous students, faculty, and others.

This is a book about my own position as a white woman invested in teaching in ways that challenge whiteness. While white teachers need to do this work, our ability to do it has many limitations. I am grateful to people of color who have honestly challenged me and/or collaborated with me. I appreciate and value the feedback I have received from colleagues of color at St. Johns and beyond. I am also grateful to other white people for the opportunity to learn alongside you as we share our struggles to see, understand, and address racism, especially our own.

Several students have kept me informed about the ways that they navigate the issues we raised in class after graduation. This has been a deep gift. I am particularly grateful to Priscilla Agyeman, Kiah Lashley, Nicole Lawrence, Gabriel Lopez, Victoria Natanova, Richée Reeves, Dannie Rouse, Chriss Sneed, Miguel Vasquez, and Tahmir Williams for sharing some of your journey with me, offering me inspiration and new perspectives.

My daughters Miriam and Rachel helped me talk through and reconsider my students' perspectives when I was stumped. They also encouraged me to lighten up, which is challenging but essential to the heavy work I ask my students to undertake. I learn tremendously from their insights into the extraordinary impact of race, class, and geography on our lives and their schools. In addition, they have both offered me meaningful help with my teaching and this book. I am grateful for Rachel's technical assistance with the online components of my teaching and for Miriam's help with citations in my final draft.

My husband, Joseph Entin, offered compassionate and perceptive readings of every chapter, as well as consistent and persistent support for this project on all levels. He is a stalwart comrade-in-arms through decades teaching and learning, hope and pain, trail and error, and a whole lot of excellent debriefing. His own determination to contribute to the world in a positive way, and his extraordinary ability to find interesting arguments lurking in thorny places, make him a staunch ally in writing this book, and in our mutual struggle to lead joyful, useful lives together in and out of classrooms.

MAPPING RACIAL LITERACIES

Introduction

GROUNDINGS
Racial Literacy and Racial Geographies

This book argues that early college classrooms can provide essential opportunities for students to grapple to describe and contend with the racial geographies that shape their lives. Based on a mixed methods study of my students' writing over four years in a First Year Writing (FYW) course themed around race and language variety, the book argues that college student writing that directly confronts lived experiences of segregation—and increasingly, of resegregation—makes a useful tool in helping college-age students see, explore, and articulate the role of race in determining their life experiences and opportunities. I begin and end each semester asking students to reflect on their racial literacies, which I define on my syllabus like this:

> Racial Literacies: This course encourages you to assume a "race aware" stance this semester, rather than a "colorblind" approach. This involves the following practices, as well as a commitment to continually educate yourself about racial matters:
>> The ability to recognize and articulate the role of race in your own life.
>> The ability to recognize and articulate the role of race in the lives of people around you.
>> An understanding of the systemic, institutional nature of racism.
>> A sense of personal agency to fight towards ending racism in personal and institutional areas where you encounter it. (First Year Writing 1000c syllabus, "Writing Across Difference: Race, Language, and Digital Composition")

Throughout this book, I explore student responses to this challenge. Before laying out the terrain of the book, I will begin with some student responses to identifying and engaging their own "racial literacies."

In his introductory letter to me, a white student from a majority-white neighborhood in Queens responded to the idea of "racial literacy" by describing race talk as "taboo" and abstractly reflecting that racism

DOI: 10.7330/9781646421107.c000

should end: "I believe that all human beings of all races deserve equal opportunity and deserve to be treated with the equal respect, love and dignity. I'm not very sure on the steps needed to take in order to work towards that goal."

At the end of the semester, his writing was quite different:

> I was asked by a friend if I think that white people really do have white privilege. If you would have asked me this question a few months ago I would say heck no! I would get very defensive and begin a whole big spiel on how my grandparents came to this country with nothing but the clothes on their back, and had to work hard to provide for their family and get them to where they are today. However, when my friend asked me recently, my answer surprised him, and would have surprised myself a few months earlier. I said to him, yes, we do have white privilege. This is not to say that because we are white, everything in life is handed to us, and we never have to work hard for what we want. That is not what white privilege means. White privilege is the fact that we as white people benefit from being white in ways that we don't even understand or even realize. We will never have to deal with the stereotypes or negative connotations of being black. My friend disagreed, and wasn't able to understand.

This student had gained sight of the previously invisible forces sheltering him from harm as he navigated the world as a white person. He could also talk about his views with a friend from his neighborhood, and acknowledge their disagreements about what it means to be white.

In contrast, an Afro-Latinx student from the Bronx predicted at the beginning of the semester, "It will be easier to write about the role of race in my everyday life because it plays a significant role especially being where I'm from, how it affects me and how I look." She entered the class listing topics she was used to discussing: "institutional racism, cultural appropriation, police brutality, etc." She was "racially literate." However, she was on academic probation when she entered the course and struggled to complete her writing assignments in my class and others. At the end of the semester, however, she completed all her missing work with success. Her final reflection identified learning about school segregation as a transformative moment for her as a struggling early college student, explaining, "I've basically been a part of the educational achievement gap for the last four years of my life and I didn't even know."

She elaborated:

> One thing that I learned this semester that really impacted me and has stuck with me was when I learned that New York City schools are as segregated today as they were forty years ago. Learning this fact has really made a huge impact on everything because I feel like it was the missing link. After I learned that, everything that I noticed in high school started

to make sense and I finally understood what I was missing. My high school only had teachers that were white and from Long Island and the demographics of the student population were predominately Hispanic and Black. My high school was basically the standard of a segregated New York City school, and I felt like I knew this because it bothered many of us that our teachers were only white but we never really thought much of it. Learning that really changed how I view New York and its school system as a whole.

In her final conference, she told me that many of her high school friends had either not attended college or had dropped out during this, their first year. Ironically, she was able to end the semester successfully as a result of grappling with the systemic nature of the racism that led her to be "academically underprepared" for college.

A third student, a Chinese American woman from a mixed-race neighborhood in Queens, initially approached racial literacies as skills for better self-defense:

This summer, a man started tailing me on my way home from work, repeating "ni hao" and "konichiwa" to me over and over. I possess the skill to ignore people like this and continue to move on with my life. This time, the man got angered that I was ignoring him and attempted to trip me as I was walking. . . . I want to improve on my skill to speak up when situations like this happen to me.

She did not return to this desire in her end-of-semester reflection. Her focus has shifted from being a target of racism to a burgeoning curiosity about the linguistic dimensions of her Chinese identity. Instead, she wrote about her racial identity through the lens of language:

I realized that I love talking about my racial identity. . . . To me, calling yourself Chinese is quite vague, not that there is anything wrong with that. It is just that, China is such a large country made up of so many different people that speak different dialects. I really enjoy the fact that I am able to speak one of the dying dialects. . . . Being Chinese is a part of my racial identity, but being Fujianese is what I truly am. What language I speak plays a bigger role in my racial identity than how I look and the color of my skin.

Having explored her marginalized ethnic identity within Chinese American culture, she then looked at a controversial New York City debate in which Asian Americans are being enlisted into becoming proxies for anti-Black and anti-Latinx policies—admissions policies at the city's "specialized high schools." Her research helped build the capacity for a wide-ranging conversation about student experiences with race in segregated New York City schools across multiple semesters in my class.

I begin with these student perspectives to highlight the wide range of concerns and strategies students use to approach intersecting questions of race, class, and geography in my course. This book draws from qualitative and quantitative work in a digital archive of student writing from 2014 and 2018, collected from over 1,000 students and including over 600 student texts. The project is in large part a textual ethnography, embedding my students' writing in deep historical and theoretical contexts and looking for new ways that their writing contributes to and reshapes contemporary understandings of the ways in which a new generation of US and global citizens are thinking about race. In addition, the book is framed as a teaching narrative, tracing a roughly chronological teaching journey that considers student writing not only in the moments it was assigned, but also in the ways I continually revise the course in response to student writing. I hope this book will contribute to scholarship on race and writing pedagogy, as well as encourage teachers of early college classes to bring such issues center stage in the classroom, on the page, and on campus.

This introduction sets the scene for analyses of early college students' writing on race through (1) my own autoethnography as a white teacher concerned with exploring, and asking my students to explore, the racial dynamics of our lives and geographies, and (2) a critical ethnography of the university where my students and I met and produced these texts. The introduction dips deeper into my racial history and geography—and that of my university—than I do elsewhere in the book, which I might describe as an "ethnography of texts," along the lines of Sara Ahmed's formulation in her study of university diversity work and racism. I begin with these personal and institutional histories to explain some of my own opportunities, sightlines, and blindnesses.[1] In doing so I also invite readers to consider their own personal and institutional histories and how those histories shape the work they are doing and want to do in their classrooms and scholarship.

This book is thus less focused on pedagogical "success" or "failure" than one might expect from an account of teaching. This is strategic. Sara Ahmed warns of the ways in which institutional research findings on diversity are often co-opted into narratives that focus on the *appearance* of success in promoting diversity, rather than the highly uneven and always incomplete work of institutional equity that is more realistic. She writes, "Too much research in this field is premised on findings that institutions *want found*: from toolboxes to good practice. Too much research thus becomes translated into mission speech, turning stories of diversity and equality into institutional success stories. There is much less research describing the complicated and messy situations in which diversity workers often find themselves" (10). As Ahmed writes, "When description gets hard, we need description" (10). Such hard description is the goal of this book.

As a white writing teacher, I began this work tentatively, with little sense of authority to teach about race effectively besides my conviction that doing so ineffectively would be better than not doing it at all. Although I initially thought my job was to push students into "better" racial understanding, as I focused more on racial issues in my classes I began to see that my own understanding needed to grow at least as much in order for the course to function. Indeed, the course's evolution has been largely driven by students' responses to and interventions in the curriculum and pedagogy I have introduced. Assignments have included personal narrative essays about race, ethnographic research on racial issues on and off campus, peer exchanges of writing, spoken word performances, interviews, infographic essays, multimedia presentations on racial issues, public letters written to important parties on racial issues, and profiles of antiracist activists. In addition, this work has led me into a range of collaborations with other colleagues interested in overlapping issues, who have provided sail, rudder, and lighthouse in navigating the waters of teaching, race, and writing.

White female faculty have a ubiquitous, often unquestioned history of teaching students of color in highly inequitable settings. Laura Wexler lays out a centuries-long history of "sentimental imperialism," in which white female teachers have been tasked with training people of color to serve in industrial, domestic, military, and colonial positions. These teaching situations combine a rhetoric of educational "uplift" with a reality of education for subordination and servitude. It is thus imperative for white teachers to analyze the very real ongoing and historical ways in which we participate in Kynard's succinct observation that "American schools and universities, through their scholarship and instructional design, have often upheld a racial status quo *alongside a rhetoric* of dismantling it" (*Vernacular Insurrections* 19). Foregrounding and interrogating our whiteness in the classroom are together a crucial step in removing ourselves from that equation.

It is difficult to do so, since beyond the ideological work white women have done to promote educational agendas that reinforce racial inequality, teaching has also been a relatively secure source of employment for white women. The fact that teaching careers have historically been a means for women in my own family to find meaningful work and economic security is a function of those women's whiteness. In contrast, tens of thousands of Black teachers were fired as a result of the integration of schools in the South (Detweiler et al.—mentioned in Ladson-Billings). The teaching force remains, and looks to remain, majority-white and female.[2] The same is true in college composition.[3] The demographics of the teaching force contribute to the opportunity gap that faces young people of color in this country, where a recent study found that having one Black teacher in elementary school signifi-cantly improved Black and low-income students' chances of graduating from high school and aspiring to attend a four-year college (Gershenson et al.). It is white teachers' important task to recruit and support faculty of color in order to intervene in this history. Further, we must do our own racial identity work in order to stay cognizant of Ahmed's point that our whiteness protects us—as she puts it, our "residency is assumed"—and obscures from us the harmful practices in which we participate in edu-cational institutions.

Composition scholars who explore the role of race in writing instruc-tion have been crucial to my development as a teacher, specifically to the ways I have designed and analyzed the assignments discussed in this book. Scholars who illuminate the racial history of composition's growth in universities, especially since the Civil Rights Era, and its connec-tions with Critical Race Theory (Kynard; Martinez; Prendergast; Reed; Trimbur), the politics of language diversity and assimilation in this uni-versity gateway space (Smitherman; Villanueva; Gilyard; Guerra; Horner, Lu, Royster, and Trimbur), and emergent methodologies for reinvent-ing the role of race in core practices of writing pedagogy—assessment (Inoue and Poe), peer review (Kerschbaum), research (Flower), and listening itself as a rhetorical act (Ratcliffe)—have all been what I will call my "racial literacy sponsors." The most sustained racial literacy sponsor-ship for this project has come from Beverly Daniel Tatum's work on racial identity development and Lani Guinier's work on racial literacy, which inspire and inform my goals and practices in the course and the book.

Mapping Racial Literacies contributes to the important and exciting body of scholarship on antiracist pedagogy in composition and beyond in two ways. First, it offers (perhaps unusually) extensive close readings of student texts. This book looks very closely at the trail of clues stu-dents' writing offers about their racial identity development and racial literacy. These readings are highly alert to students' uneven responses to the opportunities for racial vision, insight, exchange, and growth that the course aspires to offer through writing. Further, my readings of student texts also account for the ways that student resistance, revision, and re-creation of assignments has guided the course's development.

Second, the book looks in depth at the rhetorical strategies students adopt for talking about their lives under resegregation, that is, a period in which educational segregation has actually been on the rise. These students had unique situations and perspectives, but they share this context: they have grown up under the dismantling of integration, and they make their way onto college campuses from highly segregated elementary and secondary schools. They have had a mixed-race president whose election inspired claims of a "postracial" era typified by colorblind racism, followed by a white president who espouses anti-immigrant, anti-Black, anti-Muslim views openly and who has ushered in a resurgence of white nationalist policy and discourse and white supremacist activism.

When I began collecting data in my classes about students' writing on race in 2014, the Movement for Black Lives was well underway on a national level, but it had not yet impacted my campus directly. It wasn't until late 2014, when the failure to indict Darren Wilson for Michael Brown's death in Ferguson, and 2015, when Freddie Gray was killed in police custody in Baltimore, that the "full-blown, Black-led resistance movement" emerging nationally began to show up on this campus (Ransby xi). Student protestors, a new presence in our campus's racial ecosystem, swiftly connected violent attacks on Black people through policing and mass incarceration to other systemic forms of racism. Black and Latinx student activists challenged university leaders to make our campus culture more welcoming and safe for students of color, calling out small and large acts of university racism, and demanding a concrete institutional response—which is still unfolding (Vasquez). In turn, faculty of color, and some white allies, have organized to promote institutional change. As a response to student and faculty demands, university leaders have created new infrastructures. For the first time, the institution at which I teach now has a chief diversity officer who leads an Office of Equity and Inclusion, charged to improve hiring and retention of under-represented minoritized faculty, create a more inclusive campus climate and curricula, and implement ongoing professional development for faculty and administrators to build our capacity to participate in and help lead these changes ("Equity and Inclusion Council"). New institutional spaces for promoting equity work are all led by women of color, who put themselves on the line daily to go up against individual and institutional racism, and occupy important sites of struggle. In analyzing the impact and experiences of leaders in diversity work, Ahmed talks about the ways in which "[d]iversity workers acquire a critical orientation to institutions in the process of coming up against them." Thus, "[t]ransformation, as a form of practical labor, leads to knowledge" (173–74). This important, difficult work, and the transformational knowledge it generates, requires a wide range of participants doing a wide range of intellectual and personal work. In what follows, I will offer a map of my own racial geographies and that of the university where I teach. I offer these extended backstories to both ground the racial literacy work with student texts that makes up the largest part of the book and to contribute to the work Ahmed calls for: generating "knowledge of institutions in the process of attempting to transform them" (174).

AUTOETHNOGRAPHY: WHITE RACIAL ILLITERACY IN RESEGREGATING SCHOOLS

The first time I walked into a school in order to work there, rather than to be a student, was also the first time I remember being the only white person in a crowd of people. I had attended six schools in the course of my education, and I had almost always been in the overwhelming racial majority. It was eye-opening to feel self-conscious and consider, for the first time, how to carry myself as a white person in a hallway full of Black and Brown people. My eyes were opened further when I made my way to the AP history and English classroom where I would work as a teaching assistant and found that almost all the faces through that door were white or Asian. Not just the teachers, but the students as well. It was actually hard to imagine how these students had arrived at this room, since I hadn't seen anyone who resembled them in my own travels through the school. Given that they were all enrolled in an academically intensive certificate program with a track record of getting students into highly competitive colleges, it's likely that they had already been in rooms like this one for quite a while.

It is only a slight exaggeration to say I've spent my subsequent twenty-five years as a teacher trying to develop the historical and institutional understanding, as well as the personal capacity, to work against the educational segregation I first perceived that day, but had been participating in thoroughly. I could tell I had neither the information, nor the intellectual tools, to understand what I was experiencing in that school building and the implications of that experience for my larger understanding of my world. I could also sense that I had a white racial identity, and that I had work to do to understand it. The view I was afforded of contemporary forces of race, class, and geography overwhelmed two vague liberal notions I had absorbed throughout my education: (1) that the Civil Rights Movement had somehow "addressed" segregation, and (2) that the purpose of education was personal and social uplift. Of course my own "apparently (but not actually) all-white" life (Frankenburg 240) should already have given me abundant information that this was so, but I had not perceived my own life as segregated until the moment that I went—with no preparation or explanation—from being a white student in majority-white schools, taught by majority-white faculty, to becoming a white teacher teaching students of color. It's not that I lived under a rock or that I didn't realize society was segregated and racism was widespread. I did. Teaching students of color was one of my goals as an aspiring teacher. I wanted to "make a difference" in students' lives. I believed then, and I believe even more now, that schools can and should be institutions for personal and social transformation. But despite ample evidence of my own racial isolation accumulated during my first two decades of life in majority-white communities, and particularly majority-white schools, I had never consciously registered my own racial isolation, its history, and its ongoing brutal enforcement in countless social practices all around me. More important, I had not previously considered how it limited my life experience and curtailed my cultural capacity to work with people different from me, especially across class and race. This was a serious deficit in my skills as an educator and one that I had barely begun to register consciously.

The first theoretical tool that I acquired in the racial project of understanding my role as a white teacher in the United States came the following year, when antiracist psychologist Tatum led a workshop for my cohort of preservice teachers. Tatum's explanation of "racial identity development" people undergo in confronting the reality of ongoing systemic racism—especially her use of the term "white racial identity development"—named the work I needed to do, and gave it a framework. Tatum's observation that teachers aspiring to antiracist attitudes and actions would ourselves cycle through the process of racial identity development in unpredictable and uneven ways has informed and followed me throughout my subsequent twenty-five years working in schools from middle school through college. Tatum's ideas are especially prevalent in a resegregating educational scenario. She writes, "In a race-conscious society, the development of a positive sense of racial or ethnic identity, not based on assumed superiority or inferiority, is an important task for everyone" (*Can We Talk* 36). My realization that I had done so little work developing such a racial identity before I became a teacher meant that it was particularly important for me to do so while teaching.

Once I became a middle and high school teacher in my twenties, I revisited the kinds of physical racial separation I had participated in as a young person and thought further about how my experiences navigating segregated educational spaces caused me to internalize ideas, attitudes, and practices that would interfere with my goal of teaching students of all races. I offer some memories of my own segregated education to exemplify how many white teachers, in particular, internalize muted messages about the interacting forces of race, class, and geography long before taking charge of classrooms. These messages, which took place in the context of my hypersegregated white life in the 1980s and 1990s, impacted my intentions and behaviors as a white teacher, consciously and unconsciously. I continue to reflect on these experiences to deliberately interrogate the impact of these experiences on my approach to my classroom and my students.

COMING OF AGE IN RESEGREGATING SCHOOLS: MY RACIAL IDENTITY DEVELOPMENT

> *Remaining vigilant toward our own orientations to difference*
> *is important for us as teachers because our vantage points lead*
> *us to see our students in particular ways—some of which can be*
> *harmful and damaging.*
>   Kerschbaum, *Towards a New Rhetoric of Difference* 9

I was born in 1969, the year following the assassination of Martin Luther King Jr. and the election of Richard Nixon. I was a teenager in the early 1980s, the beginning of a period of racial and economic retrenchment in which wealth was transferred rapidly into the hands of a very few people, anti-Black policies focused on dismantling the social net for poor people, mass incarceration increased exponentially—in large part due to the War on Drugs—and recently implemented school desegregation programs began to be systematically dismantled.

When I consider how this larger context of racial and economic retrenchment impacted my particular life story, the most salient form it took appears to be segregation. While this is true on many levels—housing and family chief among them—it is especially apparent in my education. It's not that I lived in one particular kind of segregated community or attended one particular kind of segregated school. Instead, while moving and changing schools frequently, I navigated discrete locations in a network of schools that were either quietly and definitively segregated or integrated in highly provisional ways. Almost always, a few things were true: I was white, the overwhelming majority of my classmates were white, and my teachers were white. It was true in five out of six schools I attended from nursery school through college. My memories of students of color in elementary and secondary school are generally about a sea of white faces in all aspects of my life; a very few Asian American students in my classes, study groups, and friend groups; and Black students who were on the periphery of my schools, rarely in my classes, study groups, or groups of friends. Looking back on the racial milieu of each school I attended (a Catholic elementary school, a private middle school, a private high school, and a public high school), I remember Black students most clearly on the modes of transportation to and from school.

Two things happened in 1985. First, my affluent, majority-white sub-urban high school won a national Blue Ribbon Award, which was widely referred to as a "Ronald Reagan School Award." These awards by Reagan's Department of Education were almost always given to affluent schools, rewarding high test scores that have been definitively linked to the socioeconomic status of students' families (Rampell). In addition, the majority of students were white. I remember that school being set back from the main street of town with a parking lot for student driv-ers and a network of school buses that pulled directly up to the school. Black and Latinx students from the neighboring city who attended this school through a voluntary integration program were dropped 100 yards from school on city buses, and walked up an otherwise unused stretch of sidewalk to approach the school. The main times I saw Black students during the school day—with the exception of one or two stu-dents in my honors classes—were in the cafeteria, on sports teams, and in the typing class, which met in a room off the main hallway, away from the clusters of classrooms in the back of the school. I didn't know any-one who took typing.

Also in 1985, a regional magnet arts school opened its doors in the city bordering my suburb. Designed as a desegregation initiative, this arts program was somewhat out of step with its cultural moment of the "Reaganomics of race and literacy" (Prendergast 100). In my senior year of high school, I applied to the afternoon program, meaning that I drove into the city every afternoon to join urban and suburban students in arts programming after a morning spent completing our academic courses in our home districts. This pilot program was responsible for my single year of geographically and racially integrated education—which was distinctly "unacademic" in focus—during thirteen years of private, religious, and public schooling. We all had circuitous routes to this program on mini school busses and in our own cars. It's the one time I myself traveled across town lines as part of a public education and the only time I can remember having more than one or two Black class-mates. I was not at the academy to integrate my life, or fight segregation.

Those were dim benefits to me at the time. I was there to take theater and dance classes. That arts program received further funding after the 1996 ruling in the *Sheff v. O'Neill* case that schools in Connecticut supported "racial, ethnic, and economic isolation," a ruling that led to the opening of many regional magnet schools (*Sheff v. O'Neill*). The program is now a full-day magnet high school. The continued support for regional school integration in Connecticut is an exception to the national pattern of resegregation, which has been driven by judicial reversals and neglect of court-ordered integration. Unsurprisingly, this voluntary integration program is under constant fire.[4]

The other force for geographic and racial integration in my teen years was my urban church, whose children's choir drew teens from the suburbs and the city. To get to choir practice, I took the only public bus I ever rode as a teen. By participating in this school program and programs at my church, I traveled routes in and out of the city, meeting people who lived there, as well as people in other suburbs besides mine. As a result, I had something of a counternarrative to the fear of the city that the divided geography of my life encouraged. When my suburban classmates locked their car doors as we drove across the town line between city and suburbs—as their parents had instructed them to do—I spoke up against that move, and I saw their behavior as racist. It is good for me as a white person that I had these experiences. They insulated me from the whole-hog suburban paranoia that growing up in a Connecticut suburb was actually engineered to produce in the second half of the twentieth century—a network of economically devastated cities and some of the wealthiest suburbs in the nation. However, the side effect was a complacent feeling of "I'm not racist" when compared to other suburbanites, without an acknowledgment of the impact of segregation as a deep shaper of my life. I may have been less isolated than my suburban classmates, but the ways in which my life was integrated were all outside the academic core of my life—in the arts and in church.

While I was in college, this trend continued. Students protested the university's investment in South African apartheid, a lack of faculty of color and inclusive curricula, and racist events on campus. I was sympathetic but largely uninvolved. My studies were increasingly focused on slavery, imperialism, and feminism, but these were historical, textual, or intellectual phenomena for me, rather than part of my still nearly exclusively white social life.

When I decided to follow in both my parents' and both my grandmother's footsteps to become a school teacher in the mid-1990s, I entered a school I could *tell* was segregated for the first time. That is, few people who looked like me attended it. This moment, which I referred to earlier, marks both the beginning of my active pursuit of my own racial identity development and my first job as an educator.

In each school where I taught after that, racial geography continued to determine school demographics and priorities. At an urban high school in Boston, the student body was half what it had been before mandatory desegregation in the 1970s and 1980s, which resulted in massive white flight and general depopulation of the public schools. At a suburban middle school in Connecticut, grandchildren of white people who had fled cities in the 1970s exhibited even more racism against the South Asian grandchildren of immigrants who came to the United States after the 1965 Immigration Act than they did against the Black and Latinx grandchildren of the people their own grandparents had fled. In an ex-urban charter school, the original charter did not include money for transportation. The founders chose to use those funds instead for enrichment activities and supplies. This meant that the school, distant from public transit routes, was accessible only to families with the resources to transport teenagers to and from school themselves. Thus, positioned among several white and wealthy communities, the student body was even whiter and wealthier. In an urban magnet high school in Connecticut, funding from the *Sheff v. O'Neill* lawsuit meant a small number of suburban students were voluntarily bussed to a well-resourced urban high school much like the one I had briefly attended in the same state. In a decade of secondary school teaching in a range of settings, the common denominator was increasingly segregated conditions structuring daily life, educational opportunity, and social contact.

As I experienced the racial geography of each of these schools, and its impact on the educations of the students in each school during my first decade of teaching in the 1990s, the funding for schools became increasingly tight. National leaders of school reform spoke out about "taking over" a moribund system (in truth defunded by their predecessors to undermine mandatory legal integration), rather than reinvesting in the system that they were systematically trying to dismantle. Through attacks on teacher training, teacher unions, and schools themselves, neoliberal undermining of public goods and services could be felt viscerally in public schools. It exacerbated the deepening racial divisions these schools faced and in which they participated. By the time I began teaching college in the early 2000s, I had been deeply impacted by geographies of racial division made ever deeper by systemic resource scarcity.

To make sense of the forces of resegregation that I could discern shaping the conditions for learning in every school I was part of from the 1970s through the early twenty-first century, I have been strongly influenced by powerful scholars of race in education. These scholars have helped me map out the history in which I was participating in as I participated in it. Jonathan Kozol's perspective then and now has continually laid before me the "savage inequalities" of urban and suburban school funding, fleshing out broader systemic causes of the divisions I saw in my schools. Jean Anyon offers a clear-eyed history of how racial and economic oppression in urban schools and neighborhoods remains unaddressed by school reform efforts, and then presents local efforts that make significant differences by taking on poverty as well as race. And Tatum offered an analysis of the increasing racial isolation of our time in *Can We Talk about Race? And Other Conversations in an Era of School Resegregation*, mapping modes of action in a resegregating context for schools.

As I returned to this scholarship in order to theorize the impact of segregation and resegregation on my college students, Gary Orfield and John Kucsera at the Civil Rights Project / Proyecto Derechos Civiles actually made headline news in 2014, publishing a report that New York schools occupy "the epicenter of educational segregation for the nation" (iii). Kucsera and Orfield attribute this dubious distinction to three factors: New York state's legal court delays in implementing integration with "all deliberate speed" so that legally mandated integration began later in New York than the rest of the nation, New York's focus on implementing integration in southern states, and the dismantling of New York integration laws as early as the 1980s (iii).

Such measures to delay and dismantle school integration efforts were employed nationally over the last sixty years but were especially destructive to integration efforts in New York State. The report finds that in the New York City metropolitan area and its suburbs, during the short period during which legal programs to promote school integration were active, efforts were highly circumscribed. Programs tended to be small and local; hampered by fragmentation of school districts in the city and outlying suburbs; and resisted by elected officials, school administrators, and white parent groups. This district decentralization and fragmentation took place against a national Cold War backdrop of white flight into suburbs typified by legal and extralegal practices of housing discrimination and segregation, such as restrictive covenants and redlining. While the most egregious of these practices are no longer legal, the segregation of communities and schools that they established endure with very few exceptions. Perhaps Kucsera and Orfield's most damning finding was that in New York, as elsewhere in the country, efforts at large-scale integration had been largely given up. "Over the last 20 years, most desegregation efforts of the state of New York and [its five largest urban] public school districts have been abandoned, as minority proportions continue to rise and leaders shift focus onto neighborhood schools and the provision of equitable school funding or resources" (25–26).

While education scholars offer rigorous histories of failures to curb resegregation and build schools that promote racial and economic equity, they consistently articulate a case for the benefits of integration to students of color and white students alike, including themselves (Eaton and Chirichigno; Frankenberg and Orfield; Johnson; Noguera). Kucsera and Orfield cite "60 years of research showing that school integration is still a goal worth pursuing for a multiracial society. Research shows that integration serves white students and students of color: '[f]rom the benefits of greater academic achievement, future earnings, and even better health outcomes for minority students, and the social benefits resulting from intergroup contact for all students—like the possible reduction in prejudice and greater interracial communication skills'" (vi–vii). Despite its abandonment as a widespread educational policy, integration remains a significant, well-documented benefit to white students and students of color. Clotfelter points to its correlation with "outcomes of considerable social value," such as "academic achievement, job market success, and racial tolerance" (5). Amy Stuart Wells et al., in a study of adults who graduated high school in 1980—just before integration began to be undone by policies implemented during the Reagan administration—found that these graduates reported numerous benefits. "Attending desegregated schools dispelled their fears of people of other races, taught them to embrace racial and cultural differences, and showed them the humanness of individuals across racial lines" and provided "highly valuable preparation for an increasingly complex and global society" (5–6). According to Rucker Johnson at the National Bureau of Economic Research, "desegregation plans were effective in narrowing Black-white gaps in per-pupil school spending and class size and decreasing school segregation" (2). Benefits for Black people were significant and far reaching: "[F]or blacks, school desegregation significantly increased both educational and occupational attainments, college quality and adult earnings, reduced the probability of incarceration, and improved adult health status; desegregation had no effects on whites across each of these outcomes" (2).

Education scholars hold up numerous instances in which local schools and communities have made inroads against the historical trends (Noguera; Solorzano and Ornelas) as they call for more effective systemic change (Anyon; Ladson-Billings; Solorzano and Ornelas). Perhaps the most productive model for witnessing the bleakness of this period of resegregation in schools without giving up on integration comes from Gloria Ladson-Billings, who offers a metaphor for thinking about *Brown v. Board* as "landing on the wrong note" in the jazz tune of the United States—discordant and unsuccessful in the short term but potentially transformational in the long run. None of these scholars lets educators, policy makers, families, and communities off the hook but neither do they suggest despair.

My background in these secondary teaching contexts, and the formative role educational scholarship has played in my understanding of those contexts, means I bring four priorities to my teaching of early college writing:

1. Combatting racial isolation.

2. Creating a space to debrief almost-universal experiences of segregated elementary and secondary schooling.

3. Bolstering positive racial identity development for students of color and white students.

4. Learning from and contributing to theory and practice that supports university composition as a space of access to higher education, rather than gatekeeping.

DESCRIBING AND ASSESSING RACIAL UNDERSTANDING: RACIAL LITERACY

I begin the course's interrogation of race with an assignment I call the Racial Identity Narrative Essay, which came straight from Tatum's discussion of the importance of racial identity development. (See appendix for the full assignment.) I asked students to narrate and analyze a specific moment when they realized that an identity they held was not understood by someone else in the way they wished it to be understood. I wanted them to identify the times when they experienced what I had in my first teaching job—a confrontation with the ways their racial identities impacted their experiences—but from numerous different perspectives—when they realized they were part of a larger matrix of US social dominance and resource allocation that privileges and norms whiteness, pathologizes and targets Blackness, and asks all other racial groups in this country to contend with this dualism, "choosing" how to affiliate and where to make common cause. I wanted them to articulate where they were in the complex struggle to confront the existence of an inhumane racial hierarchy that has a deep psychological, interpersonal, institutional, and systemic impact on their lives. I have taught this assignment to jump-start conversations about race for many semesters. I now introduce it with a "One-Minute Stories" exercise from Maurianne Adams, Lee Anne Bell, and Patti Griffin's *Teaching for Diversity and Social Justice* that puts students in quick conversations about their early memories related to race. I emphasize that sharing these stories reduces racial isolation and allows students to hear, and enter into the perspectives of, students who are different from them. The question that emerged as I read and responded to these essays was—how could I assess students on their understanding of race?

Around this time, I encountered the term "racial literacy" in Larry Blum's book, *High Schools, Race, and America's Future: What Students Can Teach Us about Morality, Diversity, and Community* about teaching a mixed-race class on race to advanced high school students for college credit. Blum used the term to put racial awareness and understanding on a par with the kinds of "literacy" that high school students are tested on to assure they have achieved basic knowledge in essential areas of learning. His choice of the term "literacy" appears pragmatic, a means of asserting the "academic" nature of learning about race, as well as its essentialness to a "good high school education."

Blum writes, "High school subjects are generally seen as building blocks, defining a basic level of knowledge every citizen and worker must have to contribute to society and to understand the world around them. I thought of my course the same way. There is a basic level of knowledge about race, and specifically race in American history, that every American should have—a kind of racial literacy—even though most of them don't" (8).

After reading Blum's account, I added the "racial literacies" that appear at the beginning of this introduction to my syllabus, in order to explain the basic skills of the FYW course. (I also lay out "rhetorical literacies" and "digital literacies" the course will give them opportunities to practice.) Blum's useful concept gave me a framework for articulating and assessing how I expected students to engage with race in class. However, it lacked a theoretical grounding and genealogy that would give it the legs to ground a larger book project.

More recently, I have been introduced to Yolanda Sealey-Ruiz's practice of naming and promoting racial literacy in educating preservice teachers. Given the overwhelming whiteness of the teaching force, this is a particularly important population to reach. For Sealey-Ruiz, teachers must be able to "probe the existence of racism and examine the effects

of race and institutionalized systems on their experiences and representation in U.S. society" (129). She promotes these abilities through the
dynamic, growing Teachers College's Racial Literacy Roundtable series.

Sealey-Ruiz's conception of racial literacy draws from Critical Race
Theorist Lani Guinier's use of the term "racial literacy" in 2004 as a
"thought experiment" to reveal, and envision an alternative to, the limitations of racial liberalism, particularly as embodied in the mid-twentieth-
century legal strategy of *Brown v. Board of Education*. As opposed to liberal
racial reform, which Guinier describes as insufficient, driven by elite
agendas and top-down strategies for social change based on a constricted
view of racism as "a departure from the fundamentally sound liberal
project of American individualism, equality of opportunity, and upward
mobility," she envisions racial literacy as "a more dynamic framework for
understanding American racism," one that would keep an eye on race's
connections to the unequal distribution of resources and would look at
race intersectionally, with a particular eye on its interactions with geography and class. For Guinier, racial literacy is "the capacity to decipher
the durable racial grammar that structures racialized hierarchies and
frames the narrative of our republic" (100). The concept of "racial literacy" is finding its way into education, composition, and diversity work
in productive ways. While some scholars promote racial literacy among
preservice (mostly white) teachers to improve their teaching of students
of color (Sealey-Ruiz; DiAngelo; Grayson), other researchers use "racial
literacy" as a term to describe and analyze the tools people of color use
to name and counter the racism they encounter, from daily microaggressions to large-scale historical and institutional racism (Twine; Stevenson;
Kynard).[5] My hope, in *Mapping Racial Literacies*, is to listen for, support,
and promote racial literacies in both of these analytic frames—a tool to
combat white racial illiteracy and a tool to heed and amplify the critical
racial literacies of students of color.

Although I was not introduced to them in this way, the two most
influential frameworks guiding the evolution of my course—Tatum's
use of racial identity development and Guinier's thinking on racial
literacy—both ground their analysis in the context of school resegregation post–*Brown v. Board of Education*. Tatum and Guinier each propose
modes of forming cross-racial alliances in an era of deep and deliberate
racial isolation. For most white students, this change most often means
new vision and new interpretation of their experiences, something like
what I experienced when becoming a teacher. For students of color,
it can mean a range of things. Perhaps it can mean validation of their
experiences and an understanding of how those experiences fit into

systemic patterns. Or, if that is already part of their understanding, it can mean an institutional space where that understanding is validated and attempts are made to bring it into interracial discourse. In addition, as Pedro Noguera described the long-term benefits of his experience in a majority-white school, attending racially integrated schools "provided me with a valuable form of social capital that made it possible for me to advocate for myself and others, navigate rules and barriers to pursue my goals, and form strategic alliances with mentors, friends, and associates based on recognition of our common interests." For all students, I hope it will create a roadmap to action.

RACE, CLASS, AND GEOGRAPHY AT ST. JOHN'S UNIVERSITY

Having mapped my own racial geography through a lifetime spent in schools, I will next offer an institutional racial history of my university. I do so to surface the racial histories that surround and determine my current teaching context. This kind of personal and institutional work is especially important in college composition, since the history of that discipline is an (often unacknowledged) racial history.

Many scholars locate the origins of contemporary composition at the City University of New York (CUNY) in the 1960s and 1970s, and describe the activism of Black and Puerto Rican students and communities as the impetus for its origin (Reed; Kynard; Prendergast; Trimbur). In what follows, I will lay out some of the corollary history of my own institution in the same period. Efforts to better understand that history are currently underway among St. John's faculty. St. John's is often ranked among the "most racially and ethnically diverse" national universities in the United States.[6] How did St. John's become "diverse"? How does its diversity interact with racial histories of New York City and with universities across the country?[7] The research I've been able to conduct suggests that two key moments stand out in this history, which cut against the larger narrative of integrating universities in the nation and in New York City. The first moment occurred in the 1960s, when the university rejected racial integration as well as liberalization and secularization of its student body, curricula, and governance, setting a course in opposition to that of most New York City and national universities in that period. The second moment grew from legislation that was passed at that same time but that only impacted the university twenty to thirty years later, when students of color entered the university in significant numbers in the 1980s and 1990s.

The whiteness of university student bodies, curriculum, and governance were all challenged by community and student activists in the

1960s. New York City was one of the epicenters for this activist work, most notably on CUNY campuses. Due to activism led by a coalition of Black and Puerto Rican student and community groups, the City University of New York opened new campuses, changed its admissions policies, and underwent radical transformation in the 1960s and 1970s. Activism at CUNY spurred transformations of universities, and academic work itself—as well as significant backlash—that scholars are still unpacking. The study of writing is central to that history, as academic programs designed to control, mediate, and mitigate the qualities of these new students' writing immediately exploded at CUNY during this time, and many professors in these new writing programs participated in this activism, while theorizing approaches to Black and Puerto Rican student writing that were inevitably also approaches to racial justice. As Composition scholars and teachers forged new policies and pedagogies, the College Composition and Communication's Language Policy Committee authored the 1972 Resolution "Students' Right to Their Own Language," which Catherine Prendergast has referred to as an "antidiscrimination measure" fighting the history of literacy's uses to exclude and disenfranchise people of color and immigrants (96).

Unlike CUNY, St. John's University, a Catholic institution in the same city, repressed pressures for more inclusive governance, admissions, and curriculum in the 1960s. The university's response to Civil Rights activism was influenced by a related set of forces transforming Catholic universities' place in US higher education. Founded in 1870 to educate Catholic minorities, who were either unwelcome or threatened in public universities including CUNY, St. John's initially served an excluded minority. When CUNY opened its doors in 1847 as the Free Academy, graduates of Catholic parochial schools were not admitted (Trimbur 220). Unlike other private colleges and universities, which largely secularized beginning in the late nineteenth century, St. John's continued to embrace its identity as a Catholic institution, even as in underwent tremendous growth in the 1960s, with enrollment doubling between 1955 and 1965.

A few years before CUNY made history through activist-led admissions and curricular transformations, St. John's garnered media attention by doubling down against such liberalization and transformation. In 1965 the university earned censure from the American Association of University Professors and probation from the Middle States Association of Colleges and Schools, when St. John's president and trustees refused to renew the contracts of thirty-three junior faculty rather than negotiate over their right to unionize. Twenty-two of that number were not allowed back in their classrooms for the final three weeks of the semester (Morris 25). Two hundred faculty, many of them non-Catholics recruited from graduate schools around the country to serve the growing population of students at St. John's Brooklyn and Queens campuses, went on strike in support of their fired colleagues (Scimecca and Damiano 26). Striking faculty received little support from the student body, a largely white and Catholic group at the time. Scholarly accounts of the strike are generally partisan, either supporting the Catholic mission of the university in that era of change, or coming out against the university's resistance to falling in line with modern secular university practices. Ultimately, most of the striking faculty did not return. The university liberalized its governance system sufficiently to satisfy the Middle States Association's charge to "bring the university more fully into the mainstream of American higher education in the twentieth century," and St. John's retained its university accreditation (Morris 274).

If one sticks to the record of the scholars who have written about the strike, this does not sound like a racial history at all. Instead, it sounds like a story of white faculty defeated by a white administration in an attempt to gain more control over their teaching of a white student body. Unlike a few years later, 1964 was not a time of much publicized racial unrest on university campuses. Further, St. John's racial demographics remained largely white throughout this period. Enrollment reports from the 1950s through the 1970s report that students were 98.4 percent "White" and 1.6 percent "Colored" in 1950. In 1974, the total enrollment of students of color had increased only to 7.9 percent.

However, if one reads what was dubbed the "crisis at St. John's" geographically, St. John's role in this history was to hold the line not just against liberal reforms of curriculum and governance but also—though this is muted in all accounts I have seen—racial integration. The campus's original location in Bedford-Stuyvesant (a German-Irish neighborhood when the university was founded in 1870) put it in the center of Civil Rights protest and activism in New York City ninety years later. In the first half of the twentieth century, multiple migrations of Black southerners and Caribbean migrants to the neighborhood made it the second-largest Black neighborhood in New York City. The year 1964, when St. John's notorious labor conflict began, coincided with not only the passage of the 1964 Civil Rights Act but also with the first of a series of racial uprisings in cities across the United States. When an off-duty white police officer killed James Powell, a Black teenager, community outrage spread in both Harlem and Bedford-Stuyvesant. Robert Kennedy visited Bed-Stuy in 1966 and made it the testing ground for

Table 0.1. Annual enrollment reports, St. John's University Office of Institutional Research, 1950–2015

	Amer. Indian	Arab	Asian	Black	East Indian	Hispanic
1950	Not used	Not used	Not used	Not used	Not used	Not used
1974	0.1%	Not used	3%	4%	Not used	1%
1987	0.1%	1%	3%	5%	0.7%	4%
1991	0.4%	Not used	8%	9%	Not used	9%
2001	0.0%	Not used	11%	12%	Not used	13%
2015	0.0%	Not used	14%	13%	Not used	13%

Source: Goodwin and Roseland-Brenton and "University Factbook."

his response to urban Black poverty, working with Bed-Stuy residents and community groups to found the Bedford Stuyvesant Restoration Corporation in 1967 (Woodsworth). Just two years earlier, Kennedy had offered to intervene in St. John's labor dispute, perhaps seeing himself as an Irish Catholic leader invested in Civil Rights, and thus holding expertise (Morris 280). The university declined his offer.

It appears the university quietly sidestepped 1960s Civil Rights activism, and students of color themselves, by moving its programs out of Bedford-Stuyvesant throughout the mid-twentieth century as people of color moved in. The move was gradual, beginning with construction of a new building in downtown Brooklyn for graduate programs in 1928, followed by the purchase of the Hillcrest Golf Course in Hillcrest, Queens, in 1936. Construction didn't begin on that property until 1954, and the campus opened in 1956, with more programs moving there through the next two decades. In its final years, the Bed-Stuy property housed only the St. John's Preparatory School, which temporarily closed its doors from 1972 to 1981 due to a "changing society and resultant decreased enrollment in the late 1960's," according to the school's website ("School History"). When it reopened, the prep school was in Queens, which at the time was a largely white borough. (According to the US Census, Queens was 92 percent white in 1960, 85 percent white in 1970, 70 percent white in 1980, and 58 percent in 1990.)

While St. John's was charged by the Middle States Association of Colleges and Schools with a need to enter "the mainstream of American higher education" in terms of faculty governance and curricular control, it was well in the mainstream of white American institutions leaving the urban centers during the same period. Not only did this era explicitly

White	Other	Unknown	Non-Res. Alien	Nat. Haw. Pac Isl.	2 or more races
98%	Not used	("colored" 2%)	Not used	Not used	Not used
Not used	92%	8%	Not used	Not used	Not used
60%	5%	23%	Not used	Not used	Not used
70%	Not used	Not used	4%	Not used	Not used
49%	Not used	11%	4%	Not used	Not used
42%	Not used	8%	6%	0.2%	4%

cement the university's resistance to faculty governance by academics outside the St. John's milieu, it also saw the repositioning of the institution away from centers of urban Civil Rights organizing by people of color. Unlike the mid-sixties, the late 1960s and early 1970s—so electric on other campuses around the country—were quiet years at St. John's.

By 1971, two years after CUNY began its policy of Open Admissions, the Bedford-Stuyvesant property was sold and all programs were moved either to Queens or to another campus on Staten Island. Barbara Morris, whose 1977 dissertation narrates the crisis as a rite of passage for a modernizing Catholic university, explains the decline of Brooklyn enrollment as an explicit function of CUNY's acceptance of more students of color: "[L]ocated in a highly urbanized area, [St. John's enrollment] had decreased sharply as a result of the Open Admissions Policy of the City University of New York which was effected in 1969" (301). In effect, St. John's repositioned itself in opposition to Open Admissions, which brought students of color to CUNY in significant numbers for the first time. St. John's maneuvered through New York's geography to avoid Civil Rights and Black people. In fact, enrollment data show that St. John's only significant demographic shift in the 1960s and 1970s came with the admission of women as undergraduates in 1968.

Despite the limitations of this data, particularly the "unknown" category, a few trends are clear. Student demographics became slightly less white in the 1980s. Enrollment of Black, Asian, and Hispanic students climbed slowly, and in rough parallel, during the last thirty years. According to St. John's data collection, between 1987 and 2015, Black student enrollment went up 8 percent, Asian student enrollment went up 11 percent, and Hispanic student enrollment went up 11 percent. With its white student population below 50 percent since the turn into the twenty-first century, the St. John's student body is no longer predominately white.

It is an historic irony that—despite St. John's evasion of Civil Rights Era reforms, of students of color, and of other liberalizations of university study and governance—there are a significant number of students of color at St. John's today. The university is in the top 40 most racially and ethnically diverse national universities in the United States, according to US News and World Reports ("Campus Ethnic Diversity"). Unlike many public and private universities around the country in the 1960s and 1970s, this change in student demographics was not the direct result of student, community, and faculty activism to change enrollment. Students of color appear to have begun attending St. John's in the 1980s, during a very different cultural moment, and not as the result of student activism.

In the 1980s and 1990s, Black, Latinx, and Asian American students entered St. John's at roughly the same time. A commuter school until the 1990s (and still largely one, with over 70 percent of students commuting), St. John's has experienced shifting demographics as the demographics of Queens have shifted. The resulting historic irony is that students of color entered this university during a historic moment of resegregation due to erosion of Civil Rights victories such as *Brown v. Board of Education* under Nixon and Reagan. Integration of Black and Latinx students into formerly white schools was actually on the wane nationally as Queens became more racially diverse due to new immigration and white flight (UCLA report). Thus the new commuters integrated the school as part of the same racial geography that caused the university's leaders to move it out of the city. White flight continued and made people of color the majority in Queens for the first time.

A second contributing factor to the university's racial and ethnic integration in the 1980s and 1990s was a different piece of Civil Rights legislation—the Immigration Act of 1965—which lifted the ban on immigration from Asian and Latin American countries that had been in place since 1924. This law impacted St. John's in two ways. First, according to Miyares, while "this law transformed the ethnic geography of the United States, . . . few areas were as affected as Queens" (474). The 1990s saw particularly dramatic population growth in Queens, largely due to "either new immigration or internal migration of immigrants" (475). Second, according to Chang et al., St. John's was strongly impacted by a national trend in which Asian American college student demographics increased in the 1980s and 1990s, as the children of new immigrants admitted since 1965 began to attend college (1).

The increasing racial and ethnic diversity of St. John's students began during a national period of retrenchment in integration, largely despite, rather than because of, the will of the institution. Thus, the demographic shift in the student body was never associated with reforms of faculty governance or curriculum in response to activism. Its story looks different, therefore, than the perhaps more familiar narrative of the struggle to institutionalize student and faculty demands for inclusive student bodies and curricula. For example, many universities in the 1960s opened ethnic studies programs—interdisciplinary programs of study intended to offer critical perspectives on race and other social differences—in response to student activism. Until very recently, almost no ethnic studies programs existed at St. John's. There have been a women and gender studies minor and an "area studies" programs for the study of geographic regions. After a brief period of existence, a Black Studies program shut down.[8]

While individual professors teach courses that would fall under the purview of ethnic studies—as called for by Black, Latinx, and Asian American college students across the country in the 1960s and 1970s, and again by Asian American students in the 1990s—the only programs of study listed under the university's offerings in "Multicultural and Multiethnic Studies" were "global" in conception, rather than focused on the US experiences of people with global heritages. These minors include the study of the regions of Africa, Asia, the Middle East, Latin America and the Caribbean, and Europe, rather than the experiences of Americans with diasporic histories in those regions. The exception to this rule is the minor in "Italian American Studies."

This is a very particular way to approach "global" education in Queens, the New York City borough best known for racial and linguistic diversity. It foregrounds international relations, but forecloses study of people of color in the United States, US Civil Rights, and immigration—the issues most prominent for its students and community. Curricular reform has thus been out of step with the enrollment of students of color at St. John's. The diversification of the university's student body, brought about by movement of immigrant populations to Queens following the Cold War and white flight, has been accompanied by little to no activism or curricular reform at the university until the current moment. Very recently, faculty of color at St. John's have begun organizing an institutional home for race and ethnicity studies. In spring 2020, a full slate of classes is running in the new Critical Race and Ethnic Studies Program. This tremendous step, long overdue at our institution, has been driven by student of color activism and faculty of color leadership.

DIFFERENCE AS A RESOURCE FOR BUILDING RACIAL LITERACY IN A NON-INTENTIONALLY INTEGRATED UNIVERSITY

I write this book at a critical moment for my university. We currently have, through an accident of the forces of segregation, a racial balance of students that looks highly inclusive. In a potentially bitter irony of the current neoliberal moment, the very students of color the university first avoided and then absorbed have become valuable—their "diversity" now acting as a global commodity. Will the institution increase its capacity to serve these students? Or will it instead attempt to profit off their presence on campus, marketing them as a sign of being a "diverse university" with "global" investments?

As students, faculty, and administrators work to determine the course our university now sets, it is essential that student perspectives and experiences inform and drive institutional change. This textual ethnography, and its extended close readings of student work, aims to model methods for listening to students and creating conditions for them to listen to each other, in support ultimately of building campus capacity to recognize and value the experiences and priorities of students of color. To do such work, rhetoric scholars have begun developing models for listening to "difference" that are transformative, rather than co-optive. In this book, I aim for something like Krista Ratcliffe's "rhetorical listening," a stance of openness to difference, or Stephanie Kerschbaum's call to "resituate the problem away from *learning about,* and thus needing to know students, toward *learning with,* and thus always coming-to-know students" (Kerschbaum 57). Viewing difference in this way holds out hope for ethical teacher-student relationships and constantly evolving identities and relationships.

While I am highly aware of the resegregation of US public schools and differential access to privileges and resources through higher education along racial lines, schools have nevertheless been the places where I have experienced the greatest awareness of and access to information about segregation, and, ironically, where my own life has been perhaps most integrated. My university, despite a history of avoiding antiracist curricula and people of color themselves, finds itself—through accidents of geography and history—educating a relatively diverse student body. And recently, faculty and students of color have organized themselves to demand the university institutionalize its commitment to serving those students well. This book traces my attempts to build individual and collective racial literacy to increase my—and my students'—capacities to support such larger institutional change in our university and beyond.

STUDY DESIGN AND IMPLEMENTATION

To lay the groundwork for this book, I created an archive of student writing about race in my class. My methodology is textual ethnography, embedding my students' writing—and my intentions in assigning, responding to, and analyzing it—in broader pedagogical, institutional, historical, and theoretical contexts.[9] Throughout my data analysis, I have looked for new ways that student writing contributes to and reshapes contemporary understandings of the ways in which a new generation of US and global citizens are thinking about race.

Before I began collecting this archive, I applied for and received Institutional Review Board approval from my institution to use student writing for research. For eight semesters, I asked students for consent to use their writing in my research. I have included writing only by students who gave consent during that time, and I have changed all of their names to maintain anonymity.[10]

Using a sabbatical to collect and code the data, I read thousands of texts written by the 512 students I taught during this time period. These texts had been stored by students on password-protected websites used in class. I uploaded 690 selected student texts to a similarly data-secure archive. These texts offered the most salient insight into my research question: What did students do with the specific opportunities to write about race they encountered in this class? What could I learn from their responses?

I reviewed each text that consenting students had written in response to assignments asking them to write about race. In 2012, this was one assignment per semester, but between 2014 and 2016, it became the majority of course assignments. I coded each text I entered into the archive. Because I developed themes and patterns as I read texts, I used an open-coding approach, taken from grounded theory (Oktay; Bryant and Charmaz).

My approach to and understanding of this project evolved through extensive note-taking while assembling the archive. These notes discussed

- the categories I was developing;
- verbal and written exchanges in particular classrooms that potentially impacted one or more pieces of student writing;
- what was going on campuswide or nationwide during a particular semester;
- teaching opportunities I felt I had seized or missed;
- how what happened in a particular class or semester led me to revise the course in subsequent semesters.

My notes acted as a site for what Kerschbaum calls "incubation" of data generated in classrooms, separating insights best suited to helping me improve the class from insights best suited to sharing with an outside audience about the work done in the class (24–25).

Several areas of work collected in this archive did not prove germane to my ultimate approach and will not be considered in the following chapters. First, a set of categories emerged to collect and codify students' engagement with their own racial identity development (102 texts), their encounters with other people's notions of what one or more of their racial identities "means" (65 texts), or direct forms of racism (502 texts). Initially, as I created the archive, I expected to focus on student writing about the performance and perception of racial difference, as I had in my first time writing about my students' writing on race ("Whiteboys"). This student work remains valuable in creating a classroom in which students practice disclosure of personal experiences with race in order to lay the groundwork for naming and analyzing systemic forms of racism. (See my discussion of Marc Lamott Hill and Beverly Daniel Tatum's call for this work in the same piece.) While I certainly have many questions about their work and the conditions under which I assign it, these questions did not rise to the top in this research data. It may in the future.

In addition, there were robust categories of student writing about areas of the course that are aspirational. As I try to bring intersectional analysis into my class's approach to racial inequality, I collected 111 student texts that explored the intersection of race and a range of other social categories: class (36), gender (35), ethnicity (16), religion (11), and sexuality (13). In addition, students wrote a small number of texts related to activism (15), another area of the course I would like to develop. While it is useful to see what students are writing in those areas, the data analysis I did there marks future areas of inquiry for me, hopefully with student and faculty collaborators. It is not ready for external publication, as I still have more to learn than to share.

In contrast, the intersection of race and geography emerged as the most salient category for answers to my research question, yielding information ready to be shared externally, as well as being fed back into improving the class. This was the area of inquiry in which students came closest to my goal for them: to generate writing that leverages personal experience around race in the direction of large social insights about patterns of racial inequality. Racial geography is a milieu in which *all* students hold expertise. Paradoxically, segregation impacts everyone by the fact of holding them apart from each other. Geography is tangible and physical, which makes for good writing. It engages what C. Wright Mills calls an individual's "sociological imagination," that is, the observation of large-scale social patterns in concrete, observable moments of lived experience. In my experience, students are interested in mapping and sharing the racial geographies of their childhoods and adolescence as part of entering a new community in college. And at a majority commuter school, students are often exploring racial geographies they still inhabit.

ORGANIZATION OF THE BOOK: CONSTRUCTING PERSONAL AND INSTITUTIONAL RACIAL GEOGRAPHIES

This introduction has focused on racial geography from the 1960s to the present—with a particular focus on resegregation. These geographic frameworks are central to two histories that frame these classroom exchanges: (1) my own racial identity development as a teacher and (2) the racial history and milieu of my university. The rest of the book is organized around the affordances of my compositions course's focus on racial geography at this particular moment at this particular university. Each chapter focuses on a key moment in my efforts to use my classroom as a laboratory to find ways of supporting the work of racial identity development and racial literacy. In each moment, a focus on geography became the hinge in those efforts. Racial geography, especially that of resegregation, cuts against the colorblind narrative of "progress" on Civil Rights, enabling students to see the ongoing, even intensifying, segregation of their current lives, and those of other students. I explore key moments when students attempted to gain such vision in chapters 1 and 2, which are grouped together in section 1, "Mapping Racial Geographies." Racial geographies intersect with linguistic geographies, allowing students to connect their experiences navigating race and language to their experiences navigating race and space. I speculate on the potential of these parallel geographies in chapter 3, which occupies its own short section, "Mapping Linguistic Geographies." Racial geography offers a sightline into institutional racism, where I'm working to develop the course's potential to be a "community literacy think tank," along the lines of Linda Flower's work. In chapter 4, I look in-depth at one student's effort to use racial literacy sponsorship to move toward institutional analysis of racism. In my epilogue, I bring these forays into racial geography back to my own institutional context, my development as a teacher, and my ongoing goals for the course. Chapter 4 and the epilogue occupy the final section, "Mapping Futures."

Chapter 1—Mapping Whiteness: Hypersegregation, Colorblindness, and Counterstory from Brown v. Board *to Michael Brown*

This chapter describes writing about race and space done by my students beginning in the fall semester 2014, when the state of acute racial segregation and inequity that characterizes life in Ferguson and St. Louis County began to stand for the racial divides that characterize the nation at large. The chapter lays out histories and critical standpoints that inform my readings of student texts and my shaping of this book, including Nikole Hannah-Jones's journalistic work connecting Michael Brown's experience with police violence to the history of school segregation in Ferguson and the nation at large; Eduardo Bonilla-Silva's sociological work analyzing colorblind racism; and Aja Martinez's work developing counterstory as a critical race theory tool for combatting colorblind racism in composition pedagogy and theory. The chapter then analyzes students' rhetorical strategies for representing hypersegregated white communities as a potential tool for developing racial vision and promoting cross-racial dialogue.

Chapter 2—"It's Real": Peer Review and the Problems of Colorblindness and Empathy

This chapter extends the work of chapter 1 through a deep dive into a series of peer review exchanges among three students who wrote about their local experiences of segregation: a biracial student who moved to a white community and faced school segregation, a Chinese American student who faced both hostility and friendship from white neighbors and classmates when she moved out of Chinatown, and a white student from a gated white community who attempted to expand her racial vision through writing. I analyze these writers' individual and collaborative insights, the limits of their interactions, and the ways they productively resisted writing, responding to, and revising assignments. Throughout, I am invested in understanding their responses to the assumption, embedded in this series of assignments, that empathetic "rhetorical listening," in the spirit of Krista Ratcliffe, can be a tool for building racial literacy and resisting colorblind racism. In analyzing the dynamics of this group's exchange, I develop a new term—the "emotional imperative"—to describe the limits of empathy in such exchanges. Finally, I describe revisions I made to the course after seeing such limits on leveraging personal geographies into a robust critique of colorblind racism.

Chapter 3—"Your Grammar is All over the Place": Translingual Close Reading, Anti-Blackness, and Mapping Linguistic Geographies

This chapter marks a detour from the book's focus on racial geographies, interrogating how racial ideology impacts student writers who also navigate linguistic geographies. Here, I analyze student responses to my invitation to consider more deeply—and wield more consciously—the language resources they bring into classrooms. I seek to understand the potential for their often deeply racialized assessments of their own language resources, and those of others, to enable them to build common cause across language communities and racial communities. In particular, I look at the role of Black language as a recurring trope in multilingual students' writing about their experiences navigating the designation of "ESL" in schools.[11] I argue that the volatility of this trope—Black language serves in their work as a call-to-arms, stumbling block, source of strength, or taboo—poses a challenge to contemporary scholarship on language diversity. Ultimately, I locate this volatile trope in the emerging discussion of translingual writing in composition studies, arguing that these students do the work Keith Gilyard has called for in connecting global and local US language struggles.

Chapter 4—"Saying Honest Things We Wish Weren't True": Racial Literacy Sponsorship and Challenges to White Hypersegregation

The final chapter focuses on a research assignment into institutional racism that I have developed recently in response to the limits of student writing discussed in earlier chapters. The chapter discusses that project's impact on two levels. First, I address the larger picture of trying to promote transformative learning across differences of race, class, and geography in the class. Second, I look close-up at the "racial literacy sponsorship" of a white female student who used the course to look at racism in law enforcement and in her own family. This student's personal racial geography—she is a future educator from a hypersegregated white community, with close relatives in law enforcement—offers impediments to racial literacy that stand in for broader patterns of racial illiteracy on our campus. Her idiosyncratic attempts to overcome impediments to seeing and speaking up against personal and institutional racism are important in terms of my goals for my class. Ultimately, I find the winding course of her racial literacy learning results in her own ability to contribute to the learning of other students.

Epilogue: Mapping Countergeographies in "How Racism Takes Place"

The epilogue maps ways forward for both myself as a white teacher, and my university as an institution newly committed to equity for all students across intersecting lines of identity and oppression. I end by sketching out two countergeographies emerging in my class, where I have just started asking students to contemplate and analyze, first, "where they are coming from"—a deeply divided racial geography that will give them a lifetime of reflection and reevaluation—and, second, "where they are headed"—the deeply inequitable educational and professional land-scapes onto which they are moving and which they can enter with eyes wide open, ready to collectively and individually counteract inequity. My hope going forward is to help students develop capacity and tools for a lifetime of critically engaging—and combatting—the (re)segregation and racial inequities that surround us all.

SECTION 1

Mapping Racial Geographies

1

MAPPING WHITENESS

Hypersegregation, Colorblindness, and Counterstory from Brown v. Board to Michael Brown

It is certainly ironic that while race relations in America have changed significantly since 1954, . . . our public schools increasingly reflect enrollment patterns reminiscent of the 1950s. In order for us to avoid further societal regression, the social implications of this enrollment pattern require our attention—for White students who are racially isolated in predominantly White schools; and for students of color who are trapped in segregated schools with limited resources.

Beverly Daniel Tatum, *Can We Talk About Race? And Other Conversations in an Era of School Resegregation* 15–16

This essay is an exercise in SEEING race. That can be very uncomfortable, especially since many of us were taught that NOT to see race was a way of "not being racist." This essay asks you to take a different approach. Look at a space you know well, and look for race within that space. See what you notice. See what questions you have about what you see. See what you think. See how uncomfortable you are, but keep looking. The goal is the same as that of not seeing race—you are trying not to be racist! But the approach is different—instead of being colorBLIND and kinda hoping racism goes away because we refuse to see it, you are trying here to be colorAWARE and to name what is out there in an effort to understand it.

"Race and Space Essay" assignment, First Year Writing 1000c: Writing across Difference: Language, Race and Digital Composition

Coming from a predominantly white neighborhood and a very sheltered home, race was not a significant part of my everyday life. To me, people are people, and I never cared much about the color of somebody's skin.

Kaitlin

The population is 99.9% white, then there's us. Yup, you read that right. We are the only black family in the neighborhood. When I tell people that they say "Damn, you must live in a nice neighborhood." Microaggression much?

Ashley

DOI: 10.7330/9781646421107.c001

This chapter interrogates the potential of interracial writing exchanges to decrease racial isolation and increase students' capacity to observe the personal and systemic impact of racism in their own and each other's lives. The first half of the chapter introduces the historical, pedagogical, and rhetorical orientations that led me to ask students to write about race in their neighborhoods in late 2014. I lay out these orientations at length in order to share my process with other teachers who have embarked, or are considering embarking, on pedagogical projects such as mine. The second half of this chapter takes up student writing from my classes, first by surveying student responses, next by analyzing students' rhetorical depictions of majority-white neighborhoods, and finally by unpacking a particular interracial writing exchange between two students who grew up in majority-white communities. Chapter 2 dives even deeper into another writing exchange among three students on the same subject, exploring the questions I raise in this chapter. Together, chapters 1 and 2 trace the ways students navigate within and against colorblindness—a racial ideology that erases and explains away the evidence of their lived experiences in hypersegregated white spaces. In doing so, I offer racial geography as a critical model for moving toward antiracist composition pedagogy.

At the heart of both chapters are textual ethnographies of student writing exchanges as they attempt to map their own racial geographies, particularly in white spaces. In this chapter, I situate these writing exchanges in three different ways: historically, in the larger context of housing and school resegregation since the Civil Rights Era and in the more immediate context of Michael Brown's death; ideologically, in the context of colorblind racism, the salient racial ideology of the post–Civil Rights Era; and rhetorically, through readings of their work for elements of counterstory, a term adapted by compositionists—most notably Aja Martinez—from Critical Race Theory. While these historical and critical lenses lay the groundwork for and deeply inform my close readings of student writing exchanges, ultimately I do not use these readings to either fully critique or fully celebrate my students' writing and thinking about race. Instead, these perspectives provide me with a framework for investigating what happens in their work.

My students' lives to date have coincided with abandonment of widespread integration programs, and they thus grapple with the particular ideology that accompanies the evisceration of Civil Rights legislation—colorblindness. As a result, my pedagogical goal is to promote a culture of writing that values racial vision. In doing so, I am responding to sociologist Eduardo Bonilla-Silva's call for new qualitative methodologies for researching—and combatting—colorblind racism. At its most ambitious, this chapter looks at my writing class as an example of how writing, reading, and revising together might offer college students a map away from colorblind racism.

FROM *BROWN V. BOARD* TO MICHAEL BROWN: DEVELOPING A CONTEXT FOR READING NARRATIVES OF RESEGREGATION

Before introducing their work itself, I offer a speculative parallel between the writing and responding that took place in my classes during the fall semester 2014 and what happened in the nation during the months our class met, that is, the murder of Michael Brown in August and the non-indictment of police officer Darren Wilson for his murder in November. While I am happy to admit the stretch necessary for the parallel I am making between my students' writing exchanges and what happened, and continues to happen, in our national community through Michael Brown's story, there are some incontrovertible connections.

My students that semester were Michael Brown's peers. They were first-year college students in the fall of 2014, which was intended to be Brown's first semester of college. Like Brown, my students are almost all products of intensely segregated schools. These schools—his high school and most of theirs—went through a period of legally mandated integration that was on the wane by the late 1980s, and they have all graduated from secondary school during an era in which those schools have been resegregating.

The further parallels I draw between my students' stories and Michael Brown's are more speculative, but strategically useful. In both cases, color-aware narratives by people of color disrupted colorblind racism's ideological function and offered new narratives of stark, present-day racial injustice. I claim that students' race-aware narratives in my class, and their reception, made institutional racism more visible to students in the course. As in the national reception of Michael Brown's story, this process of increased visibility was fraught, uneven, and uncertain. It by no means led to consensus on the meanings of their stories, or on race, or on unified action by students. However, I argue that like in the national conversation, what happened in the writing relationships among these students created crises in their worldviews that had the potential to impact their racial identity development and their rhetorical practices around race.

In a final connection, the events in Ferguson during the summer and fall of 2014 caused a sea change in student activism on our campus. As far as I am aware, there was little to no student activism at the university until the end of this particular semester. The first event I am aware of on campus took place that December, when the NAACP chapter led a die-in in December. By the following spring semester, several students came into my class having attended Black Lives Matter marches over winter break, and this set the stage for a much more robust activist culture on campus than I had seen in my previous five years teaching there, including a student-led march through campus for Freddie Gray that spring. In my classroom that fall, however, these issues were largely latent, unfolding under our feet. The growing campus conversation about systemic racism was not an explicit part of these particular students' conversations, or my teaching, but it framed our exchanges.

As activists, journalists, and scholars uncover more about systemic racism in the institutions and daily lives of Michael Brown's community, the state of acute racial segregation and inequity that characterizes life in Ferguson and St. Louis County has come to stand for the racial divides that characterize the nation at large. According to Jelani Cobb, the Black Lives Matter movement "exposed Ferguson as a case study of structural racism in America and a metaphor for all that had gone wrong since the end of the civil-rights movement." While there are many aspects of Cobb's claim to explore, I will focus on how Michael Brown's story—like my students' stories—offers a sightline into resegregation. St. Louis's history of residential and educational segregation shines a light on that of the nation at large.

According to *New York Times* magazine reporter Nikole Hannah-Jones, "Few places better reflect the rise and fall of attempts to integrate US schools than St. Louis and its suburbs, [. . . since d]ecades of public and private housing discrimination made St. Louis one of the most racially segregated metropolitan areas in the country." Hannah-Jones connects Michael Brown's life and death directly to resegregation:

> Since Aug. 9, the day Michael Brown's lifeless body lay for hours under a hot summer sun, St. Louis County has become synonymous with the country's racial fault lines when it comes to police conduct and the criminalization of black youth. But most black youth will not die at the hands of police. . . . They will face the future that Brown would have faced if he had lived. That is, to have the outcome of their lives deeply circumscribed by what they learn and experience in their segregated, inferior schools.

The extreme inequity and segregation that Michael Brown endured in Ferguson and its neighboring communities exist despite the fact that greater St. Louis pioneered one of the largest, most expensive, and most controversial school integration programs in the nation between 1983 and 1999. In uncovering this history and a contemporary struggle over integration in the high school from which Michael Brown graduated, Hannah-Jones points out that Michael Brown's mother, Lezley McSpadden, was one of the children bussed out of a majority-Black school district to attend elementary and secondary school in a neighboring majority-white school district through this mandatory integration program. In fact, Hannah-Jones quotes McSpadden, in the first hours after her son's death, describing her struggle against educational injustice in his life. "'Do you know how hard it was for me to get him to stay in school and graduate? You know how many black men graduate?' she implored. 'Not many.'"

Hannah-Jones's reporting reveals that St. Louis's integration and resegregation really does show us an extreme version of the nation's post-*Brown* history. In order to avoid implementing *Brown* in St. Louis, white families fled to suburbs to start their own "de facto" segregated schools. Families of color were excluded from this large-scale relocation by racist housing policies such as redlining and restrictive covenants. When the racial disparities between St. Louis's schools and its suburbs became so pronounced that they faced lawsuits in the 1980s, a large-scale program to bus 15,000 St. Louis students to suburban schools took effect. This highly controversial, extremely effective program ended up costing $1.5 billion and was under constant fire from state officials such as John Ashcroft and Jay Nixon. In 1999, the plan was made voluntary, reducing the number of students it served by two-thirds, and enabling suburban districts to opt out. St. Louis's story of desegregation and resegregation is a particularly stark example of *Brown*'s betrayal.

So while McSpadden was able to attend school herself in a wealthy suburb of St. Louis, her son attended multiple underresourced schools in the majority-Black communities where he was raised. In fact, he graduated from a high school that lost its state accreditation, triggering new integration efforts that led to as much resistance from white parents as St Louis's 1970s integration efforts. The curious feature of these twenty-first-century white parents' objections, as Hannah-Jones reports, is their insistence that the issue is not race and that anyone who says race is a factor is themselves racist. Such colorblind disavowals would not have occurred to a white parent in the 1970s.

This backsliding away from Civil Rights in which Michael Brown's educational opportunities in 2014 were actually more constricted than his mother's two decades earlier, combined with the attitudes of white parents who fought against having students from his high school bussed to their majority-white district in 2014, demonstrates the perilous state of racial inequality under resegregation, and the extent to which this injustice is invisible to most Americans.

According to Tatum, "As a culture, we celebrate the symbolic importance of the anniversary of *Brown v. Board of Education*, without fully acknowledging the reality of K-12 public school resegregation" (*Can We Talk about Race* 12). Born in 1954 along with court-ordered desegregation in *Brown v. Board*, Tatum calls herself "an integration baby," one who came of age when formerly all-white institutions of secondary and higher education were opening their doors to Black students for the first time (1). Whereas the state of Florida paid for her father to leave the South to pursue a PhD, rather than admit him to a segregated state university, she was part of a wave of young people of color admitted to formerly all- or almost-all-white colleges and universities. She also points to the legal history that has immediately followed *Brown*'s passage and endured until today, in which integration has been delayed, diminished, and derailed in courts and communities around the country. In his 2004 book, *After Brown: The Rise and Retreat of Desegregation*, Charles Clotfelter cites four factors that "frustrated, and ultimately blunted . . . the execution of the policy of desegregation." These were the "apparent white aversion to interracial contact, the multiplicity of means by which whites could sidestep the effects of the policy, the willingness of state and local governments to accommodate white resistance, and the faltering resolve of the prime movers of the policy" (8). This is a grim counternarrative to the racial progress narrative that relies on an invocation of Civil Rights victories of the 1960s to mute allegations of systemic racism in the present.

Tatum speculates about what it means to live in an era of resegregation, in which "our public schools increasingly reflect enrollment patterns reminiscent of the 1950s" (*Can We Talk about Race* 16). She writes, "One possible outcome [of continuing residential segregation and increasing school resegregation] is that while interracial contact and more-tolerant racial attitudes increased during the last half of the twentieth century, the same may not be true in the first quarter of the twenty-first century, particularly in our public schools" (13–14). Given this context, she warns that "the social implications of this enrollment pattern require our attention—for White students who are racially isolated in predominantly White schools; and for students of color who are trapped in segregated schools with limited resources" (16). Tatum promotes an agenda for helping students transcend these legacies by (1) supporting white teachers to build their capacity to educate and support students of color; (2) forming significant interracial connections;

(3) developing positive, aware racial identities for people of all racial backgrounds; (4) building leadership opportunities and communities for young people of all races to fight against the increasing racial isolation and inequities of their lives.

This chapter charts my attempt to respond to these calls from Tatum. The historical context of resegregation that restricted and contorted Michael Brown's educational chances is the same one that determines my students' educational experiences and futures. The highly uneven amounts of access and resources that they bring to college themselves are in large part the result of their resegregated schools and communities. No matter how invisible the histories behind their schooling, that history is there, in their grandparents' "integration baby" generation, in their parents' generation at the tail end of integration, and their own era of resegregation. My students' attitudes toward race—in particular, their abilities to counter colorblind ideology by analyzing the segregated realities of their daily lives—thus matter very deeply. Despite the apparent intransigence of colorblind legislation and ideology, my students are part of a generation being led by activists of color to take a systemic look at racism after years of "postracial" discourse. Of course, my students, like all young people in their generation, have the option to ignore systemic racism. There are certainly daily encouragements for them to do so. I try to use my time with them to stack the deck in the direction of a color-aware approach to the racial injustices that face their generation.

RESEGREGATION AND RHETORIC: THEORIZING COLORBLINDNESS AND COUNTERSTORY IN COMPOSITION STUDIES

Engaging with my student's attempts to use writing to make sense of this historical context in their daily lives means engaging with the ideology of colorblind racism—a salient means of denying the present-day acceleration of racial inequality and separation. Eduardo Bonilla-Silva describes colorblind racism as "a seemingly nonracial way of stating . . . racial views without appearing irrational or rabidly racist" (48). While I do not directly apply Bonilla-Silva's framework for analyzing colorblind racism to my students' writing, or teach his work to them, his work deeply undergirds my approach to framing and responding to student writing. His thinking has helped me understand and engage my students' work, and I will lay it out before diving into that work.

In his influential 2003 analysis of the self-reported views on race of white people at several universities and in the city of Detroit, *Racism without Racists: Color-Blind Racism and Racial Inequality in Contemporary*

America, Bonilla-Silva thoroughly delineates colorblind racism as a
post–Civil Rights Era ideology. For Bonilla-Silva, its ideological function
lies in its attempt to erase racial significance from the reality of contemporary American life. While explicit racism played a dominant ideological role during Jim Crow, when national racial policies reflected explicit
white supremacist priorities, the silence and evasions of colorblind ideology fit the current disavowal of racial inequity as *racial* at all, allowing
individuals and institutions to evade or evacuate the Civil Rights legislation of the 1960s, aimed to redress racial injustices that, in this logic, are
blurred, diminished, evaded, or erased. Bonilla-Silva describes this shift
memorably, in an often-quoted passage:

> Compared to Jim Crow racism, the ideology of color blindness seems like
> "racism lite." Instead of relying on name calling . . . , color-blind racism
> otherizes softly ("these people are human, too"); instead of proclaiming
> God placed minorities in the world in a servile position, it suggests they
> are behind because they do not work hard enough; instead of viewing
> interracial marriage as wrong on a straight racial basis, it regards it as
> "problematic" because of concerns over the children, locations, or the
> extra burden it places on couples. Yet this new ideology has become a
> formidable political tool for the maintenance of the racial order. Much as
> Jim Crow racism served as the glue for defending a brutal and overt system
> of racial oppression in the pre-Civil Rights era, color-blind racism serves
> today as the ideological armor for a covert and institutionalized system in
> the post-Civil Rights era. (3)

In other words, once the law no longer explicitly endorsed white
supremacy—and racism began to be redressed through the courts—racism
had to go underground. When people can argue that the problems of
our time are "not racial," racial redress and reparations can appear un-
necessary. Wells et al. refer to this mode of thinking as "white double
consciousness" (31), and Kenneth Clark called it "moral schizophrenia"
(Duke University address 1972).

Bonilla-Silva's analysis discerns distinct patterns in the ideology of colorblindness, which offers "set paths for interpreting information [that]
operate as cul-de-sacs because after people filter issues through them,
they explain racial phenomena following a predictable route" (26). The
four principal paths, or frames, he identifies are *abstract liberalism,* in which
concrete situations of racial inequity are blurred into platitudes or doxa of
liberal principles such as equality, despite the fact that "modernity, liberalism, and racial exclusion were all part of the same historical movement";
naturalization, in which racial realities are made into nonracial "facts of
life"; *cultural racism,* in which disadvantages and obstacles experienced
by a racial group are imagined as cultural traits of that group, whereas

advantages and privileges of another group are similarly imagined as their own "culture"; and *minimization of racism*, in which the impact of racism on any group is imagined as insignificant (28–29). Together, in this model, these frames for thinking serve white people "as an interpretive matrix from which to extract arguments to explain a host of racial issues. More significantly, together these frames form an impregnable yet elastic wall that barricades whites from the United States' racial reality" (47).

Although his primary goal is to analyze the cultural logic that both promotes and disavows the systemic inequities experienced by people of color, Bonilla-Silva also depicts the dangers of segregation to the white people enforcing it. In his estimation, whites lead "hypersegregated" lives, and their racial isolation makes them particularly susceptible to colorblindness. To some extent, his analysis satirizes pathological depictions of segregation's impact on people of color, such as a "culture of poverty." However, he is also serious in finding that "whites' high levels of social and spatial segregation and isolation from minorities creates what . . . [he] label[s] as a 'white *habitus,*' a racialized, uninterrupted socialization process that *conditions* and *creates* whites' racial taste, perceptions, feelings, and emotions and their views on racial matters" (Bonilla-Silva 104). Flipping the Moynihan Report–style discourse of racial isolation and pathology on its head, he uses this tool to look at white communities. Further, he finds that "[r]ecognizing whites' lack of realization that race matters in their lives, combined with their limited interracial socialization, helps decipher the apparent contradiction between their stated preference for a colorblind approach to life (which corresponds to their perception of how they live their own lives) and the white reality of their lives" (116). The sociological distance he takes on widespread white hypersegregation exposes how white racial blindness makes perfect sense in an era of deep, unacknowledged self-isolation.

I am particularly interested in Bonilla-Silva's assertion that colorblind racism is "slippery, apparently contradictory, and often subtle" (53). This aspect of colorblindness is part of its post–Civil Rights Era ideological role in making invisible the foundational role race plays in the legal and lived realities of white people. I am looking for ways that young people maneuver in and out of the "impregnable yet elastic wall" of colorblindness as laid out by Bonilla-Silva to catch glimpses of the racial structures of their lives. While I do not ask students themselves to analyze colorblind rhetoric, I establish a stance in the class's foundational goals that is explicitly anticolorblind and advocates racial awareness. I use my readings of this student work to look for ways that race-aware practices of reading, writing, and thinking can intervene in the ways that this elastic wall "barricades whites from the United States' racial reality" (47).

Thus, although I accept Bonilla-Silva's extremely useful and thorough elaboration of colorblindness as the prevalent form of racist ideology in this historical moment, my orientation to students' texts has two differences from his approach to interview subjects' words. First, whereas Bonilla-Silva's close readings of interview transcripts use micro-instances to support the elaboration of the larger cultural formation of colorblind ideology, I propose to use close reading for more or less opposite ends. I focus on moments when the logic of colorblind racism founders or falters in fine-grained moments of textual interaction among my students. I look for aberration, static, and glitches in the patterns he describes—not to disprove his theory, but to attempt to explore the potential for disruption of the dominant ideological purpose of colorblind racism as he describes it. Thus my readings of my students' texts assume that colorblind discourse dominates classroom exchanges, and they look for moments when that dominance is challenged.

Second, I aim to reframe the conversations students have about race to increase the likelihood that they will need to square the racial reality of their lived experiences with the colorblind discourse that may seem to arrive unbidden on their screens as they type. I discuss the specifics of my pedagogy later in the chapter, but the essential elements include (1) introducing colorblindness as false consciousness early in the semester, (2) introducing assignments that explicitly encourage racial vision and awareness, (3) rarely intervening or disagreeing with students' specific racial statements in their writing and response (I stick to asking questions), and (4) not grading individual pieces of writing. Instead, I open the semester with a grading contract that stipulates a general rubric for grading in which habits of work, rather than individual pieces of work, receive grades (Danielowicz and Elbow; Inoue and Poe). In doing this, I attempt to create a minimally coercive space for students to narrate and respond to each other's stories. Thus, where Bonilla-Silva used large-scale studies to theorize the parameters of white people's active denial of race operating in their lives, my case studies attempt to set up conditions for people of all races to understand that colorblindness is counterproductive, and to help each other gain some awareness and critical distance on it, and practice operating differently.

My belief that my students may be able to fight colorblind racism through telling their stories indicates that I am probably more optimistic than Bonilla-Silva about the possibility of working against ideology in young people's thinking. However, the conditions seem fruitful enough to try. In addition, my work responds to what Bonilla-Silva, in a moment of strategic optimism, identifies as a way to disrupt colorblind racism. He calls for a "new civil rights movement" led by Black people and their allies, and my hope is that spaces such as these writing groups can be micro-instances for making those alliances. There is grounds for hope here, on a broader historical level, given the close resemblance the Black Lives Matter movement bears to the movement Bonilla-Silva called for in 2003. Despite the hopeful orientation of my pedagogy, my students' peer review groups demonstrate sharp limits on the efficacy of these reading-and-writing relationships, particularly their ability to move students of other races into alliance with Black people.

Aja Martinez's models for applying rhetorical analysis to colorblindness in student writing very much inspires what I seek to do in this book. In her 2009 *College English* article, "The American Way: Resisting the Empire-of-Force and Colorblind Racism," Martinez develops the latent rhetorical argument of Bonilla-Silva's analysis of colorblind practices. Her close readings of Chican@ student texts, analyzing them for their use of the frames of colorblind racism he identifies, inform what I set out to do here. She compassionately discerns, in the ways that Chican@ student writers in her classes adopt "a rhetoric of color blindness," a conscious or unconscious belief that in order to assume "the academic voice in higher education or what could be argued as a 'white voice,'" one must also adopt "an alignment with whiteness" (593). She concludes by calling for faculty to name and study colorblind racism to help Chican@ students avoid internalizing or fully adopt it, supporting them in "navigating through the system with their identities still intact" (595).

In pursuing this goal, Martinez's more recent work has pursued the Critical Race Theory concept of "counterstory" as a tool to intervene in colorblind ideology. Her use of counterstory has profoundly shaped the way I read my students' writing. Developed in the 1980s by legal scholars of color to counteract the attacks on 1950s–1970s Civil Rights legislation, Critical Race Theory foregrounds the colorblind logic in the legal argumentation that eviscerated hard-fought decisions promoting racial justice. Scholars such as Derrick Bell, Richard Delgado, and Patricia Williams turn to personal narrative and rhetorical experimentation in order to expose traditional legal discourse's complicity in the evacuation of Brown and other Civil Rights legal victories.

Martinez argues for—and enacts—strategic uses of Critical Race Theory methods in antiracist composition pedagogy and scholarship, joining scholars such as Carmen Kynard and Catherine Prendergast. She argues that Critical Race Theorists' rhetorical strategies such as "storytelling, family histories, biographies, cuentos, testimonios, and counterstory" intervene in "majoritarian stories of racialized privilege and . . . help to strengthen traditions of social, political, and cultural survival and resistance" ("Critical Race Theory" 23–24). In particular, she advocates the use of counterstory as a methodology "to expose, analyze, and challenge stock stories of racial privilege and . . . help to strengthen traditions of social, political, and cultural survival and resistance" (Martinez, "Plea" 38). Since contemporary racism "is often well disguised in the rhetoric of normalized structural values and practices," Martinez advocates for and models the use of such counterstories, largely but not all by writers of color, to make visible the racial realities occluded by what she calls, after Richard Delgado, "stock stories"—"those that people in dominant positions collectively form and tell about themselves. These stories choose among available facts to present a picture of the world that best fits and supports their positions of relative power" (38).

In addition to advocating for such strategies, Martinez employs narrative practices inspired by Critical Race Theory to articulate her position as a Latinx academic, writing rhetorically experimental counterstories about her experiences in the academy in the form of fictionalized dialogues. Further, Martinez analyzes elements of colorblind ideology in her students' writing and looks for conditions that would enable students to produce counterstories as well. Inspired by her work, I look for places where my students pit counterstories against stock stories in their peer review groups.

The writing and responding of the students I discuss in this chapter engages the specific rhetoric of colorblindness in uneven, unpredictable, idiosyncratic ways that require close scrutiny. Their writing moves in and out of ideological frames that support a colorblind approach. At times, students challenged each other to be more race-aware, and at other times, they encouraged each other to be more colorblind. My central interest is determining the potential of explicit conversations about race for puncturing colorblind racism and promoting racial vision and for understanding the struggles students experience while doing this work. The premise that underlies this work is that racist ideology—in particular, colorblind racism—is not monolithic. As Bonilla-Silva has written, it is flexible and elusive. This means it is hard to counter with direct argument, despite the profound ways it operates on people's thinking as they make meaning of the world. While this is part of its durability and strength, it also leaves room for countering its evasiveness and denial with the simple direct testimony of people's lived experiences of racial inequality and separation.

The unwieldy blend of colorblind stories and race-aware counterstories that typifies this student writing offers important opportunities. First, students can interrogate their own thinking and constantly question their accountings of their own experiences. Second, readers of this writing can observe the close quarters shared by race-blindness and race-vision in the thinking and storytelling of young people grappling to make sense of their racial realities. Tracing their intellectual and emotional journeys through the materials of their own lives offers a sight line into the ways residual, dominant, and emergent discourses coincide in the thinking and writing of young people. I am looking for ways to deploy Bonilla-Silva's tremendous insights about colorblindness to increase young people's awareness of the role of race in their lives and to give them opportunities to discuss that role in mixed-race groups. In many cases, my students have bought into at least some forms of colorblind ideology, and it is crucial for them to discern the ways in which it is laid into their thinking and that of their peers, while struggling to extricate themselves and each other from it. I believe most of my students move in and out of colorblind racism as they write about their lived realities.

COMBATTING COLORBLINDNESS: SITUATING THE ASSIGNMENTS, INVITING COUNTERSTORIES

At the beginning of the semester, I describe colorblindness explicitly and point out that it has little support as a strategy for solving racism. I say this when I introduce the course and the narrative assignments, and I have used quick plugs from a number of different antiracist activists to support this point early in the semester.[1]

My explicit message to students about colorblindness appears as an epigraph to this chapter. I use it to introduce the value of race-aware discourse. I believe this context for telling stories about race matters. It offers (1) an opportunity to discern and articulate the racial reality of one's life, (2) a push to work through and possibly away from colorblindness by telling these stories in a mixed-race group. I aim to give students as many opportunities as possible to articulate race-aware perspectives, assuming that for some of them this is new (for many of them, of course, this is not at all new) and for all of them it is a valuable practice in the post–Civil Rights Era of resegregation.

This stance on my part runs two risks for students who want to articulate views at odds with mine. First, they may want to debate whether or not it is a good idea to talk about race, and my emphasis on race-aware discourse does not make space for that debate. This risk is deliberate on my part. Through experience, I have learned that the alternative is to spend the semester on that debate itself, rather than students' ideas and experiences. I take steps to take that conversation out of our classroom dialogue, not because I don't value it but because it is counterproductive in a class whose specific purpose is to take a look at race. In this classroom, the horse is out of the barn. If they ultimately want to argue that racism is a bygone phenomenon, they have that option in their final portfolio. But they first need to tell some vivid stories about their own experiences with race that led them to this belief. This rarely happens, but it has occurred.

The second risk I run in requiring students to express their experiences and views on race is assessment. Students will naturally feel uncomfortable voicing views at odds with whatever they perceive mine to be, since I am assessing their work. Although I cannot eliminate this dynamic, I take steps to remove students' views on race from the grading structure of the course, as described earlier in the chapter. Further, in my comments on student writing, I make an effort to assume a stance of curiosity about students' views and experiences, rather than sharing my own. This stance runs the risk of leaving problematic statements unaddressed and forcing students to handle difficult or triggering statements on their own in peer review groups. I do two things to prevent this situation: (1) I ask students to email me before the groups meet if they see a "red flag" in another students' writing and they think something has come up that merits my intervention. (2) I sit with groups for their discussions if I think one or more students' writing could be triggering, and I moderate those discussions. This happens rarely. Generally, I leave the conversations to students after setting up parameters.

I have been assigning the "Racial Identity Narrative Essay" since 2012, aiming for student writers to put peer readers in their shoes through sensory and emotional description. Here is an excerpt from the assignment. See the appendix for the whole assignment.

> The purpose of this essay is to ask you to write a narrative of one very specific moment in your life that demonstrates something important about the impact of race in your life—in order to share and understand each of our stories better. One point of this assignment is to just get to work telling stories about race. If we keep chipping away at the ways in which the different forms of racism haunt all of our experiences, we have a better shot at getting as free of it as we can. A second point of this assignment is to reflect on what Beverly Daniel Tatum would call your "racial identity

development," your lifelong process of incorporating messages about race out in our world into your sense of yourself and how you fit into that world.

Students write about many important things in this essay, but for the purpose of the book it plays a simple role—a warm-up for writing about race in one's life and also for the act of sharing, and responding to, those stories with other college students. The writing that students have done on this assignment doesn't serve this book's specific goal of looking at the role of segregation—particularly white hypersegregation—as a window into patterns of racial inequality, so I will not devote as much time to it here. However, the essay is important to understanding the other writing that students do, for two reasons. First, many of their exchanges of writing relevant to racial geography refer back to these essays, since they are the first essays students exchange with their peer editors. Second, the "Race and Space Essay" developed in part to solve a problem of colorblind racism that emerged in the writing students did in these initial race narratives. I found that many students who explored moments in their lives in which they raised important questions about the social foundations of troubling moments in their families or communities would shut those moments down at the ends of their essays. This occurred so often that, as I coded these essays, I came up with the category "colorblind conclusion" to describe what I saw. In addition, students would use colorblind rhetoric in their peer responses. What I mean is that their language would follow one of the frames identified by Bonilla-Silva to minimize the impact of the insights made possible by a students' writing about race in their lives: abstract liberalism, naturalization, cultural racism, or minimization of racism. These moves, in students' conclusions and their peer feedback, concern me because of the implications for racial identity development. Most models of racial identity development theorize a hinge moment when an individual, whether white or a person of color, is confronted with evidence of racial prejudice, discrimination, or systemic inequality, and faces some pressure to "reintegrate" that evidence into their preexisting belief that racial equality has already been achieved in our current moment. The early stages of racial identity development, especially for white people, contain a possibility of *not* developing, in part because of pressure from other whites. Because the particular moments many students chose to write about were ones that challenged them to look at racial problems, a return to colorblind truisms at the end of an essay looked like it could signal such "reintegration" of colorblind ideology.[2]

In addition, peer responders, who understandably wished to sympathize with and comfort classmates who told disturbing or challenging stories, would often invoke colorblind logic to do so, with the impact of dismissing, rather than exploring, important questions raised by their peers' experiences and writing.

In response to these colorblind patterns in student writing and responses, I have developed measures to minimize colorblind undermining of potential insights throughout the writing process. Each measure makes for better writing, asking students to explore and lean into tough questions, rather than backing away from them. In addition, I encourage writers and readers to pursue the thinking that comes from confronting disturbing evidence in their lives.

In mini-lessons on framing essays, and in studies of mentor texts, I point out places where writers can raise, rather than resolve, questions that have emerged in a piece of writing. I explicitly label the "first draft" conclusion as a "colorblind conclusion" and encourage students to move past it. To frame all conversations on race, I use Glenn Singleton's "Four Agreements for Courageous Conversations about Race." The fourth agreement asks participants to "expect and accept nonclosure: This agreement asks participants to 'hang out in uncertainty' and not rush to quick solutions, especially in relation to racial understanding, which requires ongoing dialogue" (Singleton 58–65). By naming the urge to contain troubling questions about race as understandable but counterproductive, and by suggesting students resist that urge, I hope to support their efforts to be race-aware.

The final measure I introduced to extend the learning in the "Racial Identity Narrative Essay," was to begin following it with the "Race and Space Essay" in 2014, asking students to write, and respond with peers, to a second essay that looks through a racial lens specifically at their neighborhoods and to put in writing what they see. Here is an excerpt from that assignment (for a full version, see appendix):

Race and Space Essay: Write about your neighborhood with attention to race

Section 1: Description. Write an overall description of the racial groups who live in your neighborhood—get really really local (like just your block) and then, if you want, zoom out a bit to include the surroundings. Describe your neighborhood in such detail that if one of your peer reviewers woke up there, they would know exactly where they were. Is the racial make-up of your neighborhood uniform/diverse? Consistent/changing? How so? What do you think of what you notice?

Section 2: Narrative. Tell a story about a time when you noticed race in your neighborhood in some way. Or when, looking back, you see that race was a factor in something going on that you didn't notice at the time. Bring this moment to life so other people reading your narrative can walk in your shoes through that experience.

After sharing a draft of each of the two essays with a small group of peers, randomly selected by me, students revise one of the two pieces into a Spoken Word they perform for the whole class.

When I began archiving student writing, coding it, and reflecting on what I heard back from students, I found that a very high number of student essays engaged the issue of segregation, or took place in a seg-regated racial landscape. Out of 689 student texts written in my classes over the last six years, which I selected and coded for the archive, 138 texts addressed the topic of segregation. This was one of the largest topics that emerged in this collection of student writing. (In contrast, 18 student texts were about integration.) Out of 138 texts on the topic of segregation, the largest number of students (41) wrote about seg-regation in their neighborhoods and communities. Close behind was the topic of segregation in school, written about by 35 students. Of the 41 texts on neighborhood segregation, over half wrote about liv-ing in majority-white neighborhoods (26), one-third wrote about living in majority-Black neighborhoods (13), 3 wrote about majority-Asian American neighborhoods, and 2 wrote about Latinx neighborhoods. The student writers were sometimes in their neighborhood's racial majority, and sometimes not.

In addition to keeping track of the racial makeup of these students' neighborhoods, I noticed several themes emerge across the work. Fifteen students (7 people of color, 8 white) wrote about directly wit-nessing white racism in majority-white neighborhoods or schools.[3] Many students wrote about neighborhood changes, either their own move from one town or neighborhood to another, or changes in the neighbor-hood itself while they were living there. Seven students, who expressed a range of racial identities, wrote about demographic changes in their neighborhoods; ten students of color wrote about moving into white neighborhoods for the first time. No white students wrote about moving.

For the purpose of this chapter and the next, I will focus on the larg-est group of students who wrote about segregation—those who grew up in majority-white neighborhoods. Fifteen of these students were white, and eleven of them were students of color. I am interested in unpacking their observations about "white" spaces, which are often described by white students as "having no race" or not involving "racial issues." Texts that name the racial dynamics in such spaces are positioned to lend insights into students' approaches to seeing race and the ways they make meaning out of what they see. How do students account for the role of this racial geography in forming their senses of self and community? How do they make sense of segregation as an ongoing reality in their daily lives? Where are they most fully engaged in colorblind rhetoric, and where, if anywhere, do they articulate racial vision?

Once they explicitly acknowledged the whiteness of a community, no writer denied the presence of race as an issue in that community. Two white students described public displays of anti-Black beliefs at large in their white communities. One described her town as a place where Confederate flags were often used to decorate clothing and vehicles. The other wrote: "Being that my neighborhood was predominantly white and not as exposed to other races as much as other people, there were often a lot of prejudices tossed around about other races."

Seven students described the hypervisibility of people of color in their white neighborhoods in one of three ways: (1) by marking the race of people of color while muting the whiteness of other neighbors, (2) by writing extensively about neighbors of color (if they were white), or (3) describing the experience of being hypervisible in that way (if they were people of color). Ten students described brief incidents pointing to larger social inequities or prejudices under the surface of daily life. Six of these students identified as white, two as Black, and two as Asian American. Five students wrote texts that appeared to try to work out a connection between racial and economic forces at work in their white neighborhoods. The two students doing this who were white stopped short of making those connections. The students who did connect acts of racism in their neighborhoods to larger economic and historical forces they saw themselves as part of were all students of color.

"OUR HOUSES WILL ALL LOOK SIMILAR TO YOU JUST LIKE WE ALL LOOK SIMILAR TO EACH OTHER": MAPPING WHITE HYPERSEGREGATION

In this section, I will introduce the writing three students did in response to the charge to describe the racial dynamics in their largely white neighborhoods. Two of the students identify as white and one describes herself as a white-appearing Latina. All are female. For each student writer, the whiteness of her own community created a clear conflict with the privileging of "diversity" as a positive feature of communities. However, while I have often heard the colorblind phrase "My town didn't have much race" used by white students to describe their all-white communities, these students used this assignment to attempt to describe living in a white neighborhood, not as a *non*-racial experience, but as a racial one.

I will use Chris's and Maja's work to demonstrate common rhetorical strategies that emerged for looking at white communities. Students who undertook describing the whiteness of their neighborhoods often adopted an ironic tone, often one that became elementary in diction and repetitive in rhythm. For example, Chris's description drew on the parallel racial, economic, and architectural uniformities of her neighborhood as she answered the charge to "show me your neighborhood." She condensed many forms of homogeneity into one brief description of suburban whiteness.

> The first thing you may notice is the street is much quieter, you may see someone jogging or walking their dog. You may notice that they all look the same. Chances are he or she would be White. In fact, I'd make a bet with you for 100 dollars that they are. You may notice some older people, or some families with minivans or strollers parked in their driveways or cars packing to bring their kid back to college. Our houses will all look similar to you just like we all look similar to each other.

In Chris's description, whiteness is part of a uniformity she describes as both superficial and deep. Race is one aspect of excessively homogeneous middle-class suburban life outside of New York City, designed to facilitate white affluence. Her peer reviewers, both women of color from the city, pushed her to weigh in on what she thought of her neighborhood's whiteness. One of them referred to that level of segregation as "white supremacy." Chris's response to this description is hard to track, as her revision of this piece was minimal. However, two rhetorical clues suggest a level of self-awareness and ironic engagement in her initial draft: her offer to make a bet with her reader about her neighbors' whiteness, and her inclusion of whiteness in a larger homogeneity of economic class and lifestyle. She included this piece in her final portfolio, and when reflecting on it in an end-of-semester reflection, wrote, "although it wasn't any easy task, I learned a lot about myself and my neighborhood when I had to write about it." She suggests a struggle and engagement with racial vision that she connects to the process of coming to a college that is less segregated than her home. Being around people of color for the first time in college, she writes, "has only opened my eyes."

Chris embeds her neighborhood's whiteness in a racial geography in which planned suburban homogeneity is contrasted with urban "diversity" in New York City, thirty miles away. In contrast, Maja, a white student from Queens, portrays both her urban neighborhood's whiteness and its homogeneity as surprising, given that Queens is a famously diverse borough of the same city.

At first, the whiteness of her neighborhood discouraged Maja from writing about it. She met with me after writing a first draft of a "Race and Space Essay" in which she explained that she lived in a predominantly white neighborhood so had nothing to say about race in her neighborhood. She had written instead about her experience with customers of different races in her retail job in a more integrated Queens neighborhood. When I asked her to speak about her own neighborhood in terms of race, she started to talk about it in this way. I asked her to write it down, and she wrote a new essay that became this poem.

While her block sounds similar to Chris's in its whiteness and affluence, her rhetorical presentation of her neighborhood uses even more irony, contrasting what one expects in a Queens neighborhood with what one sees in hers.

My White Walls

I live in Queens.

The most diverse city in the world.
Let's imagine all the towns that would make up this city;
You must think,
that a block,
of about 30 single family homes,
equates to 30 different countries.
You must think,
that every ethnic cuisine,
is represented in restaurants on the main road.
You must think,
that everyone,
is so used to looking different,
different skin shade or face structure,
that they embrace it and get along.

But I live in a small neighborhood in Queens.
You would expect,
each neighborhood
to be diverse like Queens,
but it's not.
The 30 houses,
that should resemble the 30 countries,
just resemble 30 shades of white.
There are no ethnic cuisines,

Only iconic New York food joints
McDonald's,
Diners,
Pizzerias
Chinese food.

Are people used to looking different from one another?
No.
Why?
Because they all look the same . . .
My neighbor is white,
The family that lives on the block behind mine is white,
The family members and friends that come to visit are white,
The mailman is white,
The UPS guy is white,
The FedEx guy is white,
The garbage men are white,
The principal in the local elementary school is white,
The principal in the local junior high school is white.

But I do see some other races.
The Chinese food places are run by Chinese people,
The delis are run by middle eastern people,
The dollar stores are run by Korean people,
The warehouse employs black people.
Those races work here,
but they don't live here.
Why?

May it be
because Whites just want the goods those races bring, and nothing else?
Or may it be
because the others want the benefits of the "white and wealthy" area?
Which is it?
Why are we taking advantage of each other,
but are not together?

That's like asking how many licks does it take to get to the tootsie roll center of a tootsie pop, the world will never know . . .
because I live in Queens.

It is interesting that she writes this as a Polish immigrant who arrived
in New York as a young child and might constitute a form of "ethnic diversity" in her "white" neighborhood. However, she does not make that
argument. Instead, she focuses on the "whiteness" of her neighbors as
an odd phenomenon that cuts against the expectations of a reader who

knows she lives "in the most diverse city in the world." Like Chris, her descriptive language is somewhat stripped down and repetitive. This appears to echo her goal of describing the repetitive nature of her white landscape.

It is difficult to say what rhetorical meaning Maja is giving the relations among races in her neighborhood. She constructs the poem around the contrast between what "you would expect" to see in a Queens neighborhood (a different ethnicity in every house in every neighborhood, a kind of United Nations representing many countries of origin) and what the neighborhood actually looks like (everyone who lives there is white). Her observation goes on to explain that people of many races come through her neighborhood because "they work here, but don't live here," and she tries out different ways of imagining that economic relationship. Because the neighborhood is wealthy as well as white, she tries out different ways of imagining the economic "taking advantage of each other" going on between white residents and people of color coming into the neighborhood for work. While she clearly sees that there are racial patterns at work, she ends up depicting the nature of the relationships between white people and people of color as unanswerable, obscure (like how many licks to get to the center of a tootsie pop). The elementary rhetoric she slips into—with very simple diction, repetition, and the tootsie pop analogy—keeps this all superlight and echoes Chris's similarly supersimple diction. Are they going back to beginnings to resee things? Are they mocking the assignment? Are they uncomfortable? Are they ironizing the segregated reality of their lives with the postracial expectation that segregation is "over"? Chris and Maja did not choose to revise these pieces in their work with peer reviewers, so there is not enough evidence of the thinking that underlies the ways in which they represent their white neighborhoods. Whatever the underlying causes were, both writers break through colorblind rhetoric to describe the whiteness of their communities but stop short of exploring the roots of that whiteness.

Cassandra, whose essay begins with a scan of neighborhood whiteness very much along the lines of the essays I quote above, lifts up the rug of white hypersegregation in ways that Chris and Maja do not. Cassandra describes living in a wealthy, majority-white neighborhood in Queens, where she witnessed the following incident when stopping at a real estate agency with her mother on a series of errands.

> A black couple, probably in their early 30's, walked into the office. They went up to one of the agents and inquired about any houses for sale in the area. The agent, a white male, probably around 50, said, "No I'm sorry, we

don't have anything available right now." The couple looked a little disheartened, accepted his answer, and wrote their phone number on a piece of paper so that when something did become available, the agent could let them know. I thought to myself, *It's pretty strange how there's no houses on the market here. I wonder what the agents do all day then?* I looked to my left and saw that my mom was still talking to her friend about good allergy doctors. I glanced back to my right, and I saw the real estate agent take the paper with the phone number, crumple it up, playfully hit his coworker, and say "Don't they know this is [a white neighborhood]?" They both started laughing, like little kids who were being tickled.

We left shortly after I witnessed and heard this situation. I'm not really sure if other people around the office heard the comment the man made, because no one reacted. *Was it because no one thought there was anything wrong with what he said?*

Cassandra's direct witness to the well-documented practice of real estate agents refusing to sell houses to Black people isolates her. No one else seems to see it. Her mother is otherwise occupied, and Cassandra can't tell if anyone else heard. If they did, she questions whether they would think anything was wrong with it. She is left questioning the extent of the racism she had witnessed. As she tells it, her glimpse into the systemic racism underlying that segregated neighborhood is isolating. Her image of isolation and silent questioning resembles the stage of racial identity development in which an individual perceives racism around them for the first time and is discouraged from holding onto that perception.

However, by the time Cassandra revised her piece to present it to the class, she became more definitive, adding two lines:

People heard. People saw. People didn't speak up.
And you would think living in the most accepting time period probably in history, things like this wouldn't happen anymore but concealed things happen all the time to keep certain colors in and others out.

In her final portfolio, Cassandra identifies her portfolio theme as "sight and voice." This rhetoric of vision and voice shows one writer trying to amplify her act of witnessing, to both share, and also distinguish herself from, active racist practices underlying the hypersegregation of her neighborhood.

While Chris and Maja demonstrate the sometimes uncomfortable results of segregation, Cassandra's glimpse leads into more systemic insight. She was aware of the history of systemic housing discrimination because of films and readings in class, and she had an opportunity to connect those histories to her own community. However, none of the three writers I've cited so far chose to dig deeper into the personal impact of growing up in segregated neighborhoods. I will cite a pair of students who do more of that work and who do so while reading and commenting on each other's work.

KAITLIN AND ASHLEY: "WE AREN'T UNDER JIM CROW LAWS YET PEOPLE STILL HAVE THAT MENTALITY"

Kaitlin, who identifies as white, and Ashley, who identifies as Black, both wrote their initial "identity" essays about a moment when they were deeply shocked by an unexpected encounter with racism in an all-white setting. When students in Kaitlin's seventh grade history class articulated Islamophobic stereotypes in a discussion of the anniversary of 9/11, she was taken aback. Kaitlin articulates a colorblind perspective that she explicitly links to her hypersegregated white childhood—"Coming from a predominantly white neighborhood and a very sheltered home, race was not a significant part of my everyday life. To me, people are people, and I never cared much about the color of somebody's skin." Confronted with her classmates' ideas about Muslims, she had a crisis. "I couldn't believe how ignorant about the world I was. I thought that racism wasn't as extreme as it once was in our country but I was terribly and embarrassingly wrong. From that point on I promised myself that I had to grow out of that ignorance and I had to get a true understanding about what was going on in the world."

Ashley comforts Kaitlin in the margins: "It's okay! You don't have to beat yourself up because everyone has things they aren't aware about. I think since you weren't aware of how alive racism still is[;] you didn't really notice or care if someone looked different than you, you just accepted them for who they were."

In her own "Racial Identity Essay," Ashley characterizes her knowledge about race differently. She describes her awareness of racial issues as a result of attending a diverse high school while living in white communities: "My friends and I are good kids who never got in trouble and were at the top of our class. We are aware of race and what goes on in the world. However it was never a big deal because our high school was so diverse that being different wasn't a big deal."

Ashley identifies herself and her friends as Black early in her essay, taking pains to clarify for readers in her class—Kaitlin among them—that she was causing no trouble as a Black person in white space. Walking into a pizzeria in a small mostly white town "after a great day of good clean fun at the bowling alley next door," Ashley foregrounds the ways in which her racial awareness was not on high alert because of two things: (1) her experience in interracial settings and (2) her merit "at the top of her class" who's having "good clean fun."

The only other customers in the pizzeria were "a cute little family [who] were sitting enjoying their dinner. It was a mom and dad with two young children. The family was white." While she describes the father and baby brother as "distracted," she notices the mother and daughter looking at her.

> I was admiring the cute little family until I heard, "Mommy, they don't look like monkeys." At that moment I think I stopped dead in my tracks because I couldn't believe what I just heard. The mother quickly shushed her daughter and looked me dead in the eyes and gave me a guilty look. This little girl couldn't have been older than 4 or 5 maybe even younger yet she could disagree with her mother about my friends and I looking like monkeys. There was no one else around; it was just the family, my friends, and I. The moments after were just a blur.

Kaitlin sympathizes with Ashley, writing: "I can't believe how cruel and inconsiderate people can be. That is not right to judge people and it is such a shame how one person can ruin your day and in this case, leave an impression/burden on you that you have to carry around now."

In Ashley's account, she and the little girl are silenced—the girl by her mother, and Ashley by her friends, who don't believe she could have heard correctly. She concludes, "I can't blame that little girl for what she said because she is just repeating what she heard from her parents. No one is born being racist. It is something that is taught. I have to blame her parents because they are the ones that have to instill good values in their children."

As Ashley's peer reviewer, Kaitlin highlighted this passage and responded: "This is so true! 'No one is born racist' really hits the nail on the head. In this case it is nature vs. nurture and as you said, racism is something that is taught and the only way to fix it is for people to change their mindsets about certain things." Kaitlin firmly endorses Ashley's refusal to blame the young white person being exposed to an over-the-top racial stereotype. It is tempting to imagine Kaitlin putting herself in the position of this little girl, particularly because her next essay focuses on memories of her mother's messages to her about racial difference when she was a young child. Both writers, raised in majority-white communities, share a concern over the racial messages young white people are absorbing.

After reading Ashley's essay, Kaitlin wrote about her own mother's role in forming Kaitlin's views about race in a segregated white neighborhood. Kaitlin begins her essay with similar suburban iconography as other student writers. Dog walkers, joggers, and lone families of color punctuate a uniform, and uniformly white, landscape. She very clearly links her community's vigilance against outside influences to its whiteness.

> Everyone who lives on my block is white. . . . In my town, we tend not to get a lot of new neighbors, so once again, everyone knows everything. If someone on my block gets arrested, gets into a car accident, is getting divorced, or someone needs to seek medical attention and they call an ambulance we all will find out by the next morning. We also know who has which car and if any car is not from our block, we all go on alert, watching the foreign object to see who claims it. However, once you branch out even farther and start going to different towns, you can see the diversity. For example, if you go to neighboring towns, . . . there are a significant number of middle-eastern people, and once you go even further than that, and go into [X], there are a huge number of African Americans and Hispanic people. Those areas are deemed as bad neighborhoods due to the high crime rate and poor financial standings of the individuals who live there.

Racial and economic segregation are etched into the geography of Kaitlin's childhood experience. Thus, everything in her neighborhood seems not only white, but fixed in place, unchanging. The "foreign" object she imagines sending them into hypervigilant surveillance is a car, but it signals a rhetorical shift from describing people doing things to people being observed from a distance. The farther she moves from her own white block, the farther her sentences distance the subject from the people she sees. She shifts from first-person plural in her neighborhood, to second-person singular in "neighboring towns," to third-person plural when naming "a significant number of middle-eastern people" and even "a huge number of African Americans and Hispanic people." As she describes these large groups, apparently ringing her white neighborhood, people of color are relegated to grammatically remote parts of the sentence—objects and prepositional clauses. This dynamic picks up when she tries to explain the poverty and violence she perceives in Black, Latinx, and "Middle Eastern" communities and shifts to passive constructions such as "these areas are deemed as bad neighborhoods." For Kaitlin, as she tries to describe her community with a racial lens, whiteness and subjecthood are linked, and people of color are rhetorically as well as geographically remote.

    After setting this scene, Kaitlin spends most of her "Race and Space Essay" describing her own white mother's comments during rare moments when she encountered people of color during her childhood. Writing in response to Ashley's account of a white mother actively teaching a young child a deeply racist stereotype, Kaitlin likely intends to endorse her own mother as a model of tolerance, a kind of counterstory.

Kaitlin recalls specific moments when, as a young child, she observed individuals of color in her neighborhood, and asked her mother questions about race and language differences:

> Whenever a person who was not white walked by, I would, as any child, stare. I recall this one time, when I was in elementary school, this man would speed walk past my house every morning before I got on the bus. What struck me as strange is that he wore this long garb and a hat while he ran (which I later found out was called Pathani Kurta Pajama and a skullcap) since if I were to go outside, I would probably put on shorts and a t-shirt.
>
> So I asked my mom one day, "Why does that man wear that same outfit every day when he walks by?"
>
> She said, "I do not know, that is what some people do," and since my mom gave me some sort of answer, my justification became "just cause" and that was it.

Kaitlin's intention appears to be to depict her mother as neutral toward this man. Her mother's lack of hostility operates as a sign of tolerance—a contrast with her seventh grade classmates' parents (who presumably pass on stereotypes about Muslims to them) and the mother in the pizza place (who tells her daughter Black people look like monkeys). Kaitlin's mother certainly offers Kaitlin no negative views of the man. A second way of reading this scene, though, focuses on the impact of Kaitlin's mother's incuriosity. Through the phrase "I do not know," Kaitlin's own curiosity is deflected. His differences thus become illegible to Kaitlin. While the fact that he speed-walks by every day suggests he lives somewhat nearby, he doesn't register for her as a neighbor about whom her family knows and monitors everything, but rather as an outsider, someone beyond their purview. Since Kaitlin began elementary school in 2001, this conversation likely happened soon after 9/11, and the man is wearing clothing associated with Middle Eastern countries and the Indian subcontinent. Kaitlin's mother offers neither racist ideas about the man, nor any way of understanding him that would help Kaitlin see race, ethnicity, or nationality. A similar moment reinforces this point:

> I was a little older, but still in elementary school, and I was playing outside on the front lawn with my brother and my parents watched from the stoop. A man with a darker complexion (I cannot remember what his race was) walked by and he was speaking a language that I couldn't recognize. I tried to listen in case I was not hearing him right, but I still could not understand him any better. After he walked by, I turned to my mom and asked, "What did he just say?"
>
> She said [,] "I do not know, I couldn't understand him."
>
> I responded, "Why not?"

> My mom replied, "I don't know what language he was speaking."
>
> Once again, as a child, I thought that everyone in America spoke English, it didn't process that people from other countries do not speak English as their native language and I went on playing with my brother.

Kaitlin's attention to the details of this childhood moment incorporates an attitude toward difference that promotes a pronounced lack of inquiry, an incitement to colorblindness. In her memory, her mother—on a block where everyone knows everything about everyone—again models blankness about the dark-skinned man who walks by. His language and skin mark him as different, and her mother's brief comments suggest he remains outside their concern, outside the circle of their close-knit white community. Tellingly, Kaitlin's memory, which is otherwise quite vivid, cannot call up his race or identify the language he was speaking—in her memory, she is already blind to it. She cannot describe her neighbor of color because she is unable to see him.

Whether Kaitlin is endorsing her mother's tolerance, critiquing her colorblindness, or both, she ultimately questions the adequacy of her own ability to see race in her essay's conclusion. She describes traveling—in fifth grade—to a high school in a nearby town for a singing audition. This experience inspired the title of the essay, "Out of My Realm":

> Upon arriving, a couple of red flags went off in my head. First off, I had to go through a metal detector to enter the school. I never had to do that before. Another red flag was how dirty and run down the school seemed, like the people there did not care about it. Finally, as I walked into the waiting room to get called in to perform, I realized that I was one of the only white people in there. I was so confused because I had never been in the minority before. I was used to being in the majority of the school population. At that stage in my life I also had never been in such a diverse group before and I needed a moment to take it all in.

Kaitlin's first memory of being in a majority-Black and Latinx high school does not involve any descriptions of the people she saw or the emotions she experienced. Instead, she remembers visual details of space that signal an underresourced school as "red flags"—metal detectors and "dirty and run down" conditions. She does not describe any of the people of color she encounters or probe her initial impression that "the people there did not care about" the school. She describes herself as "confused" and needing "a moment to take it all in." Despite how little she gets on the page about this experience, her attempt to describe it looks like a move against the lifelong training she has had in muting her vision of people of color.

In the margins of this first draft, Ashley encourages Kaitlin to keep working on this:

> I want to know more about how you felt when you felt like a minority. This could be really personal and you might not want to talk about it. I can see that you were not only shocked but also mesmerized by the surroundings you were in. Did you ever feel uncomfortable? Whenever I'm in a new environment I'm more aware of what is going on since I'm uncomfortable and feel like I don't belong.

Ashley asks Kaitlin to reverse her learned habit of being *un*-observant about race, encouraging Kaitlin to use her discomfort as a resource for heightening her powers of observation. Ashley marks discomfort as an opportunity for better vision. Kaitlin does revise this piece slightly—emphasizing the shock of realizing the proximity of communities of color to the community where she grew up—when she selects it to perform as her Spoken Word for the class. She adds this brief reflection: "The most shocking part for me was that I wasn't even that far away from home. . . . I was only a few towns over and I was shocked at how the composition of the towns changed within miles of each other." She compares this startling revelation to her current culture shock as a freshman at St. John's, the first integrated space where she has spent time.

> Thus having seen what a few miles difference could expose me to in terms of race and the people around me, imagine what the over twenty mile drive that I do every day in order to get to school exposes me to. Every day, I feel as though I cross those invisible barriers temporarily, not just at school, but also going from town to town. It has helped me to realize that there was a life and a society that is outside of my own and I know that the older I get, the more I will be forced out of my comfort zone and really embrace the world around me.

Kaitlin describes her discomfort crossing the boundaries surrounding hypersegregated white spaces and suggests that her growing ability to handle these crossings is part of growing older. However, she completes these assignments without analyzing either her inability to see the people of color around her, or a sense of why her life is so segregated. While I read Kaitlin's early instruction in a tolerant brand of colorblindness by her mother as a shaping force in her current inability to see people of color clearly, it is unclear whether she is defending the "tolerance" of her early instruction, exploring the colorblindness it has created, or both. However, it does seem that Ashley's narrative has inspired her to focus on her mother's role in forming her attitudes toward people of color.

At the same time that Kaitlin wrote "Out of my Realm" for Ashley to read, Ashley wrote her "Race and Space Essay" titled "Where the Black

People Are" for Kaitlin to read, describing her small-town New England neighborhood. Ashley opens with the same ironic presentation of white uniformity used by white students describing white neighborhoods but continually reflects on the ways that whiteness impacts her family, as the "only black family" in that community.

> Our neighborhood consists of the pharmacist, police officer, landscapers, bankers and parents of lawyers. The population is 99.9% white then there's us. Yup, you read that right we are the only black family in the neighborhood. When I tell people that they say "Damn, you must live in a nice neighborhood." Microaggression much? We have some nice houses but they aren't million dollar mansions with butlers and maids. I live in a normal suburban neighborhood with white picket fences and families with 2.5 children.

Ashley leans even harder into the ironies of white suburban life that Chris and Maja employ in their writing. Labeling the response that a "99.9% white" neighborhood must be "nice" as a "microaggression" disrupts both the racial wealth gap and assumptions that her proximity to white people makes her rich. In addition, she disrupts neighborhood "normalcy" itself. Her use of "white picket fences" sounds racial in this context, and "2.5 children" sounds strangely disembodied. Leading with her own race enables her to throw the whiteness of her neighbors into more relief.

Ashley uses two different modes to represent her racially isolated white neighbors, and her family's treatment by them. First, she minimizes the danger she faces due to white hostility in descriptions such as that that of her older neighbor, whose more obvious racism she codes as a concern over "safety" and "security," much like Kaitlin describes her neighbors vigilant behavior towards "outside threats." Ashley identifies his concern over "security" as racially coded, but also discounts the threat he represents:

> On the right side is a sweet old man who is stuck in the "olden" days but he's our little "security guard" who isn't afraid of anything and won't hesitate to ask someone why he or she is on the street when they don't belong. He always makes sure that my family and I are safe. His wife who died a couple years ago was the sweetest woman you ever met and would always keep him in line. When we moved many years ago, she even told my parents where the best schools were located and started us in the right direction.

She minimizes her neighbor's racism, depicting it as dying out with her dying neighbors and enclosing euphemistic prejudices in quotation marks: "'Olden' days," "'security guard.'" She does not deny the reality of her elderly neighbor's views, but she describes them as historical liabilities, almost as an affliction of old age. Further, she offers the image of her neighbor's deceased wife struggling to "keep him in line" so that his current antics are actually signs of his loss. Ashley appears to domesticate this man and shrink him down to a size she can deal with. The image of a rogue "security guard" with ideas from the "olden days," keeping track of all the comings and goings in a suburban neighborhood post–Trayvon Martin and George Zimmerman could actually be fairly terrifying, but she brackets off those fears from her representational frame in offering it to the class.

The trope of the older racist white neighbor or family member (usually in the writer's grandparent's generation but sometimes in their parent's generation) that Ashley invokes here appears in several other students' descriptions of their majority-white neighborhoods. A white student from a small New England town described her older neighbor complaining to her mother about people of color moving in with the euphemism "the neighborhood is changing." Although her mother is unsympathetic to the neighbor's views, she remains silent. Another writer describes his white father's anger at new Asian neighbors in a majority-white neighborhood in Queens. Having been hit by another car in a neighborhood fender bender, the writer's father steps out fuming at "Asian drivers," then changes his tone when he sees the person who hit him is another white neighbor. The drivers share a laugh, then amicably work out a plan for addressing their accident. Several other students write about moments like this: an older white neighbor accuses Latinx workers of stealing a basketball hoop, and the thief turns out to be white; an Indian American student, whose family moves into an otherwise welcoming white neighborhood, is harassed by the older white woman next door who shatters their glass doorbell and leaves the shards on their front porch. By acknowledging racism in white neighborhoods but only in the views and actions of older people, student writers simultaneously acknowledge and sideline white racism, making it a problem that is on the way to solving itself. This trope's elastic ability to at once expose racism and displace it onto the receding "past" is a hallmark of the logic of colorblind racism, as analyzed by Bonilla-Silva.

In contrast to these descriptions of white behavior that read as potentially "postracial," Ashley's narrative also describes the impact of a more subtle form of hostility as her family moves around their neighborhood. Her description makes this behavior appear much more threatening.

> We often get those stares where you can see them peek through the corner of their eye. Their eyebrows scrunch together and their smiles wipe off their faces. Some stares would make your hairs stand up and chills run

down your back especially if you were a young girl like I was. Sometimes we would even see them turn around and walk back in their house if they saw us coming.

In this passage, Ashley strikes a very different note from her indulgence of an older neighbors' residual racism. Furtive looks, from neighbors and strangers alike, cause her physical fear. This undercurrent of fear and hostility belies apparently congenial neighborly dynamics, revealing tensions and prejudices that can easily remain invisible to white people such as Kaitlin who inhabit the same white landscape but have been trained not to see exactly these moments. Kaitlin has a carefully cultivated blind spot when people of color appear in her frame of vision. In fact, it's possible Kaitlin would make precisely the faces that frighten Ashley, given her self-described difficulty seeing people of color.

In contrast to Kaitlin, Ashley describes how she has developed a necessarily hyperaware vision, honed through her neighbor's constant low-level targeting and occasional outbursts of explicit racism. Both writers identify silent moments of tension when white people look at people of color on a largely white landscape, much of which occurs without actually naming race.

Against this backdrop of silent racial fear and hostility, Ashley and Kaitlin both make moves toward racial vision, and they respond to each other's stories in modes that endorse such vision. What they both describe throughout is a racial geography saturated with white people's racial isolation and attention to the symptoms of that separation—silence, confusion, and perpetuation of racist ideas promoted and left unchallenged in hypersegregated white communities.

When initially asked about their personal experiences with race, Kaitlin and Ashley narrated dramatic moments when they were confronted with long-standing, deep-seated racist ideas held by people around them, that they were not expecting. When asked about their neighborhood experiences with race, they talked about much smaller, incremental experiences with race—ideas and attitudes accrued through multiple, daily contact and sedimented into their consciousnesses. Both describe the harm of white hypersegregation. Kaitlin's classmates alarm her with their prejudices, and she then alarms herself with her own lack of knowledge to combat them. Ashley describes the daily stress and unpredictable crises of being surrounded by white people whose prejudices are largely silent.

Ashley and Kaitlin use the opportunity for a cross-racial exchange of stories about the impact of living in a hypersegregated white landscape to explore the ways colorblind racism works: the quiet ways that racial vision is curtailed, racial prejudices are sustained on mute, and intermittent eruptions of deeply rooted racism seem to arise from nowhere. This portrait of colorblind racism raises questions and offers some potential for change based on the critical distance enabled by naming a phenomenon.

While these students created meaningful, mutually informative portraits of the harm of colorblindness in white communities, their takeaways were different, and tentative. Kaitlin vowed to be more aware of the world around her, to see more. Ashley appeared to ask young white people such as Kaitlin to learn to see race better. While these moves are symmetrical and potentially useful, there was little space in the assignment and their responses to each other to begin making sense of the conditions of extreme segregation under which they both grew up.

Their exchange leaves me with questions about the impact of the racial vision afforded by these writing assignments and in these exchanges. Have these incursions against colorblindness made lasting impressions, or does the elasticity of colorblindness cause it to bounce right back? My most ambitious goal for counterstories is to generate a map away from colorblind racism. On this front, the results were disappointing. What students generated instead was an X-ray of the personal harm done by segregation and the culture of largely unspoken fear and prejudice engendered in highly segregated white neighborhoods. While this activity translated into cross-race agreement that white people need to see race better, and generated some efforts on white students' part in this direction, these peer review exchanges did not result in deeper understandings of the roots of this ongoing segregation. Many students referred to their surprise at the whiteness of their neighborhoods; some explored how white hypersegregation impacted them; but few generated robust explanations for it. They all seemed to take segregation as a natural feature of the racial landscapes where they were raised. In their groups, they observed it without questioning it.

The question going forward is whether student exchanges such as these can do more. Can they help students both with their racial identity development (which seems a readier target) and with their understanding of institutional patterns and structures of racism (which seems harder to achieve)? The following chapter takes up an extended exchange among three students to probe this question further.

Meanwhile, the attitudes fostered in hypersegregated white communities take a much more visceral toll on students of color than on white students. As Kaitlin struggled to see people of color, pushing lightly against her lifetime of colorblind education, Ashley concluded this unit with a

Spoken Word performance that she wrote after her peer exchange with Kaitlin. She asks the questions that this unit of study left unanswered:

Why?

Why do I always notice things that I wasn't looking for? Why did I hear the little girl say, "Mommy, they don't look like monkeys." At that moment in time the whole entire world stopped, I was completely stunned by what I just heard. Why? Why did that nun tighten her purse strings and double check if her car was locked? How are you a child of God, but quick to judge? Why? Why doesn't the neighbor at the end of my street like me? Why? Why did that mother not want her daughter to hold my hand in dance class? Why? I always ask myself these questions. Is it because of the color of my skin or did I just take it the wrong way? I should be mad, furious actually. But no, I am sad for them. No one is born hating another race it is something that is taught. We aren't under Jim Crow laws yet people still have that mentality.

I take Ashley's question "Why?" as a challenge to keep deepening this work. How can an exchange of stories about racial geography promote racial perceptions that lead to productive racial identity development? How can such exchanges fortify students to push past the incitements to turn a colorblind eye to the racial inequities around them and support their efforts to identify, analyze, and debunk those inequities in our classroom and on our campus?

2

"IT'S REAL"
Peer Review and the Problems of Colorblindness and Empathy

This chapter takes a deep dive into an extended peer review exchange among three students in the fall of 2014. It follows them through the process I describe in chapter 1, in which students write about the racial geographies of their lives, share that work with other students, and revise their writing in response to peer feedback. By tracing the ways peer responses impacted students' writing, I interrogate my assignment design's underlying assumption that empathetic cross-racial storytelling can combat colorblindness and promote racial vision. I interrogate this assumption in two ways. First, I seek to understand the ways in which these exchanges did, and did not, transform writers' and readers' understandings of racism and segregation—in particular, how it fostered racial literacy and made inroads into colorblind racism. Second, I hone in on the specific limitations of "empathy" in these exchanges and how those limitations suggest new directions for peer review in my classes.

These three students completed all the assignments I describe in chapter 1. The first, the "Racial Identity Essay," was an account of a single moment that impacted or illuminated their racial identity. The second, the "Race and Space Essay," was a more targeted look at the role of race in their neighborhoods. These two essays are shared with peer reviewers. The third text is a Spoken Word performance developed from pieces of the first two essays and performed for the whole class. (All three assignments are available in full in the appendix.) My primary interest in this chapter is in the second essay, which focuses on racial geography, but I will discuss all three assignments since the work they did there is embedded in this other network of assignments and responses.

This chapter looks in at least as much depth at the writing students did *in response to each other's writing* as it does to the writing to which they responded. I am concerned with what Krista Ratcliffe calls "rhetorical listening" in their responses, that is, a stance of openness to difference, of attunement to experiences, understandings, and orientations with which one is unfamiliar. The goal in both their essays and their responses to

DOI: 10.7330/9781646421107.c002

other students' essays—a goal I share explicitly with students throughout this process—is to write and read well enough to create a crisis in the narrowness of one's own worldview and that of one's readers. I include myself in the audience positioned for transformative understanding through reading and writing. I read each student's description of their particular lived experiences of racial difference and how they respond to the meaning-making of others, as what Stephanie Kerschbaum calls "dynamic, relational, and emergent . . . rhetorical performance" (57). Thus, I expect students, and myself, to make and remake our positions in and on difference as we all write and respond. The chapter's extremely close-up tracing of each student's rhetorical moves allows me to speculate on the ways in which they impact each other and the course.

All three students described growing up in highly segregated communities: Danielle, a student who identifies as half-Black, and moved from Queens to Long Island to discover that segregation was alive and well in what she expected to be an integrated community; Grace, a student who identifies as Chinese American, and moved from Brooklyn's Chinatown to a predominantly white neighborhood in Brooklyn; and Andrea, a student who identifies as white and was raised in a majority-white gated community in a racially mixed town in southern California.

The most provocative element of this group's work together was the way that one student rewrote the rules of peer engagement, challenging my assumption that effective personal storytelling inspires empathy, and asked her peers to confront white racism directly. The ways in which she short-circuited their exchange of stories and analysis provided useful moments in the exchange but also revealed the limits of the exercise itself. Ultimately, this proved a valuable contribution to the growth of the course.

"IT'S REAL . . .": DANIELLE WRITES IN
THE EMOTIONAL IMPERATIVE

Take a minute and let that dissolve.

In the first sign that she would adapt the course's assignments to her own goals, Danielle skipped the racial identity narrative altogether. While that assignment asked students to focus on a personal experience first and to slowly build social vision from it, she jumped right into the social, ignoring individual interactions. She wrote about the racial dynamics of her neighborhood right away in her first essay, without waiting for me to specifically assign that topic in the second essay. Because of this, we decided together that she would revise the essay about her neighborhood as her second assignment, rather than writing a new one, since she had already begun on that topic. I thus frame this account of her writing group's peer review exchanges with her first and second drafts, since she kicked off the discussion of racial geography early.

Danielle spent most of her childhood in a largely Black and Latinx urban neighborhood near our university. However, she writes about moving to a majority-white suburb of the city for her last three years of high school. Despite the fact that the majority of people in her new town were white, her new neighborhood in that town was what she termed "Afro-Latino," due to historical redlining practices in that community and in Long Island more generally.

Ironically, Danielle opens her essay by stating that segregated neighborhoods can promote racial harmony, as she experiences in both her urban and suburban neighborhood where people of color predominated. "When you grow up in a neighborhood where everyone is the same race you don't really have to worry about someone being 'racist.'"

She follows this with a caveat about venturing into spaces where white people live: "When going outside of your neighborhood you can see the difference and sense some sort of racism." While Danielle's new segregated neighborhood felt familiar and comfortable, the segregation of her new high school came as a shock. Knowing the town she had moved to was majority white, despite the lack of white people in her neighborhood, she asked, "'Where are all the white kids?' 'Why are there so many black kids?'" She learns the answer from teachers and students at her high school: "Turns out that all the white people that lived in the area, on the 'white' side, had taken their kids out of the school system. All of the white kids everyone was so worried about were now in private schools. . . . As outrageous as this sounds, these parents took their children out of the school system because there were too many black kids."

Danielle's title "It's Real" testifies to the intensity of her confrontation with white supremacy alive and well, embedded in this community. New in town, but also participating in the situation unfolding around her, she is much less concerned with her own emotional response to this knowledge than that of two other groups: The first group is her readers. She repeatedly conveys to readers the importance of themselves absorbing the difficult reality of what she is describing. For instance, after she reveals that white parents pulled their children from the public school system in her town once it was forcibly integrated, she instructs readers: "Take a minute to let that dissolve."

The second group whose reaction Danielle is concerned about is the group she calls "the white kids everyone is so worried about":

> I thought that stuff like that only happened in movies or down south, but right here in [our state] we have such ignorant people that will pay money to keep their kids away from people of color. Which I think is sick. I feel that people, children especially, should be opened to diversity. What are you teaching your kids? To not feel comfortable around black people, or to not associate themselves with blacks.

Throughout her narratives and peer responses, Danielle wants to understand how segregation impacts the young white people who have been segregated away from people of color, and how they reconcile themselves to this separation, or don't.

"WHAT ARE YOU TEACHING YOUR KIDS?" DANIELLE, ANDREA, AND WHITE RACIAL IDENTITY DEVELOPMENT

I believe this question—"What are you teaching your kids?"—is not merely rhetorical. I see Danielle looking for answers to this question in several places over the course of the semester. She consistently asks Andrea, her white classmate and peer review partner, to elaborate on Andrea's efforts to explain how a young white person forms their ideas about race, particularly as taught to them by white parents. (I will discuss Andrea's narrative itself soon.)

Danielle's comments in the margin amplify Andrea's race-aware stance in Andrea's first essay, "Categorized." In this essay, Andrea alternates between raising questions about her first confrontations with the biological and social fictions of "race"—including the peculiar puzzle of her own whiteness—and a recurring habit of dismissing those reflections in a colorblind intellectual shrug about how we are all part of the "human race." However, if you read only the section of this deeply ambivalent essay highlighted by Danielle, you see a much less equivocal model of a white writer interrogating her position within racial identity and racial injustice.

Nowhere, when Andrea displays colorblind thinking, does Danielle display any interest in her margin comments. Instead, she responds to and asks for more information only in the places in which Andrea articulates her very young struggles to understand racial identity, both her own, as a white person, and also those of people of color. When Andrea makes her strongest statement of awareness of the systemic and historical nature of racism, asserting that "discrimination has become a part of life due to the strong presence of ignorance within society throughout history," Danielle responds in all caps: "THIS IS SO TRUE." She continues: "Society has installed ignorance in people who have passed it on through generations. Discrimination is a part of life that needs to be stopped." Thus her revision takes Andrea's statement of racial injustice—"Discrimination is a part of life"—and turns it into a call for action against such injustice. Danielle reinforces and amplifies Andrea's moves toward color-aware discourse.

Danielle expresses particular curiosity about the process by which Andrea has formed her ideas about race as a white person and asks for more information there. When Andrea sheepishly describes having wondered, at age five, if Latinx people are darker because they fell in the mud, and then says that probably sounds "racist," Danielle responds: "I like how you said that you thought they were the color they are because of the mud. I giggled, but it attracted me because although you didn't mean to be racist it was a racist comment." She neither comforts nor condemns Andrea. Instead, she "giggles," marking this moment as both uncomfortable and important: "[T]hat is going to be the most memorable statement to me from your essay."

A final place that struck me in her feedback is her follow-up question to Andrea: "It made me wonder do all white kids ask [why some people have darker skin than them?] And what is the answer their parents give them?" Danielle uses Andrea's anecdotes to deepen her initial question about the ways that white parents instruct their children about race.

"I CAN RELATE": DANIELLE RESPONDS TO GRACE'S RACIAL IDENTITY ESSAY

In contrast to her feedback to Andrea, Danielle's margin comments to Grace focus on expressing solidarity as people of color who move into majority-white communities during adolescence. Grace quotes racial slurs from white students at her middle school, after attending a racially homogeneous elementary school in Brooklyn's Chinatown. Her new classmates make comments such as "What is that chink doing there?" "Ching chong." "Chow-fun." She then describes how she dealt with those slurs in forming her current attitude toward her racial identity. Danielle writes that Grace's piece

> made me think of my topic in another point of view. I'm sorry that that was something you had to go through during your transition, but it is good that you did. It was an experience that made you realize who you are as a person and made you more confident about who you are and where you came from. . . . I as well grew up in an area where the people were the same race as me, so I can relate.

Danielle finds a commonality here between herself and Grace growing up in racially homogeneous communities of people of color, then being thrown into a mix with hostile white people.

Like Danielle's essay, Grace's text maps the jarring changes of leaving a racially homogeneous community of people of color for a majority-white community. Her Chinese American identity is marked by ease and unselfconsciousness in her elementary school, in which she was in the racial majority: "It was easy for me to wear red on Chinese New Year, easy for me to bring a lunch box packed with all my favorite Chinese dishes, easy for me to exchange little phrases in Chinese with my friends, and most importantly of all, easy for me to walk down the hallways without feeling like I'm the odd one out." In her middle school, where she is in the racial minority, she is targeted by white students' racism and isolated: "I wasn't like them. They don't eat with chopsticks, or drink soup after their meals, or think red is a lucky color. They didn't know of side dishes, just like how I didn't know of dessert. It was just me." In response, she learns to reject anything "Asian"—"No more glasses. No more 'China bangs.' No more chopsticks. No more fish." She identifies this decision as a source of loss: "I changed. And I deeply regret it to this day. I couldn't hold chopsticks the way I used to when I was younger since I've adapted to using the fork and spoon. I couldn't eat fish because I would cringe away from it due to my mentality of being judged as an Asian again." Additionally, she realizes that rejecting her "Asian" identity to protect herself from racism will always fail: "I couldn't change the fact that my parents spoke Chinese at all my parent-teacher conferences. I couldn't change the smell of incense on my shirts and hair every time there's a Chinese holiday. I couldn't change the fact that I think in Chinese almost all the time. And most importantly of all, I couldn't change me." She concludes by asserting that she reclaims her identity as Asian. "No matter how I attempted to alter my appearance, and change how others view me, I knew that I've always been and always will be Asian. And quite frankly today, I am fine with that."

As with her comments on Andrea's draft, Danielle both affirms the value of Grace's struggles to develop a positive racial identity and pushes her to explain her thinking on race more clearly. When Grace asserts that she is reconciled to being "fine" with being Asian, Danielle says: "[I]t takes a matured individual to come to an understanding like that. It's nice that you learned from your experience. You should be comfortable with who you are no matter what anyone else has to say." However, she also pushes her to elaborate: "I was confused as to how you were able to change all of these things? And did it take you long to realize that you were still Asian?" She asks Grace to think harder about both her earlier disavowal of her Asian characteristics and also her lukewarm re-embrace of that part of her identity.

"REMNANTS OF THE ASIAN BUBBLE": VISUAL EFFECTS IN GRACE'S RHETORIC

Am I fond of being Chinese? I guess so.

Because Danielle essentially wrote her "Race and Space Essay" early, both of her group members read her neighborhood piece before writing their own. Before moving on to each of their "Race and Space Essays" to flesh out the range of writing on personal racial geographies that took place after reading hers, I begin my analyses of their writing with their comments on her first draft.

While Danielle's comments offer Grace connection through their shared experiences as people of color either kept apart from whites or put into adversarial relations to them, Grace places her connection with Danielle on very different ground. She repeatedly refers to the strength of Danielle's feelings as the most striking aspect of her work—"I found this essay so emotional and strong at the same time"; "you have very strong feelings about this topic and you show it clearly in your essay." Grace then describes those feelings themselves as her tool for understanding Danielle's experiences. She never mentions or responds to Danielle's assertions of commonality of experience as women of color. "[Y]ou clearly show how you felt and that allowed me to understand how you felt," she writes. In contrast to Danielle's assertions of connection through their shared identities and experiences, Grace maintains a kind of distance on Danielle's writing, despite Danielle's assertions of closeness in their identities and experiences. Refusing to acknowledge any part of Danielle's experience intuitively or through her own experience as a person of color, Grace relies on Danielle's words for understanding. If Danielle's logic is not clear, Grace is able to point it out. This occurs most clearly when Grace questions Danielle's concluding sentences, whose colorblind rhetoric appears to conflict with Danielle's race-aware writing elsewhere.

Danielle writes: "I've always been proud of my race and nationality. I never felt insecure about being half black. I never discriminated against people of a different race than me. I believe that at the end of the day we all bleed the same so skin color means nothing to me." Grace asks, "Do you think race is something we can live without noticing (I'm asking this question only because I think the last sentence of your essay is a very thought-provoking statement)?" Although I can't tell if "thought-provoking" has a negative or positive connotation here, Grace's response points out the incongruity of Danielle's last sentences in the essay in which they appear. They certainly bear the hallmarks of colorblind logic—"We all bleed the same" and later "race means nothing to me." But Danielle's statements of the meaninglessness of race do not seem to mesh with her exposé of present-day racism elsewhere in her piece, as Grace may be suggesting. Nor does this passage ultimately do the usual work of a colorblind conclusion, which makes racial vision / racial awareness / racial categories into the "real" racial problem, rather than racial injustice. Such a postracial disclaimer would cut sharply against Danielle's racial rhetoric elsewhere in her text.

Grace's refusal to identify herself with Danielle's narrative, or to respond to Danielle's assertion of a connection with her as women of color, echoes the distance Grace describes herself experiencing from her own Asian American identity. Her second essay, about her adolescent move from Chinatown to a predominantly white urban neighborhood, expresses multiple conflicting attitudes toward the white and Asian American people in her new neighborhood, including her own family. Her short essay articulates at least three different modes of racial vision, which I read as experiments in seeing race, attempting to discern patterns and changes in her rhetorical stances toward racial identity. I will describe the three modes of seeing in terms of camera lenses in order to capture how I understand them to influence her thinking throughout the piece.

Lens #1: Sepia—Normative Whiteness

First, when discussing her friendly white neighbors, she normalizes and ironizes whiteness, offering cross-racial observations and critiques in an even-handed way as someone who can compare white neighbors to her own experiences of Asian American family and neighborhood life. Grace's opening paragraph asserts, "there is nothing unusual about the block I live on"; there is "nothing uncommon" there; "nothing you can find here that you won't find somewhere else." According to Grace, the only unusual feature of the block is its "lone-standing houses." Perhaps "lone-standing houses" here suggests her family's upwardly mobile move there from the denser architecture of Chinatown.

Grace spends the most descriptive energy in this piece on her immediate neighbors in the new white neighborhood—an "Irish family." They are highly visible and audible to her, always outside in their yard. Their music, barking dogs, nightly basketball games, and regular barbeques bring constant sounds and smells through Grace's window. She describes them as extroverted, unselfconscious and open. Grace is "amazed and curious" at their pets, and those of her other "friendly neighbors who own dogs, and snakes: one even owns a parrot." "Coming from an Asian family," she writes, "I never got into such a close range with all these animals before, and I was amazed and curious. My mother likes to call them 'of the same kind as rodents,' but I love them." In this passage, Grace seems amused and interested in new white habits, while her mother is more dubious. She contrasts the white family's habits to her own family's, and her conclusions seem comfortably even-handed. "Asians do quite a few things differently than the Irish family next door. For one, we don't BBQ every Friday, and another, instead of playing basketball, my brother was trained to study at home almost every day. They play loud Dubstep music when they eat while we prefer to eat in peace." She weighs in on these as relatively innocuous and positive differences, claiming, "[B]eing part of this neighborhood allows me to learn from others who are different from me. I believe that learning from others is the key way to expunging racism." Her light tone and focus on innocuous details of daily life resonate with a colorblind approach to integration as natural, easy, and not a big deal.

Lens #2: Out of Focus—Selective Colorblindness

Undercutting this light-hearted and positive insistence on whiteness as benign normalcy, Grace inserts a layer of unease. In her first paragraph, sandwiched between her claims of "nothing unusual," she describes her block as "eerily quiet." She also describes her move from being "stuck in a predominantly Asian neighborhood" to being one of two Asian families on an otherwise white block as "sort of nerve-racking."

The main embodiment of this "eeriness" is actually another Asian American family in her new neighborhood. Her descriptions of this family undermine her dominant narrative of cultural harmony and suggest a strain of internalized racism. Having described her Irish neighbors at length, she turns her gaze to the other side of her house: "On my other side live Asians, the same kind as I am. They don't care much for anything really, and like to just go about their life the way it is." These neighbors might just be quiet, but her line "they don't care much for anything really" makes a strange and brief companion to her initial descriptor that they are "the same kind as I am."

In a passage where she ostensibly reinforces her message of self-growth through exposure to residential diversity, Grace dramatically contrasts her impressions of her white and Asian neighbors: "Altogether, race in my neighborhood isn't very diverse. However, it still opened me up to new experiences. I came to love the lovely and vibrant music that the

Irish family plays every night, and the delicious smell of BBQ chicken that is blown through my window sills by the autumn chills. Meanwhile, the Asians next door seem dark and sometimes, I even get the feeling that they don't exist." These descriptions undermine her claim that her neighborhood is a place for people to share experiences. Questioning her Asian neighbor's existence may be a way of saying they don't spend much time outside, but it is quite a dramatic way to put it. Why does Grace have trouble describing, even seeing, her Asian neighbors?

Lens #3: Shaky Camera—Race-Aware Discourse = "Playing the 'racist card'"

Grace herself explains how "it's funny how I never noticed" that her own family and their next-door neighbors are "the only Asians on the block" until it was pointed out by her friend, who occupies a space of problematic racial interlocutor in her text, and whose own race she never reveals. "'You know, shouldn't you make friends with the Asians next to you? Asians stick together,'" he goads her. This unnamed friend—whose views she sprinkles throughout the text, deeming them sometimes so racist that she is tempted to "play the 'racist card'"—reads like an import from her first essay, in which she experienced a crisis in her unassimilated Chinese identity when targeted by the racist comments of white middle school classmates. She does not identify this friend by race, but she continues to quote from his off-the-cuff, sometimes bizarre racial essentialisms, such as "Chinese people steal and lie," "I love Koreans," and his assertion that her Asian neighbors don't associate with her because she is "white-washed." He is an unstable source of racial awareness, since his comments always come freighted with racist baggage, or freely shared stereotypes. She describes herself as "in awe" of the things that come out of his mouth. Her friend's pronouncements simultaneously make race visible to her and introduce racist stereotypes into the narrative, an unwieldy rhetorical package.

Her friend's wildcard comments appear to highlight the unresolved dilemma of Grace's first essay—how to forge a positive Chinese racial identity after needing to jettison it in the survivalist assimilation of middle school. Challenged by his loaded comments, Grace began to reflect.

> I started to think about race very intently. I looked at the things that the white people did and the things that our Asian families did and I compared them. There wasn't much diversity where I used to live and there isn't much diversity where I live now. Yet, I feel like I have a whole different perspective of life outside of Asian neighborhoods. In places like Chinatown, where everyone was the same, of course I felt like I blended

in and felt like I was part of the "norm." However, moving to a predominantly white neighborhood showed me that sticking with the "norm" isn't all that great. . . . I hear lots of other things about Asians, particularly the Chinese. Am I fond of being Chinese? I guess so.

This ambivalent passage, coupled with her finding that the "norm" of her childhood was less than great, leaves Grace with plenty of critical insight but little sense of belonging. She appears to be using her considerable powers of observation to forge an image of her white neighbors' benevolent whiteness that she can relate to better than that of her hostile, antagonistic middle school classmates, but this process has dropped some kind of barrier between her and her ominous "Asian" neighbors, who remain largely invisible and silent in this ostensibly benevolent white neighborhood.

Distinguishing herself from her friend's assertion of racial solidarity among Asians, Grace asks herself, "Should I have made myself known to them just because they're the same race as I am?" She decides she should not have. She describes the benefit of "moving to a predominantly white neighborhood," saying it "allowed me to learn and break out of my 'Asian bubble.'" Her goal is to "preserve my culture while realizing the importance of stepping out of your comfort zone to experience new things." Tellingly, Grace uses the first person—"my culture"—then switches to second person—"your comfort zone." This suggests a split in her perspective as she tries to adapt her experience to this assignment. The language of "comfort zone" itself seems to draw from the assignment's language, while the second-person pronoun suggests her distance on that imported term for describing her experience. Such split thinking appears to be occasioned by her attempt to see other Asians in this new space of whiteness.

RESPONDING TO "REMNANTS OF THE 'ASIAN BUBBLE'": ANDREA AND DANIELLE PUSH BACK ON GRACE'S "WHITE-WASHING"

While Andrea and Danielle both offer positive feedback to Grace about her connection with the white family next door, they both also question Grace about her Asian neighbors and her racial identity. Andrea latches onto Grace's most optimistic message of melting pot happiness: "I really admired your interacting with the Irish family because it showed how beautiful it is when cultures are able to integrate peacefully in society even if they do things differently." However, she notes Grace's distance from her "Asian" neighbors: "[E]ven though you are of the same umbrella as the Asian people that live close you still do not identify with them personally" and suggests Grace look at her friend's allegation that Grace has been "white-washed," calling it "an interesting topic for you to investigate in more writings that we will do in this class." Andrea lightly marks this hesitation in the midst of joining Grace in what looks like a celebration of integration on her block as a *fait accompli.*

Danielle's letter to Grace also draws a largely positive racial message from Grace's piece, based on its vision of peaceful integration. She emphasizes her solidarity as another person of color doing the hard work of integrating white communities: "I too started off in a neighborhood with not many other races, everyone was just like me. . . . So I can definitely relate to the changes and adjustments of a new neighborhood. . . . It's people like us that move into diverse communities who are more open with the concept of diversity." She then prods Grace to explore the invisibility of the other family of color on the block, commenting after Grace introduces them: "'On my other side live Asians, the same kind as I am.' I would really enjoy having the honor of knowing what exactly it was you meant by that." When Danielle asks this same question in the margin, Grace responds—one of two moments in this peer review group when a writer responded directly to a margin comment on Google Docs. Although it is easy enough to respond directly to these comments, students generally don't, and I believe it shows a particular investment in the response process when they choose to do so.

Danielle highlights Grace's phrase "Asians, the same kind as I am," and comments, "Hm this is interesting. What kind is that?" Grace replies:

> I'm Asian but specifically, Chinese. My neighbors are also Chinese but they are Hong Kong citizens. I was born here but my parents like to say that I'm a "Hong Kong" person instead of "Chinese" because they are both from Hong Kong. This is because historically, there was a time when Hong Kong was also a part of the UK. Even today, some Hong Kong people (despite them also being Asians) like to think of themselves as part of the English/British. It's like categorizing a race within a race.

This opens a window into the relationship between Grace and her neighbors. On the one hand, her distance from the identity "Chinese" makes more sense. She has been raised to think of herself as Chinese and also not-Chinese, even before she distances herself from being "Chinese" when taunted in middle school and when her parents moved their family from Chinatown. Her parents were born in a Hong Kong that was not part of China until 1997. On the other hand, if her family and her neighbors are both from Hong Kong, and share the legacy of British imperialism as well as US immigration, why does that not create a bond? Danielle's question prompts Grace to explain more connections to her neighbors that might promote solidarity among families of color in a majority-white neighborhood. However, no sense of connection accompanies this revelation that her parents and her neighbors both came from Hong Kong.

GRACE'S REVISION: ASSIMILATION, INVISIBILITY, AND REDEFINING COLORBLINDNESS

In her final piece for the narrative writing unit, a Spoken Word performance in front of the class, Grace revised her first piece for performance. In this revision, Grace explains where the experience has left her: "Just another Asian, they said. She's so good at math because she's Asian, they said. I hate defining myself as an Asian. No, don't get me wrong; I don't hate my own race. I'm angry and frustrated, and maybe I'm just a little disappointed."

In this revision, I see Grace revising the notion of colorblindness to fit her specific experiences. She describes other people as blinded by color in ways that limit her life. It's not her racial identity itself that bothers her. She describes wanting to reclaim that identity, though somewhat ambivalently. Instead, she fears the invisibility that awaits her if she does re-embrace "Asian" attributes. Ultimately, Grace describes being on both ends of colorblindness, in which her neighbors are invisible to her because of their Asian identity, and she has experienced her own invisibility behind the stereotypes people associate with the cluster of behaviors she grew up with, labeled "Chinese." "Race? I feel like race is a barrier, a huge one. One that blinds the people who are different from you. One that's so enormous, it shies you away from taking chances because you're afraid, afraid of being defined as that race instead of who you actually are. And it's hard with the world being this way." She articulates how white students could see only her "Chinese" attributes, not her. However, when she strategically distanced herself from those attributes, she describes a sense of loss. Unable to be seen by whites and be Asian at the same time, she describes experiencing a kind of colorblindness to herself and others, one different than Bonilla-Silva and others theorize. The pressure Grace experiences externally and internally to identify with white normativity may symptomize the pressure on immigrants to value and assume the characteristics of "whiteness," which after all was invented to limit the allocations of the privileges of US citizenship, a practice that continues to this day. (Later in this chapter, I discuss this in greater depth.)

Grace's writing exhibits both fine-grained analysis of her own and her peers' experiences with race, and moments of invisibility and resistance to seeing. To some extent, this strategy allows her to closely observe white normativity while inserting rhetorical distance between herself and other people of color. She thus subtly reframes colorblindness as it impacts her adolescent experiences of assimilation to white culture.

"THE LANDSCAPERS AND THE WALKERS": ANDREA'S RHETORIC OF EMERGENT VISION

Eyes slowly open and I awaken.

In Andrea's first essay, the "Racial Identity Essay," Danielle has asked her to explain how white people develop their attitudes toward race. In her own margin comments to Danielle's first draft, Andrea's questions seem to mirror Danielle's questions to her. Andrea seems specifically interested in Danielle's attitudes toward white people. She asks, "Do you like Queens better or do you like living in Long Island better?" Given the racial geography Danielle has laid out, Andrea seems here to ask Danielle how she feels about being around white people. Given Danielle's consistent expressions of greater comfort with people who share her racial background through all her varied experiences of segregation, these questions make sense. Andrea's questions attempt to bring white people into focus, as viewed through Danielle's lens. Andrea could be said to be trying for a glimpse of whiteness through Danielle's eyes.

One of Andrea's questions causes the second occasion in this peer review exchange when a writer responds directly to a peer comment in her own margin. When Andrea asks, in the margins, "Did the white parents make the argument that [racially integrated schools] wouldn't be safe for their children?" Danielle replies simply, "Yes they did." I think this short sentence echoes Danielle's direct address to readers throughout her piece—"Let that dissolve"; "It's real." She repeats her habit, in her essays themselves, of writing short sentences emphasizing the presence of racism and segregation in the current moment. I take this as Danielle's challenge to Andrea to absorb the information Danielle has recently had to absorb herself about suburban racism. Specifically, Danielle challenges Andrea, her white reader, to face the racial views of white parents who won't send their children to school with Black and Latinx children.

Although my primary interest is Andrea's "Race and Space essay," I will also spend time on her description of her own white racial identity formation in her initial "Racial Identity Narrative Essay" because of the care she took in articulating it, the value Danielle found in responding to it, and my own focus on racial identity development as potentially enabling to these exchanges. Unlike the dark skin of Latinx children, Andrea did not question the physical fact of her own light skin as a child. However, she did puzzle over the cultural meaning of her whiteness. She described being unable to match her whiteness neatly with language, culture, and place until her girl scout troop chose a Dutch theme for a performance, and she believed she finally understood. "I remember this being the most confusing thing ever because in my mind I thought that all black people were African, all Brown people were Mexican, and now all white people were Dutch." When her mother explained that she had no Dutch ancestry but rather had ancestors who are Italian, Irish, and Greek, she could make little sense out of this. Whiteness thus remained blank, a false or absurd category of identity for her, one she uses for comic purposes in her essay.

Andrea appears to be at a tipping point between seeing white privilege as a social problem, and seeing the naming of whiteness as itself a social problem. She concludes her piece by asserting connections across race—"Racism dissolves when you spend time and care about people who are not of the same race." However, this assertion is undermined by the hierarchical nature of the "loving" relationships she has described with Latinx people in her childhood. She cites her relationships with domestic workers in her home; classmates who she asked for help understanding their language; and members of her integrated church youth group, one of whose mothers works for her family. The unexplored hierarchies in what she describes as loving interracial relationships appear to employ colorblind racism's minimization of the role race plays in explaining racial phenomena in a society. Rather than interrogating the contradictions of her own white middle-class identity, Andrea's last word describes racial identity itself as an inherent absurdity or a burden placed on her and other humans, driving them apart: "We can categorize people into almost endless types of groups but we cannot categorize people out of the group human." This phrase encapsulates colorblindness's erasure of racial realities with great efficiency.

This struggle between competing racial logics animates her writing, and in this first essay colorblindness appears to win the day. However, I believe the peer review exchanges she had with Danielle and Grace impact Andrea's precarious placement on the brink of antiracist rhetoric, even as she continues to articulate colorblind doxa.

I believe Andrea's feedback from Danielle on her first essay influences her to articulate the role of race in her home community more clearly. This second essay she shared with the group is titled "The Landscapers and the Walkers." There, she explicitly focuses on white privilege and the Latinx labor that makes possible her affluent lifestyle. Her first line—"Eyes slowly open and I awaken"—celebrates awareness and vision. Andrea then describes a scene of Southern California gated community affluence made possible by immigrant labor:

> The sun beams through the shutters and outside I see neutral colored houses atop of rolling hills. As I look left I see freshly cut grass which shines from the park surrounded by peppertrees. I hear the sound of weed-whackers and lawn mowers from below. I see elderly neighbors taking their morning walk, hispanic men in large straw hats working hard in the yards of my neighbors and on the park, and children walking to the bus stop.

Tellingly, Danielle comments on this opening sentence's celebration of awareness and vision: "This is really a great way to start off your essay. It really pulled me in."

After describing an extremely racially divided neighborhood, Andrea then describes her more integrated church as a complex space of both cultural mingling and division. The congregation featured a Spanish mass as well as an English mass, which created a linguistic and racial divide. "[D]ue to the language chasm there was a segregation between the adults in the church but the teens and children were integrated because we had all gone to the same youth groups and confirmation classes."

The intercultural friendships Andrea asserts between young people is thrown in crisis when her mother hires one of her friend's mothers as a second housekeeper. Furious after walking downstairs one day to find her friend's mother folding clothes in the living room, she describes herself as "sort of confused" and "guilty."

> I thought my mom assumed that since she was Mexican she would hire her to clean our house. I stomped upstairs to my parents' room and said, "Why did you hire Julio's mom to housekeep for us, he's going to think we are a bunch of racists!" My mom giggled and then explained to me that she offered to because she needed some extra money in order to send her third son to college. I felt relieved when she told me this and happy that we could contribute to the education of her son.

"Giggling" has been invoked earlier by Danielle, when she responds to Andrea's childhood theory about Mexicans being covered in mud as "racist." Uncomfortable laughter appears, for both writers, to mark places of discomfort when allegations of racism arise but are then retracted. Andrea's relief at her mother's explanation, and her apparently immediate acceptance of the situation, is undercut by her mother's uncomfortable giggle.

Andrea's essay goes in two directions after this. She unproblematically asserts her new housekeeper's love for her, the affluent child of her new employer: "She loved me so much and always told me that I was beautiful and that she would pray for me. I cherished the moments that I saw her folding laundry or swiffering [Swiffering] the floors because she always had something so positive to say." "Cherishing" and domestic labor make an uncomfortable combination here, one that went unremarked by me or either peer reviewer. Andrea articulates no tension in that relationship, despite the fact that this essay opens with the invisible labor of Latinx landscapers. However, Andrea expresses more discomfort and disappointment when her white family and friends ignore her housekeeper's family at her high school graduation party:

> [T]o be honest I was most excited to see them out of the sixty guests that attended. As I mingled with long-time friends and distant family members I saw the Hernández family secluded and not being interacted with by other guests. It made me really upset because it showed me how my guests weren't willing to converse with them because they were the only hispanic family there. It opened my eyes that even that the people I associate myself closest with act nothing how I would at all.

This passage alternates between colorblind rhetoric—"I wish we lived in a world where race wasn't such a big concept and we could all just mingle freely and not worry about miscommunications or the status quo"—and an ability to apply her local situation to larger contexts. She equates the segregation of her graduation party with the segregation at her church and in her gated community.

> I wished most that my party guests would have interacted with the Hernández family but that was not the reality of the situation that day. That situation deeply hurt me and as I look back it still hurts me because I see that setting in a broader perspective and compare it to how America and how our world works. My community and the world around needs to view their actions regarding race at face value and not view themselves as a segregated community just as the adults at my church act or as the walkers [in the gated community] disregarded the Hispanic Landscapers who worked tirelessly on their own property.

Grace's feedback pushes her to consider her privilege and agency more carefully: "The mentioning of how no one interacted with the Hernández family because they were the only Hispanics there made my heart sink, and I completely understand how you feel. I think that you shouldn't take this to heart, because you know that if you were put back into the same situation today, you would've done differently and possibly introduced them to everyone at the party." Andrea's text had not expressed any guilt or questioned her own role at the party, so Grace's comment is the first place it comes up that she had a role to play in that situation. If Danielle asks Andrea to keep digging into the origins of her white racial identity development, Grace here challenges Andrea to consider her own agency as a white person to act against segregation. Andrea did not respond directly to this specific comment, but I think Grace and Danielle's challenges may both have contributed to Andrea's final Spoken Word, which opened with a revision of her "Race and Space Essay." This final version foregrounds an interrogation of her white privilege in a larger analysis of the racism she observes in others and in herself:

> Am I just white? Am I just a white girl? A white girl existing in a society of ignorance swallowed whole by quicksand that is the fear of black men on the street, Chinese on Canal, women concealed head to toe in garments. At home I see a yellow room, yellow walls, yellow bed, and am awakened by a yellow sky. Pale face residents flaunt their ethnocentricism taking walks with their pure-breds, driving their beamers and benzs to their private schooling, participating in their frivolous social affairs within this gated community. While there are migrant workers anonymous by straw hats and tirelessly cultivating the appearance of this shallow environment of geometric shrubbery and sharply cut grass. While these workers go unnoticed.

Over the course of rewriting and revising, Andrea intensifies the rhetoric aimed at showing the landscape of her childhood as one shaped by racial and economic inequality, something Danielle and Grace's comments may have helped her to see. Further, Andrea appears to be scrutinizing her own role as a "white girl" in this landscape. Three features of this final Spoken Word piece provide clues about how she engages that struggle. First of all, her attempt to remap her world, most notably symbolized by her assertion that she has moved to New York "honestly attempting to shatter the previous sphere of ignorance," leads this final piece to maintain a bird's-eye view on the racial landscape she inhabits. Other than her opening, contrasting what she sees on the street in New York with what she sees out her bedroom window at home, her perspective stays global. She describes the segregation of water and land by imagining the United States as seen through Google Maps: "The view from Google Maps even identifies this as an unjust microcosm engulfed in obtuse speculation. Yet we are all of the same geographic compass. Sun beams overhead, the great Pacific crashes on the shore to the west. Just as the coast is separated by the inland so are we." This passage strikes me as productively incoherent. I read vestiges of colorblind logic here— "segregation" between water and land could point at the arbitrariness of "naming race," or a way of dehistoricizing difference. However, she could be looking at the global landscape as fundamentally segregated as her vision shifts to see race better. The cry for unity suggesting that we are all really unified, "of the same geographic compass," echoes her earlier assertions that racial divisions keep people apart, rather than race-based laws. However, it could also point to the social construction of race. The huge geographic scale of her landscape, and the stormy vocabulary she uses, suggest to me that she is bashing her thinking against the limits of what she can see. Her bird's-eye view may also preserve some distance for her as a white writer trying to articulate a manifesto about race.

She returns to interrogating her white privilege later in the performance, listing the messages she has received as a white person, and trying to imagine a fitting response:

> I am told I don't need to worry about my financial future, I am told that I am bound to be stable nonetheless, I am told that I am admitted to the peak of the food chain, I am told that the person I am is reflected by my skin tone. Society embeds this in us with a deafening scream of this stereotypical thinking. I don't want to scream back, I want to solve this with graceful understanding.

In order to imagine a response, she returns to metaphor, portraying herself as one kind of paint on the canvas of humanity. This extended attempt to capture an aesthetic image to express her proper place in an interracial national community captures the crisis that appears to be occurring in both her racial identity development and her racial vision. Her metaphor aspires toward ease and harmony. She rejects a fundamentally unblendable "oil and water palette . . . categorized in the culture of the same paint" for "effortlessly blended" watercolors, where she could "softly and smoothly fuse —— with bountiful other paints in an honest attempt to generate unity." She wants to be part of the composition of an "exquisite image of pure humanity."

In the paragraph in which she describes this aesthetic ideal of white people blending with people of color as paint, Andrea uses the word "honest" three times—twice in the phrase "honest attempt," and once in the phrase "in all honesty." It is a striking term here in its repetition, and tempts me to speculate that it betrays a kind of discomfort that also causes her imagery to continually threaten to unravel. She uses the word again in her final portfolio when she asserts that she has matured as a writer through writing about difficult topics: "I am confident in knowing that I have become a more impressive writer this semester because of the spark and honesty I put into all of my work despite the intensity of what the instructor has asked us to discuss through words."

The fact that discomfort and incoherence surface in Andrea's prose late in the semester strikes me as a good sign. There is a dizziness in reading her attempt to reframe her worldview. It is not certain where she is headed. But a necessary disintegration to her previous racial vision appears to be underway. In her final portfolio, she identifies the act of reflecting on her early experiences with race as a deliberate "metaphor for growing up." She has set herself a potential path for further growth and clearer vision through writing. Contending with race and "growing up" are parallel activities for Andrea.

"IT'S REALER": DANIELLE REVISES AND TURNS UP THE EMOTIONAL IMPERATIVE

It's sort of like you're watching one of those old documentaries on the civil rights movement, and you're just in utter disbelief that something like this happened. But this isn't a documentary or movie where you act the parts out. This is real life. 2014 raw and unedited.

I conclude with Danielle's revisions to her first "Race and Space Essay." Her second draft contains her research findings—mostly, but not exclusively, from a source we found together online during one of her writing conferences (Singer, *Civil Rights Movement on Long Island*). In addition to this source, I believe she also responds to Grace's question about her first draft's colorblind conclusion and to Andrea's desire to understand white parents' motivation in keeping their children out of the town's public schools after they were integrated.

When revising, Danielle added new sections, rather than discrete line-edits. This section appears early in the revised essay. I have removed specific references to her town.

> I noticed the racism in school when people and teachers began to fill me in. Being new to the school and neighborhood I had a lot to learn. First off taking things back decades prior; my school was an all-white school. [The current] library, on my side, was the "black" high school whereas my school was an all-white school. The town was completely segregated. The demographic differences between [my side of town] and [the other side of town] date from the 1950s when middle class black families were "redlined" by banks and mortgage companies. It was to the point where Dr. Martin Luther King Jr. marched in front of my school. The [town] area and school district have had a racial history since the 1920s. According to [a local paper] (March 1925), ——, a [local] farmer and real estate developer, was grand kleagle of the —— chapter of the Ku Klux Klan. Yes you read that right, and he was a leading state level Klan official. Much of that history is told in an online curriculum guide *The Civil Rights Movement on Long Island*.

The history of white resistance to school integration that Danielle describes here was typical on Long Island and across the nation during Civil Rights–Era mandatory integration, even though it arrived late and did not last long in New York State. Reverting to "back in the day" stories could fit into a colorblind logic that would say these problems existed in the past but not anymore. In fact, Danielle mentions that we all expect to have moved past this kind of segregation. Coming from Queens as a teenager, she herself couldn't believe it "was real." Instead of relegating such segregation to the historical past, however, she uses this history to amplify the shock of present-day racial segregation in her new town.

Danielle's second draft describes a 2011 lawsuit by Black teachers and students in her school district, quoting in particular a white parent's response to this legal action quoted in the *Long Island Herald*. The parent writes, "'This is EXACTLY the reason that a large number of white parents in the district would prefer to send their children to private schools. . . . The racial garbage that the —— community brings to the schools interferes with providing children with a good, solid, learning environment'" (Landor). Danielle's revisions—perhaps in response to Andrea's question about white parents—place the racist views of white parents in their own mouths in the present day.

Andrea and Grace both comment on these revisions as places that reinforce their understanding of Danielle's community. Andrea writes: "This is now why I understand the great separation of white and black people in your environment." Grace replies to the "racial garbage" quote: "These quotes allowed me to understand how you felt at the time. No one should be targeted because of their skin color and I think that because of these direct quotes, your strong emotions about this topic got through to me as the reader." Andrea's comments indicate an increased understanding of the reality Danielle is telling her group about. She no longer questions white parents' motivation in removing their children from school with Black children. Instead, she is able to reflect back her understanding to Danielle and to question the larger implications of seeing what's happening in this one town: "I like how you provided the rich history of where you live because it gives me a lot of insight why your town is like this. Is it segregated like this a lot on Long Island or really only the part where you live?" Andrea's search for a larger map of racial vision, evident in her own late-semester writing, appears here to be in sync with Danielle's message confronting readers with the geography and history of racism in her community.

Danielle's moment of colorblindness in her first draft's conclusion disappears in her second. Her new ending returns to emphasizing the "realness" of what she describes. "I hate to say this but the white people and racism around my neighborhood is real." Danielle directly invites readers, as she puts it, to "look more into the racism and background of my school." She wants readers to face what is happening, as she had to face it three years earlier. "When you look . . . you will see," she commands and predicts. She also ironizes the lack of progress since the Civil Rights Movement. The same "little kids holding signs about stopping segregation" in "old pictures back from in the day" are now sending their children to her high school, which has been abandoned by the whites who were keeping them out. She interrupts Civil Rights nostalgia for the ease of condemning black-and-white photos of white people holding up white supremacist slogans on signs, and challenges readers to absorb the failures of integration. She directly challenges the color-blind truism that racism is a thing of the past and acknowledges the difficulty that colorblind readers will have in accepting what she is saying.

Danielle is potentially rewiring the empathetic equation that I attempted to calculate in this peer review assignment. My assignment asks them to "focus on helping your peers understand how they can tell their stories so that you can step inside their experiences," (see appendix) and the peer review assignment asks readers to describe places where they felt themselves move "inside" of the writer's experience and to comment on places where they could not make that move. The assumption behind this model is that writing can create an emotional echo for readers that breaks down barriers between readers and writers. A problematic corollary assumption in the assignment became evident to me when I spent time analyzing Danielle's response in particular. That is my assumption that students raised on different sides of segregation lines can break down these barriers by hearing each other's stories and to some extent "entering" each other's stories. My problematic demand that students cross lines in a story while those lines remain intact in their lives ignores the very different stakes of students' experiences with segregation. In particular, the white-dominated spaces these students describe navigating are not so different from the white-dominated space of our institution, or our class. The student body of the class, and the exchange, was not majority white, but I was a white woman in charge of that space, and being asked by a white woman to "share" the (very recent) experience of experiencing white domination is a wildly different undertaking for someone such as Danielle, who has been directly targeted by a white-dominated community, than it is for someone such as Andrea, who's been buoyed by white privilege she's just starting to see, or someone like Grace, who's alternately targeted and welcomed in white-dominated spaces, leaving her in an ambivalent, insecure position. As I read and reread Danielle's response to this story, I began to see a "racial liberalism" in my assignment that was not previously evident to me. I also saw Danielle develop a unique set of strategies to negotiate the demands and assumptions of the assignment.

Danielle's rhetorical strategy to respond to my call for telling stories with emotional impact on peer reviewers—which I am calling "the emotional imperative"—is very direct. She (1) presents the alarming facts she faced when confronted with this reality, (2) acknowledges that her reader will likely share her initial disbelief that such active school segregation could be ongoing in 2014, and (3) asks her audience to take it in and accept this reality. Instead of depicting her own emotions—which requires a level of vulnerability that could be quite undesirable in this uncertain context—and asking readers to empathize with them through the power of her description, Danielle uses the facts of her situation to offer readers *their own* direct emotional reaction. This is a huge challenge she offers to Andrea and Grace as her peer reviewers, and they both struggle significantly with that challenge.

Further than this local demand of her readers, I believe Danielle may have been rewiring the empathetic reading relation I asked for in this series of assignments. Her narrative and her revision spend much less energy on her own emotional journey than on that of her reader. Following her directions requires becoming outraged, and both Andrea and Grace stop short at taking on the outrage that Danielle's testimony demands. They do not fully heed her emotional imperative.

Although Andrea does grasp the implications of Danielle's piece, she does not succeed at the emotional transfer Danielle requests. She continues to hold up the emotions and thoughts in the piece as Danielle's. "*You* are fed up"; "*You* strongly believe"; "*You* have a strong-willed essay" (emphasis mine). Even when writing about her own response, Andrea does not identify herself. "*Your* point came across very clearly," she writes, avoiding any direct references to herself, and making Danielle's point itself the subject of the sentence. While Danielle rewires the assignment to call for a more direct acknowledgment of unabated systemic racism, Andrea actually uses the rules of my assignment—which creates a kind of buffering among feelings of readers and writers—to deflect the direct rhetorical impact of what Danielle is adapting the essay to do. Instead of using narrative as a vehicle for her own racial insight and action, Andrea asks Danielle to return to a narrative mode and explore the implications of her town's systemic racism for Danielle's individual relationships with white people, as in this passage from her comments:

I would have liked to know a little bit more about what it was like with more detailed imagery in the essay. I feel that you strongly believe that white people should not be trying to make themselves seem better than black because of the history between whites and blacks. Did you hang out with mainly African-American people because of this separation? If the answer is yes, how often did you interact with white people from where you live and how do they normally treat you and how does it make you feel?

She remains invested in focusing on Danielle's emotional response, and her relationships with white people, whereas Danielle attempts to catalyze a reader response. Danielle, whose essay does not tell a single story of interacting with a white person—or anyone, really—in any revision of this essay, is not concerned with the impact of school segregation on her feelings or her relationships with white people. Or, to be clear, she alludes to being harmed by daily microaggressions in her interactions with whites, but she doesn't appear interested in writing about that. She is much more concerned with the fact that white families are keeping her, and other young Black and Latinx people, apart from young white people in her town's public high school. Her concern is institutional and systemic, not interpersonal. Andrea accepts the incremental approach of the assignment's design and urges Danielle to reenter the frame of narrative, the power of description, the vehicle of Danielle's own emotion, rather than complete the emotional transfer that Danielle commands in the emotional imperative. Danielle appears to short-circuit the vicarious emotional equation of the assignment sequence—its investment in "empathy"—while Andrea embraces it.

Even more than Andrea, Grace appears to resist Danielle's "emotional imperative." Grace balks at the new, more radical ending in Danielle's second draft and at her new, more radical way of viewing history. In her response to draft 2, Grace asks: "this piece brings racial problems to a whole new level. I was never exposed to such an environment as you were, and I'm glad you wrote about it because now I feel like I would be feeling the same way you are feeling if I were in your shoes." She even voices a flicker of identification about being a person of color in a white school, writing, "I understand the 'nasty looks' that were given and how it feels like to be an 'opposite,'" and condemns the situation:

You put so much emphasis on the fact that people are paying to keep white kids away from the black kids, and that this is wrong. I think this is terrible and that it prevents society from moving forward and taking its course naturally. We can't have all these small neighborhoods where only one racial group is located; we should all be able to live as neighbors no matter the race or skin color.

However, Grace resists two elements of Danielle's narrative: first, Danielle's interruption of a historical narrative in which racism naturally disappears. Grace's tone changes as Danielle moves from historical to present-day racism. Early on, she comments, "I like how you included history: how it was back then compared to now." As Danielle moves to the present, however—"These white parents paid money to keep their kids away from black kids"—Grace responds, "This is a very acute observation, and a highly controversial one." In the same spot, Grace asks, rather than agreeing, "Do you think this is the main reason that there are no white kids in your school?" Unlike Andrea, who questions and subsequently accepts Danielle's assertion that white racism is keeping her town's school segregated, Grace leaves her questions hanging.

In addition, Grace describes discomfort with Danielle's expressions of outrage and disbelief in her second draft. While she finds the piece "amazing" and "emotionally written" (much like Andrea's ambivalent descriptions of Danielle's emotions as "fed up," "passionate," and "strong-willed"), Grace's identification of "rage" in Danielle's second draft does not translate into her own rage. Instead, she admonishes Danielle not to "fight fire with fire." What is notable about Grace's emphasis on Danielle's increased—and, as Grace describes them, even dangerous—emotions in this draft, is the *lack* of emotional description in both of Danielle's drafts. The second draft does differ from the first, adding two new elements: first, more explanation of the virulence of white racism in her town, as well its long and ongoing history in that community; second, a harder focus on her readers' responsibilities to "let [her story] dissolve" in their consciousness. A telling example of this amplification of information and confrontation is her revision of her title, from "It's Real" to simply "It's Realer." Danielle abandons any engagement with colorblind rhetoric in her second draft's conclusion, perhaps spurred to do so by Grace's comment on the incongruity of that line in her first draft.

A reader following Danielle's directions will face white racism as she has experienced it. Danielle strengthens her insistence that readers "look at," "see," and acknowledge that this "unbelievable" situation is "real." The greater emotional intensity that Grace perceives may actually reflect Danielle's great emphasis on reader's obligation to push past their disbelief about contemporary housing and school segregation and acknowledge it, directly instructing readers to experience outrage and shock at her account.

Grace, who noted Danielle's brief moment of colorblind rhetoric in her first piece, appears uncomfortable with the implications of Danielle's experience. Instead of seeing this community as indicative of more widespread patterns of segregation, as Andrea appears to begin doing, she encourages Danielle to work locally to clean up this problem in her community, so that progress can continue elsewhere unabated: "I'm interested in learning more about your neighborhood, and how you take an active role in helping your neighborhood rid itself of these racial problems that are overtaking what's really important, the generations that are following us. Do you think there's a chance that things will change for the better?"

This uncharacteristically directive final response from Grace suggests that she is struggling to honor the need for an intervention in the unacceptable situation Danielle has described. She appears to feel the need to propose a solution, since Danielle "bring[s] racial problems to a whole new level" for her. Local inoculation of the problem and keeping one's eye not on a racist present, but a postracial future, are the first weapons in her arsenal. Despite explaining in the first person that "I would be feeling the same way you are feeling if I were in your shoes," Grace brackets those feelings and shuts down the larger implications of Danielle's narrative, refusing to explore the ways in which she may be in similar shoes herself, which would undercut her apparent investment in narratives of racial progress.

"COUNTERCLOCKWISE"—THE LIMITS OF RACIAL VISION AND THE NEW CIVIL RIGHTS MOVEMENT

To return to my original goals for this pedagogical experiment, where did it succeed in countering racial isolation and colorblindness in an era of resegregation? Where did it fall short? It does appear to have provided "meaningful opportunities for cross-racial contact," which Beverly Daniel Tatum calls for in the context of resegregating schools. The exchange does also seem to have troubled colorblind vision, as students grappled with visual crises that may point to the fissures in colorblindness that I had hoped to occasion.

Despite significant challenges to their practices of colorblind racism, Andrea and Grace never fully embrace the antiracist vision and emotion that Danielle endorses. It is important to acknowledge their (very different) investments in white privilege and how those investments appear to motivate Andrea and Grace's attachments to marking whiteness as redeemable, even when confronted by individual and structural acts of racism by white people.

Whiteness, like any "racial project," functions in two ways. It is "simultaneously an interpretation, representation, or explanation of racial dynamics, and an effort to reorganize and redistribute resources along particular racial lines" (Omi and Winant 56). More specifically, in the United States, whiteness has been used to limit the access of people of color to economic opportunity, material wealth, and civic and legal rights: Indeed, whiteness has been linked to virtually every aspect of civic life, including citizenship (Haney-Lopez; Jacobson), voting franchise, property ownership (Harris; Lipsitz, *Possessive Investment*), wage labor (Roediger), and literacy (Prendergast). Even today, when many of the formal, legal privileges granted to whiteness throughout the eighteenth, nineteenth, and early twentieth centuries have been dismantled, whites continue to benefit from their racial position: on average, white families have roughly thirteen times the wealth of Black families and ten times the wealth of Latinx families.[1] One much-discussed historical trend through which whiteness maintains its gatekeeping function over basic rights in the United States has been what Bonilla-Silva calls its "malleability and porosity," through which selected groups of European immigrants (e.g., Italians, Jews, Irish) have been deemed "white" as part of a process of assimilating into "American" culture, and gained subsequent benefits (196). Bonilla-Silva describes the ways that twenty-first century whiteness's "malleability and porosity" continues to promise assimilation to groups of color with perceived "epidermic capital" so that Latinx and Asian Americans, in particular, are encouraged to buy into anti-Black policies and attitudes to cement their positions of "honorary white" privilege. He warns that a highly stratified racial hierarchy is likely to develop even as the country becomes majority people of color by mid-century (178). Through US history, the benefits that accrue to whiteness, and white people, have been secured by the refusal of whites to acknowledge that whiteness is in fact a racial identity, never mind a project of racial dominance. Thus, both Andrea and Grace, one white and the other in a position to benefit from quasi-white status, have a lot to lose by seeing the racial picture painted for them by Danielle, which asks them to interrogate the racial privileges they take for granted.

Ultimately, neither of them takes up Danielle's challenge to name and challenge systemic white privilege or endemic resegregation. Thus, the empathetic charge of this assignment met significant obstacles. Instead, they both end this series of writing assignments by grappling with rhetorics of visuality, problematizing how to see and how to be seen. This problematizing of vision is at once productive and evasive. In her final portfolio for the course, Grace offers this metaphor for understanding her own shifting vision on race in her life and neighborhood throughout the semester.

> Writing about race and language and breaking these two broad topics down to my own backyard made me decide that telescope is a perfect title to sum up all my pieces. It's so broad, yet it can be so specific. . . . This semester's writing course brought things that seemed so far away right in front of my eyes, and I knew that all of these aspects of my writing and of the world were always there; just something or someone has to open my eyes and bring it to a closer distance, very much like a telescope.

This image goes a long way in explaining the uneven stances Grace has assumed toward the role of race in her life throughout her writing. The self-described interplay of distance and proximity in her acknowledgment of the role of race in her life and community suggest her ongoing investment in trying to look. She ultimately shuts down Danielle's emotional imperative to acknowledge the "counterclockwise" direction of race relations in the twenty-first century, instead clinging to an investment in a colorblind racial progress narrative. However, Grace continues to rhetorically unpack small moments of racism and the psychological complexity of both racism and internalized racism. She can focus on race in extreme close-up, but when the lens pulls back to a global view, she balks at more systemic vision.

In contrast, Andrea's final portfolio statement consistently asks questions that will help her expand her racial picture of the world. Her desire to arrive at an aesthetic that can gracefully integrate white people into a multiracial fabric pushes back against the hypersegregated reality of her childhood and adolescence. Grace's dissociative telescope and Andrea's anxious palette of global abstraction both depict seeing racial geography as a troubling work in progress. Both students end the semester with paradoxical metaphors of racial vision.

While Andrea and Grace ended the semester grappling with intermittent sightlines on the entrenched racial segregation surrounding them, Danielle situated her final portfolio statement in the context of the emergent Black Lives Matter movement. When Darren Wilson's nonindictment for killing Michael Brown was announced on November 24, 2014, this class had one meeting left. Beyond an informal conversation in that final class, there was little opportunity to address this news in the context of the work we did that semester. However, Danielle's final portfolio reflection letter, written the following week, did connect her experience to Michael Brown's. Danielle titled her portfolio "Counterclockwise," explaining, "[A] clock usually ticks to the right, going all the way around. Well what if it went counterclockwise to bring time back, or if we can view past experiences and review and revise our lives." Revision, in this view, may be more cyclical than hopeful. Danielle wrote:

There are people in this country who just do NOT believe in DIVERSITY or CHANGE. Not everyone may be a witness to it but racism is ALIVE AND WELL. It doesn't seem like it's going anywhere. Racist white people hate the image of black children and white children going to school together. This is 2014. An entirely new generation, why is racism still an item? The crazy thing is people who do not witness it do not even realize that it still exists. The only time racism is made aware is when Black men are killed by white men or when altercations happen between blacks and whites. Well what about the silent crimes, that not do not get broadcasted all over the news and social media? Are those not as important because no one has died? . . . I tell of a story of discrimination at its best. No, no one was hurt or killed but the principle is spirits are killed, emotions are shot, and feelings are hurt. To live in a neighborhood with so much racial discrimination constantly going on is like living in an old civil rights era film.

Danielle combines her experience of unabated residential and school segregation and Darren Wilson's impunity for killing Michael Brown to suggest that no progress has been made against systemic racism. Echoing Michael Brown's mother, Lezley McSpadden, she implies things may actually be worse now, since the educational opportunities of high school graduates raised under mandatory integration twenty or more years ago were actually broader than that of high school graduates in 2014, before white divestment from those integrated schools began.

The Black Lives Matter movement, catalyzed by murders such as those of Brown and Trayvon Martin (and both preceded and succeeded by a flood of names terrifying in its length) looks strikingly like the "new civil rights movement" Bonilla-Silva originally called for in 2003 to combat the ideological stranglehold of colorblind racism in a resegregating nation, as he describes it here: "What is needed to slay modern-day racism is a new, in-your-face, fight-the-power civil rights movement, a new movement to spark change, to challenge not just color-blind whites but also minority folks who have become content with the crumbs they receive from past struggles" (268). While what happened in my class is a far cry from this collective, widespread movement, Bonilla-Silva's passage does describe what was happening across the country during that semester. When students arrived on campus in January 2015, only a month after this class ended, several of them had attended Black Lives Matter protests, and by the following fall semester, several students identified as Black Lives Matter activists, something unthinkable in this fall 2014 group, who could only identify Civil Rights activism as the work of a previous generation.

The assumption underlying my assignment—that seeing racial inequities in another student's life would stimulate an empathetic

reaction—caused me to underestimate two barriers to the transformative understanding I hope to inspire. First, while each story had the
potential to inspire deeper understandings of racism, colorblind explanations also abound for each of the experiences students wrote about.
Second, feeling bad about racism does not necessarily lead white people
to name or fight racism but can often inspire them to fight the forces
making them feel bad. Robin DiAngelo describes this dynamic of white
people's emotional resistance to the naming of racism, rather than racism itself, as "white fragility."

Empathy may set students on a path toward racial vision, but it
appears insufficient for helping students assume an antiracist stance. My
students' work does demonstrate that colorblind racism can be eroded
through reading and writing one's racial geography and those of others.
However, sharpening one's ability to describe racial dynamics appears to
be only the first of several steps necessary for embracing a more systemic
view of racial inequality. Andrea and Grace both combine counterstories
about racial experiences with colorblind stories they've received all their
lives, leaving them suspended, at the conclusion of this unit, between
racial colorblindness and racial vision. And they often deploy empathy
itself to thwart Danielle's demand that they recognize present-day, intensifying segregation.

Since teaching this group of students, I have added new elements to
this sequence of assignments to address the problems that came up in
this semester. To offer a clear historical background for stories such as
Danielle's, I now show the third episode of the series *Race: The Power of
an Illusion*, titled "The House We Live In," a film that describes the history of racist housing practices such as redlining, racial covenants, and
blockbusting, engineering by the federal government as well as housing
developers and lenders. I particularly appreciate the filmmakers' intersectional move to link the twentieth-century uses of whiteness to deny
housing rights to Black Americans and deny citizenship rights to Asian
Americans. I then ask students to briefly research and write about the
history of race in their neighborhoods and to share what they learn with
one another. These two additions deepened the institutional nature of
their investigations into their communities but still left me with two big
questions inspired by this group of student writers.

1. What could lead students to overcome the barriers established in
    segregated, unequal communities and make alliances across racial
    groups? I tackle that question in chapter 3, where I shift focus from
    geographies of racialized bodies to geographies of racialized language.
    That chapter traces and analyzes work done by multilingual students

to either forge or foreclose intersectional alliances that counter anti-Black ideology.

2. How can students see and articulate the institutional, systemic nature of the racial dynamics at work in their lives? Chapter 4 describes a new unit I've been developing since the semester when Danielle, Grace, and Andrea were my students. It is a culminating research project for the semester, explicitly focused on investigating contemporary institutional racism. This project—still very much a work in progress—is designed to give students an opportunity to research the underlying histories and structures that drive racial inequality in the social institutions that shape their lives and opportunities. Chapter 4 follows one white student through the peer review process described in chapters 1 and 2, and then into her original research on institutional racism for this project. My goal in this chapter is to understand what she made of the opportunity to investigate racism in her community and how she went about crafting her own, highly idiosyncratic antiracist stance within the context of her hypersegregated white life.

These questions leave me suspended between Bonilla-Silva's two visions for moving forward. The first is his dystopian vision of a color-blind future in which racial inequality *increases* while our capacity to address it *decreases*—a future "with more rather than less racial inequality but with a reduced forum for racial contestation" (198). The second is his call for a new grassroots, Black-led, multiracial, "in your face" movement with the capacity to "slay modern-day racism" (268). Many elements of my students' exchanges demonstrate the elasticity of colorblind racial denial. Nevertheless, their work inspires me to continue searching for routes that help them build their capacity to contribute to such a collective antiracist movement.

SECTION 2

Mapping Linguistic Geographies

3

"YOUR GRAMMAR IS ALL OVER THE PLACE"
Translingual Close Reading, Anti-Blackness, and Mapping Linguistic Geographies

This chapter represents a detour in my book's exploration of First Year Writing pedagogies' potential to mitigate the harms of racial segregation and isolation. In it, I examine writing by six multilingual college students, interrogating the ways in which their orientations to linguistic differences intersect with their orientations to racial differences. These student texts amplify the trend evidenced more diffusely in other texts in the archive: it appears that the degree to which multilingual writers engage in linguistic experimentation and translanguaging impacts the degree to which they build or foreclose interracial alliances.

I make two central claims based on the student texts I analyze. First, students of many racial and linguistic backgrounds described confrontations with anti-Blackness in their experiences of language learning, whether explicit or implicit. Students described language sponsors—whether family, friends, schools, or employers—embedding "racial lessons" (which almost always focused on anti-Blackness, whether promoting it or countering it) in a large number of "language lessons." Second, students who described more expansive opportunities for translanguaging, translation, code-switching, code-meshing, and any kind of movement among and between languages appeared to exhibit greater resistance to this linguistic form of anti-Blackness.

Paradoxically, my readings suggest that while the cultural work of translanguaging can support intersectional alliances across racial lines, it does so *despite* students' lack of buy-in to the linguistic benefits of multilingualism and translanguaging. The racial and linguistic allegiances and disallegiances my students forge in their writing are impacted by two intersecting histories: first, the Civil Rights Era fight for racial integration of schools and communities and the subsequent pushback toward resegregation, discussed at greater length in other chapters; second, the struggle to articulate and implement language rights pedagogies

DOI: 10.7330/9781646421107.c003

for racially minoritized speakers of English. Over forty-five years after the Conference on College Composition and Communication made "Students' Right to Their Own Language" their official policy, multilingual student writers in my classes tend to reject linguistic theories of the benefits of multilingualism. Even when they celebrate interpersonal and intercultural connections made possible through multilingualism, they rarely identify linguistic or cognitive benefits to these connections. In fact, despite wielding tremendous translingual resources, most of my students denigrate the specifically linguistic value of those resources. I hold that their lack of buy-in results from failures to implement pedagogies that support both language rights and Civil Rights. These failures must be countered with new pedagogies.

This chapter responds to Keith Gilyard's 2016 warning to the translingual scholarly community not to lose track of the sociopolitical context in which language debates occur. Specifically, he observes that while language activism began in US higher education with "a particular political problem, the harsh penalizing of students who were firmly tethered linguistically to an institutionally discredited heritage," the current "translanguaging subject generally comes off in the scholarly literature as a sort of linguistic everyperson, which makes it hard to see the suffering and the political imperative as clearly as in the heyday of SRTOL [CCCC's 1972 resolution 'Students' Right to Their Own Language']" (285). Gilyard describes translingual studies as susceptible to disembodied and depoliticized notions of difference. He calls for translingual scholars to realign the field with its original political commitments to racial, as well as language, justice. In particular, he argues for scholars to do so through archival work that centers Civil Rights Era Black and Latinx student activists' rhetorical practices (288). The archive of student writing I examine in this chapter responds to Gilyard's call. While he is particularly interested in writing by student activists driving radical changes in university demographics and language policies, my students write from a different, but related, perspective. They have attended school during the backlash against the landmark civil and language rights victories achieved by the earlier generation to which Gilyard refers.

My methodology in reading these texts—"translingual close reading"—is inspired by John Trimbur's recent tracing of a genealogy of close reading as an emergent strategy for discerning student negotiations of difference.[1] I perform extended close readings of texts by multilingual writers whose families immigrated to the United States recently, in their own or their parents' generations.[2] My readings bring together the analytic tools of translingual studies—in particular, its refusal to segregate languages across "error" and its embrace of difference as constitutive of all languaging—and those of Critical Race Theory—in particular, the strategy of counterstory, adapted for rhetoric studies by Aja Martinez as "a method to empower the marginalized through the formation of stories with which to intervene in the erasures accomplished in 'majoritarian' stories"—to parse: (1) the harm of racial segregation on young people's abilities to ally together across racial differences and (2) the role of translanguaging in their capacities to push back against anti-Blackness and monolingual ideology ("Critical Race Theory" 24).

My readings of student writing are particularly informed by moves such as Juan Guerra's to link linguistic, cultural, and citizenship differences in his analysis of "transcultural repositioning" (7), or Rebecca Lorimer Leonard's assertion that multilingual writers practice "rhetorical attunement" by "assum[ing] multiplicity and invit[ing] the negotiation of meaning across difference" (228). I am particularly interested in Lorimer Leonard's tentative assertion that multilingual writers' rhetorical attunement involves an element of "empathy," which is "not simply cognitive capacity, [but] a connecting quality—an ability to jump from individual literate experiences to those of many others" (244). Since a similar model of empathy proved a troubling area in student peer exchanges in the previous two chapters, I am particularly interested in how students' linguistic empathies interact with their racial empathies.

It certainly makes sense that these empathies are connected to one another, since the very act of "translanguaging" that I observe in their writing has been theorized by Otheguy et al. to directly counter the ways that language features labeled as "linguistic" are more often "socially and politically defined labels and boundaries" (298). If, as these scholars explain, translanguaging is "the act of deploying all of the speaker's lexical and structural resources *freely*," speakers and writers who push against strictures to the free deployment of their linguistic resources also push against the social and political—and thus, racial—divisions that have been constructed around language and language learning. Such connections are significant for teachers and scholars interested in the racial politics of language learning and its impact on writing instruction, and suggest the urgency of implementing curricular and pedagogical changes in order to stem the implicit anti-Blackness of language use in schools.

Within the larger archive of student writing about race that I developed for this project, a subset of student texts emerged that sheds light on the ways in which student experiences with language impacted their thinking about race. Of these texts, 79 described experiences I coded as "code-switching"; 42 described experiences as English Language Learners; 38 described experiences with what I called "racial language," or language that itself is explicitly about race; 38 described experiences I coded as "translingualism"; and 17 described experiences I coded as "multilingualism." Many of the pieces fell into more than one of these categories.

As I read and reread this body of writing on language experiences, I identified a particularly salient group of six student writers who wrote directly about the ways in which their thinking about language impacted their thinking about race. Such connections were evident for other writers, but this group wrote most directly about the connections. These students were all multilingual speakers and writers whose families carry linguistic traditions from South Asia, East Asia, the Caribbean, and eastern Europe. These students resemble Gilyard's "polyglot products of contemporary global dispersion," who write about their own language learning and attitudes in consistent, subtle, or not-so-subtle allusions to the students Gilyard identifies as crucial to, yet disappearing within, translingual studies—"the repressed indigenous ethnics overdetermined by dialect" (285).

These "translingual close readings" begin and end with a deep dive into the writing of one student, Sarah, who articulates intersectional allegiances to other marginalized speakers of English. These allegiances appear to inoculate her against assimilationist language ideologies *despite* her lack of value for her own multilingualism and translanguaging skills. Second, I briefly gloss the history and scholarship of language rights and language resources to situate Sarah's linguistic and racial attitudes, positing that she is using Black language as a "racial literacy sponsor" and that Suresh Canagarajah has done the same thing in his study of Geneva Smitherman's Black language code-meshing in her academic prose. Third, I look at two other multilingual writers, Rashad and Keren, whose elementary school misinterpellation as "ESL" causes them to critique monolingual ideas and some of their racial corollaries. Both of these writers come up against anti-Blackness as a brick wall in their otherwise fluid negotiation of multiple Englishes as non-Black people of color. Fourth, I briefly introduce two multilingual students, Maja and Anika, who do something quite different, opposing translingual pedagogies and using Black language to mark the limits of acceptable academic discourse. I postulate that this results from their lack of translanguaging opportunities and racial literacy sponsorship. Fifth, I analyze the writing of Hyun, a writer whose linguistic and racial allegiances at work are formed in highly tenuous contradiction to the monolingualism of his formal education. In my close reading of his writing, I call for better pedagogical support for students' valuing of intersectional linguistic risk-taking in order to foster their racial literacy. And finally, I return to Sarah to explore the hidden network of multilingual global languages in her apparently monolingual high school.

The student writing I cite in this chapter comes from the opening section of my First Year Writing course, titled "Exploring Language Resources." In this series of assignments, I introduce language rights and language resource issues and histories, and I encourage students to compare them to their own experiences and ideas about language. To begin, I share materials that highlight and celebrate present-day linguistic innovation and introduce a history of World Englishes and language standardization practices. In class, I use the term "code-switching" to describe the range of linguistic mixtures that we explore in this unit, referring to the phenomenon linguists have long described in which people move among languages and language varieties, generally in speech acts, but also in writing. I select "code-switching" from among a cornucopia of interesting possibilities for referring to movement among languages because in a core course teaching students from multiple disciplines, I believe the vast majority of them are most likely to pursue this topic in public, rather than academic, discourse. Code-switching seems to be a good signifier for that kind of linguistic move in public discourse. I introduce the classroom definition by using Gene Demby's 2013 inaugural post to the NPR's blog *Code Switch*, "How Code-Switching Explains the World," since his definition is quick and highlights resonances between language and culture. Demby writes that the term code-switching "arose in linguistics specifically to refer to mixing languages and speech patterns in conversation." But he elaborates: "We're looking at code-switching a little more broadly. Many of us subtly, reflexively change the way we express ourselves all the time. We're hop-scotching between different cultural and linguistic spaces and different parts of our own identities—sometimes within a single interaction."

After introducing the term and some history of World Englishes drawn from Dohra Ahmad and Shondel Nero's *Vernaculars in the Classroom: Paradoxes, Pedagogy, Possibilities*, I stage a debate among contemporary "Academic Code Switchers," inspired by my former colleague Carmen Kynard and developed with my former colleague Amanda Moulder, in which students debate the policy and execution of SRTOL. The exercise is framed as a collaborative writing and performance of a Burkean "parlor play" in which students enter, observe, and contribute to an ongoing scholarly debate on the effective role of language rights in the teaching of "college writing." Ultimately, students compose a public letter to a language pedagogy scholar, explaining how their experiences with language differences, language learning, and language resources inform their views on language variation. Most of the student writing I quote in this chapter comes from that final culminating assignment.

"I SUCK AT ENGLISH AND MALAYALAM": TENTATIVE
RACIAL ALLEGIANCES THROUGH LANGUAGE

Sarah, the student writer whose work I discuss at greatest length, takes up the most urgent question in this chapter: What is the potential for inclusive language practices to promote interracial connections and alliances? I chose her writing out of dozens of possible examples because the challenges she underwent navigating school as a marginalized English speaker inspired her to critique White Mainstream English dominance in schools *despite* her lack of faith in the rich translingual resources she possesses. I believe her writing reveals the potential of positive translanguaging experiences to promote common cause among marginalized English speakers across intersectional lines. Sarah's linguistic and racial alliances occurred in direct contradiction to the academic monolingualism and racial segregation she encountered throughout her education. Her account of her experience with language and race offers a counterstory, in the spirit in which Aja Martinez uses that term, in an era of widespread resistance to implementing pedagogies of language rights and language resources, despite research that clearly supports it. Sarah's counterstory accomplishes two of the liberatory functions identified by Martinez: (1) "to expose, analyze, and challenge majoritarian stories of racialized privilege," and (2) to "strengthen traditions of social, political, and cultural survival and resistance" ("Critical Race Theory" 24).

Sarah expresses leeriness of both monolingualism *and* language resources approaches, placing herself outside both oppressive linguicism and liberatory language pedagogies. At the same time, she articulates intersectional allegiances to fellow speakers of several languages: global diasporic speakers of Malayalam, people of color who speak an "urban"-inflected form of English, and speakers of "white suburban" English. Such allegiances appear to inoculate her against language assimilation and racial prejudice, though she identifies no investment in her languages as *linguistic* resources per se.

In a scene in the school library, Sarah describes a range of linguistic challenges she faces while describing her love for then-new British boy band One Direction. After referring to Zayn Malik as her "most favorite person out of the group," Sarah is called out by a classmate.

> ". . . Most favorite? Seriously?" Emma announced as if she was the smartest person in the world. I honestly didn't know what she was asking so I replied, "Yeah, I like him better than the others . . . So what?"
> "Didn't you hear what you've said? You said 'most favorite'. . . . that doesn't make sense." Victoria said in a pleasant tone. I said to myself, "She best not be trying to correct my grammar in front of all these people . . . Makin' me look like a fool."
> "Oh, sorry. . . . I didn't know," the innocent Sarah who doesn't want to cause a scene said.

Sarah—whose family is from Kerala, India, and is the first member of her family born in the United States—at first accepts her challenger's grasp on the distinctions between comparative and superlative adjectives as a matter of superior intelligence—"as if she was the smartest person in the world"—an expert on who "makes sense" and who doesn't. Initially, Sarah meekly assents to the correction, accepting the authority, if not intelligence, of the more "native" speaker of English, despite the quite evident sense of her own initial statement.

However, another voice emerges at the same time. In her head, Sarah begins code-switching into speech inflected by Black language even as she stays externally meek. "'She best not be trying to correct my grammar in front of all these people . . . Makin' me look like a fool.'" Sarah's internal voice evokes the history of language learning that she narrates in a side note after her opening anecdote. Sarah explains that she spoke only Malayalam until elementary school, when she entered an ESL program in a urban school system.

> [ESL class] really didn't help as much as my parents thought it would have because all the kids I hung out with spoke "ghetto" English. What I mean by "ghetto" is when a person talks with so many derogatory terms and slang in their everyday language. So instead of learning the typical "Standard" English, I pretty much learned "poor" English because of my peers.
> Being the kid who knew "poor" English was very tough. My parents didn't notice it because they don't really know the difference between types of English. Neither did my brother because he was born and raised in India for seven years. I started to notice my English was terrible when my friends in high school would always correct me. It actually started when I moved from [the city] to [a suburb], which was predominantly a white town. I was a sophomore in high school at the time and my friends would wonder why I had an accent. It wasn't a foreign accent, it was more of a "New York" accent. In the city, seventy five percent of the population had a different ethnic background, so they would all be coming in with different

types of accents. I just developed an accent, that was pretty much a mix of everything, and brought it into [the suburb].

Sarah describes ESL as a place where she picked up "ghetto English," which then appeared to symbolize for her an allegiance with Black and Brown classmates that she carried in her move to a majority-white suburb. She didn't learn what she was supposed to learn in ESL, which was access to a language of power. Instead, she learned a language she describes as one that resists assimilation to whiteness and fosters alliance with other people of color. Initially, she appears to describe this language in ways that evoke racial stereotyping and internalized racism—"'ghetto' is when a person talks with so many derogatory terms and slang in their everyday language"; the vernacular of her childhood is both "terrible" and "poor."

However, when a second suburban student joins the critique and makes clear the cultural and racial implications underlying the question of "making sense," Sarah responds quite differently. This student adds, "'Yeah, you say a lot of things differently. Your grammar is sometimes all over the place. You have an accent, not an Indian accent, but more like a 'ghetto' accent when you say certain words like coffee, or water. And you talk really fast when you talk in that accent.'" The second student clarifies that she is not challenging Sarah on her "Indian accent." Instead, she challenges her about why she "talks ghetto," which appears to stand in for both talking in a way marked as "talking Black" and for talking with a New York accent.

Unlike the previous correction, which she deferred to, Sarah takes this as an occasion for linguistic self-defense. "All over the place" does not name Sarah as a "foreign" Asian immigrant. To be clear, she is not an immigrant; she is US-born but highly identified with India. Instead, the allegation of her "grammar" being "all over the place" corresponds with Sarah's description of her accent as "pretty much a mix of everything," marked by her Malayalam-speaking family and her New York City peer group of Black and Latinx ancestry. Once this context is evident to Sarah—and through her story-crafting, to her readers—Sarah's response shifts dramatically.

> I got up because at this point I was pretty fed up with this stuck up town. My first year here and this is the type of impression I get.
>
> "I'm sorry I'm not perfect to your eyes. English was not my first language. Unlike you, I'm bilingual. If you don't know what that means, look it up. I come from a place where English is spoken differently. You can say it's ghetto, I really don't care. But don't pick on me for a flaw many people have. Just deal with it or you can just walk away because to me. . . .

you're irrelevant." I said as everyone at the table looked at me in complete shock. They never knew I was that type of person to be that blunt. But in all honesty, judging me by the way I talk was something that easily irritates me and something I had to get off my chest.

Sarah's "blunt" response, unexpected by her white peers, appears to embrace and defend all her languages. Suggesting that bilingualism is an unknown phenomenon to her apparently monolingual and mono-cultural critic, she flips the tables and establishes herself as possessing a larger range of linguistic practices and experiences than her interlocutor, regardless of her errors in any particular language. She further challenges all of her listeners to learn to deal with different forms of English and different forms of language, or face "irrelevance."

Sarah's defense of her bilingualism appears to draw from her positive experiences of alliance with other people of color against the homogenizing linguicism of her new peers. Sarah's comfort in the culturally heterogeneous student body of her early schooling (and she points out many New York City schools would not have been so integrated) meant that she wasn't "the odd girl out" since "everyone was sort of like a 'minority.'" This heterogeneous racial experience meshes well with her linguistic heterogeneity, contrasting starkly with the racial and linguistic homogeneity she describes in her suburban school. Geographic and linguistic movement and combination characterize her ability to resist a potentially meek assimilation into a form of White Mainstream English explicitly framed—by her white challengers and herself—as a disavowal of her connection to the city and the Black and Brown people there. Instead, she commands an intersectional language and accent that her classmate describes as "ghetto" and that she uses to defend her own cultural affinities. This defense of urban vernacular in turn buttresses her defense of her Indian diasporic language and culture.

Sarah's description of this encounter calls out what Nelson Flores and Jonathan Rosa call "raciolinguistic ideologies," in which listeners "conflate certain racialized bodies with linguistic deficiency unrelated to any objective linguistic practices" (150). Her classmate's white gaze both conflates Sarah's racialized body with "linguistic deficiency" and is also baffled by her linguistic and cultural practices, which don't display the appropriate code segregation, which is described as geographic segregation, of the greater New York area. Sarah's white peer literally calls her accent "all over the place," referencing her linked geographic, linguistic, and racial heterogeneity. Malayalam speakers have tripled in Sarah's suburban New York county in the last twenty years, but her family's detour into New York City's linguistic and cultural mixtures mean she can't or won't read as an "immigrant," which she isn't. Sarah's linguistic deviance from racialized expectations of language assimilation and racial segregation result from her occupation of interracial, translingual spaces—including a diasporic household and an urban ESL classroom.

Despite Sarah's staunch loyalty to marginalized forms of English—and their connections to her family, to India, and to a network of students of color in her old and new schools—it is crucial to note that she never defends her "Englishes" as linguistically rich and important in their own right. In fact, her assessment of her linguistic resources ascribes to a language deficit model: "Currently, I still have trouble speaking English and Malayalam, so you can say I pretty much suck at talking." She asserts that being multilingual impedes, rather than enhances, her language abilities. However, she "does not regret" the perceived sacrifice of precision in any one language necessary for her to build relationships across languages, whether those relationships are with her family, the global Indian diaspora, or with other young people of color in the New York area. Without institutional or pedagogical support for the inherent value of her language skills, she nevertheless makes common cause with other marginalized English speakers.

Sarah's intersectional allegiances and skills form as her family navigates a diasporic landscape that crosses lines of racial segregation. As Sarah describes it, these movements result in crossing lines of language segregation as well, fostering a sense of solidarity with other people of color, and to some extent inuring her to the pressure of assimilation. She is not exposed to any academic rationale for the value of her translanguaging skills—and she disavows the notion that there is a linguistic benefit to multilingualism. She thus makes common cause with other marginalized English speakers in the absence of institutional or pedagogical support for the inherent value of her language skills themselves. Without defending her own language resources, she does depict a focus on error as a form of intolerance or ignorance—a preservation of narrow language rules that correlate with narrow racial views.

"THE SPECIAL CASE OF AFRICAN AMERICAN VERNACULAR ENGLISH": CIVIL RIGHTS, LANGUAGE RIGHTS, AND RACIAL LITERACY

While Sarah does not attribute her resistance to raciolinguistic "correction" to a faith in her own languaging abilities, she does consistently link such resistance to her adolescent friendships and alliances with people of color from a range of backgrounds. Sarah's internal adoption

of Black language to resist segregation *and* language assimilation supports Geneva Smitherman's descriptions of the ways in which Black
language—both the language itself and the political movements around
it—has moved all linguistically and politically marginalized people's
rights forward in the United States. Smitherman explains that scholarship and activism on Black language have been central to all struggles
to democratize language instruction in the United States. She cites both
linguistic and racial reasons for this. First, she explains that "because
of —— major linguistic differences, [Black language] was, and continues to be, the most studied and showcased U.S. English variety, resulting
in numerous publications and broad-based exposure in academic and
popular venues" (vii). Next, she argues Black language occupies such a
central role in scholarship and legal rulings on language diversity in the
United States because of the history of Black activism and Black leadership in intersectional activism. "Blacks were the first to force the moral
and Constitutional questions of equality in this country. Further, of all
underclass groups in the United States, Blacks are pioneers in social protest and have waged the longest, politically principled struggles against
exploitation." Smitherman offers "an ironic footnote in American
life—whenever Blacks have struggled and won social gains for themselves, they have made possible gains for other groups—e.g., Hispanics,
Asians, gays, etc., even some white folks!" (145). I believe Sarah is a ben-
eficiary of this protest tradition. She reports turning to Black language
and to other people of color to navigate racial segregation by language
and geography.[3] Sarah's intersectional languaging practices support her
resistance to both racial segregation and linguistic assimilation.

"Students' Right to Their Own Language" (SRTOL), the document
written by Smitherman and other members of the CCCC Language
Policy Committee in 1972 and passed by the CCCC in 1974, has been
deemed by Prendergast an "antidiscrimination measure" that uses
"rhetoric to indict language discrimination based on racial discrimination and move people to combat it" (96). The policy's aim was to protect
students from (1) those teachers' monolingual approaches to writing
instruction; (2) the potential use of monolingual approaches to language instruction as screens for raciolinguism, or as Horner, Lu, Royster,
and Trimbur put it, "faux-linguistic covers for discrimination against
immigrants and minorities: in place of discrimination on the basis of
presumed national, ethnic, racial, or class identity, discrimination is lev-
eled on the basis of language use" (309).

SRTOL was a stand-out policy identifying language rights as Civil
Rights in a long and brutal history of nineteenth- and twentieth-century

deployments of literacy as a gatekeeper for the privileges of "whiteness." Literacy tests have limited the extension of citizenship rights to people of color through 200 years of US domestic and global expansion, including the Fourteenth Amendment and the 1917 and 1924 Immigration Acts, which all but halted immigration from anywhere besides northern Europe. These laws remained on the books throughout the first half of the twentieth century (Prendergast).

Even when language rights laws were passed, their implementation was undermined—in clear parallel to the implementation of other Civil Rights. A few examples:

- Despite its importance for college teachers of writing, SRTOL was never fully adopted by the larger body of English teachers of which CCCC is a part, the National Council of Teachers of English, nor was a clear curricular path ever laid out for implementing or enforcing these ideals (Smitherman).

- Although the Supreme Court ruled in their 1974 *Lau v. Nichols* decision that students have a right to instructional support in public school if they speak a language other than English, the "Lau remedies," or implementation recommendations, were withdrawn in 1981 (Ancheta).

- After Black and Latinx students pushed for Open Admissions to CUNY in the 1960s and 1970s, the institution was defunded, and free tuition was eliminated (Reed).

- Beginning in the 1980s, the evasions, disavowal, and dismantling of integration that followed mandatory school integration in 1954 under *Brown v. Board of Education* have led US schools to be more segregated now than they were in the 1950s (Kucsera and Orfield).

- When progressive immigration laws of 1965 finally removed literacy tests as barriers to citizenship, which had been on the books since the 1882 Chinese Exclusion Act, the 1980s saw the rise of English Only movements (Ahmad and Nero).

This history shows that hard-fought language and Civil Rights for Black people and for immigrants who are emergent multilinguals have been thwarted, blocked, and diverted by the very courts that made them into law. To combat the continued uses of monolingual literacy policies and practices to target racially minoritized multilinguals, translingual scholarship's strategy of moving from a "rights" to a "resources" paradigm appears a strategic tool. By aiming attention squarely at language differences themselves—rather than the rights of speakers and writers to retain those differences—translingual scholarship foregrounds difference as an essential linguistic quality. I am interested in the ways in which this investment in linguistic difference correlates with attitudes toward racial differences.

In what follows, I connect my students' experiences with translanguaging to their views on racial groups other than their own—especially through those groups' languaging practices. To focus this line of inquiry into connections between stances toward languaging and stances toward race, I connect Lani Guinier's use of the term "racial literacy"—which she uses to describe racial attitudes that are dynamic, intersectional, and account for geography and class—to my "translingual close reading" of student texts. To connect translingualism with racial literacy at a granular level in my students' writing, I add one more scholarly frame. My term "racial literacy sponsorship" borrows from Deborah Brandt's investigations into the ways that mass literacy played out in individual lives in the twentieth century. Brandt discerned "literacy sponsors" in her interviewees' lives: "agents, local or distant, concrete or abstract, who enable, support, teach, model, as well as recruit, regulate, suppress, or withhold literacy—and gain advantage by it in some way" (*Literacy* 167). Her focus "on the people, institutions, materials, and motivations that contributed to literacy learning" effectively mapped massive changes in the role of literacy throughout the long twentieth century onto individual lives while demonstrating the dynamics of those historical forces on an idiosyncratic and human scale (*Literacy* 9). By adapting this notion of literacy sponsorship to Guinier's speculative notion of "racial literacy," I hope to contribute a better understanding of how students experience racial learning while navigating multilingualism in the United States.

As a model of what I mean by "racial literacy sponsorship" through translingual analysis, I turn to Suresh Canagarajah as an exemplar. Just as Gilyard reaches across potential divisions between marginalized language communities to argue for intersectional translingual scholarship that foregrounds racial histories in higher education, so Suresh Canagarajah brings SRTOL itself to task for a failure to include scholarship on speakers and writers of World Englishes (WE) both in the framing of SRTOL and in subsequent efforts to expand academic discourse and assessment.

"SRTOL doesn't seem to extend to the use of all varieties of English," Canagarajah asserted in 2006:

> Though the statement itself doesn't make the identity of variants covered clear, the supplementary document by the committee reveals that the authors are thinking primarily of African American Vernacular English (AAVE) and what they call "Chicano" English (see CCCC, Srtol this book p 19 . . .). There are understandable reasons why the SRTOL committee mentions only the English of the African American and Chicano communities. In traditional language rights discourse, *national minorities*

(those with a history as long as the dominant groups and/or enjoying a sizeable demography and spread) have been given preferred treatment in language rights, while *ethnic minorities* and recent immigrant groups (with a more limited history, spread, and number) are treated as inconsequential (May). But this practice has been questioned lately, as the orientation to language rights based on the nation-state has become outmoded, just as the borders of countries have become porous under the influence of globalization. Now, even as Anglo American students are compelled to develop proficiency in multiple Englishes in order to shuttle between communities in the postmodern world, we must take a fresh look at the treatment of World Englishes in SRTOL. (287)

Canagarajah does not stop at naming this exclusion of World English speakers and writers in the history of Civil Rights–inspired language education reform in composition, however. Instead he deems it "a blessing to be able to cite as precedent the advances made by African American writers and to create further spaces for new Englishes in academic writing" (292). He turns to Smitherman's academic code-switching—with her encouragement—as a translanguaging model for himself and his students to emulate, rather than a rival to compete against. Extensively analyzing her use of forms of Black language in her argument for language rights, he offers himself as a "student" of that kind of code-switching, in the service of "making space for pedagogical rethinking and textual experimentation" (300). In a move that can offer a powerful model to students such as Sarah, Canagarajah develops a relationship with Smitherman as both historical actor and translingual writer, making her his "racial literacy sponsor."

Rashad, a student who was in Sarah's class, and Keren, who took my class a few semesters later, both wrote about experiences that placed them on the fault lines of linguistic, racial, and geographic differences. Like Sarah, they both spent time in ESL classes as children. Unlike her, they were both native speakers of English. They describe their experiences being misplaced in ESL classes because their elementary school teachers misperceived their forms of English (Guyanese Creole and Indian Standard English) as "foreign languages." In what follows, I lay out the ways in which Rashad and Keren confront, first, the unintelligibility of their English in the monolingual ideology of US schools, and then the invisibility of their race in the Black-white binary of the US racial scene. After exploring the critical stances toward language that they develop through the experience of being misunderstood, I explore their more direct writing about race in their lives, looking for possible transfer from their critical stances on language to critical stances on race. Both begin writing about encounters with the ways Black people are treated in the United States, and both use those encounters to mark places where they feel invisible or silenced in the US racial landscape.

RASHAD: "TRYING REAL HARD TO STAY IN THE LINES WHEN I COLOR, A FEAT I HAD YET TO CONQUER"

Rashad, one of Sarah's classmates, wrote about his school's attempt to pull him out of class for ESL instruction in his Bronx elementary school. Beginning his tale as another day in elementary school—"I was minding my own business trying really hard to stay in the lines when I color, a feat I had yet to accomplish"—Rashad is interrupted by a teacher who brings him to "a room that was decorated with simple words like hello, goodbye, bad, and good. . . . The room smelled like crayons and bad perfume. It didn't take long for me to feel queasy." Left alone in the room without explanation, Rashad does some detective work. He sees a sign that says "Team E.S.L." and checks out the other kids in the room with him.

> I was familiar with some of the kids because we were told they couldn't speak English when they were introduced by Ms. Delisee and other teachers. Why am I in here with them? Is this a mistake? As I wondered a thought occurred to me: I was such a good student that I was going to help Ms. Lee teach these kids.
>
> Boy was I wrong. Ms. Lee gave us all a book.
>
> "I am here to help you all learn English," she said. "It isn't all that difficult." She scanned the room and said, "Open to page one and let's have Rashad read. Take your time, honey. I know it can be challenging."
>
> I was stunned and confused. They didn't have me here to teach but to learn English. My English is fine, I thought to myself. Everybody can understand me. Sure there are a couple words that I can't pronounce and some that I say funny but you can understand me.
>
> "Did you hear me Rashad?" Ms. Lee said.
>
> "Why am I here? Meh nah undastan," I said.
>
> "Sweetie, you need to learn English," she said.
>
> As I stood there anger was building up in me, like a volcano getting ready to erupt. I could feel water starting to fill up my eyes. The anger had consumed me so much that I barely could open my jaw to speak. I had to pry them open and force the words out.
>
> "But I ca speak it," I said with my voice shaking.
>
> Ms. L. shouted, "STOP WASTING MY TIME AND READ." Her face turned red when she said that.
>
> The whole class was staring at me. Their stares felt like someone was stabbing a sword through me repeatedly. Each word I spoke only fueled the anger in me until I started shouting. That volcano had erupted inside of me.

"MEH NO ENGLISH. ME NAH SCHUPID. YOU FATTIE," I screamed.

I ran out the room and went back to my classroom. Ms. D. saw me and took me to the main office where my mother picked me up. I explained to her what was going on and she stormed into the principal's office where she let them have an earful. My mother's voice could be heard throughout the hallways. That was the last time I was considered an E.S.L. student.

As Rashad reflects on what happened to him, he recalls his mother's words afterward:

"Rashad, when you're at school or anywhere else speak the best English you possibly can. When you're at home you can speak Creole," my mother would say.

"Why?" I asked.

"You want to sound educated when you're in public," she replied.

She would constantly preach this to me on a daily basis. Every time I would speak at school I was always cognizant of how I said things, try my best to sound intelligent.

Looking back years later at this incident I realized that my pride was the source of my outburst. The school thought that I couldn't speak English which in my eyes meant that they thought I was stupid. Intelligence is something that I pride myself on.

Neither Rashad not his mother defends either the "intelligence" or style of Creole. However, their actions suggest a loyalty to its use, and staunch resistance to its exclusion from the lexicon of "English." Like most of the 200,000 Guyanese Americans in New York City, Rashad does not perceive himself as a speaker of a foreign language, and the only reason he is perceived that way is that his teacher has trouble understanding him.[4] Rashad and his mother demonstrate a contradictory attitude in their response to their form of Creole World English. On the one hand, they are resolute in the face of marginalization, both shouting down his teachers and principal until he is back in the mainstream classroom. On the other, Rashad tries hard to take in his mother's lesson that Creole is only for private. Shondel Nero would recognize here a practice of "simultaneously denigrating and celebrating the vernacular" (503). While Creole language is "typically denigrated because of its association with low socio-economic status and lack of education," Nero argues it is also "often used to assert 'true' Caribbean identity in informal and private domains" (503).

Rashad's greatest evidence of internalizing this contradictory message may lie in his early college essay-writing practice itself, in which Rashad writes expertly in a standardized form *about* Creole, putting actual Creole passages in highly contained quotations that contrast with the way he describes the thoughts in his head. He renders even his conversation at home with his mother, where the conversation would logically have taken place in Creole, in a standardized form. His translanguaging skills here demonstrate his intelligence and mastery of standard forms at the same time that he narrates the dangers of speaking Creole in school.

In another essay, Rashad demonstrates how the intelligence he is proud of functions outside of school, by trouncing an antagonist for their inability to accurately discern cultural differences, just like his teacher. Waiting out a hot summer blackout on the stoop with his cousin, Rashad and his cousin are surrounded by a group of laughing boys, who throw water balloons at his cousin and call her a "terrorist." Rashad stops the boys in their tracks. First, he accuses them of a ham-fisted attempt to get the girl's attention because of a crush. Then Rashad points out their cultural illiteracy, since his cousin is Trinidadian, not Arab, or whatever they presumed because of her skin tone. Finally, Rashad points out the futility of a water balloon attack on a hot day, since the balloons are actually refreshing when they explode. Rashad values his sharp wit and demonstrates here how he wields it against neighbors who can't read Caribbean races as well as a teacher who can't understand Caribbean languages.

When he can, Rashad calls out racial and linguistic profiling, as in the classroom and on the stoop. Elsewhere, however, he talks about a form of racial profiling he does not feel empowered to speak out against: "Growing up in the Bronx I watched countless times as students were stopped and frisked for no reason at all." He narrates an account in which two Black boys are patted down by the police during a neighborhood basketball game. Rashad and the other kids in the park—who read as Brown, not Black—are left alone. He does not speak back to the police officers profiling Black youth in his local park, because the stakes are too high. In that situation, he sits "stunned," commenting, "I couldn't believe that happened." This is the one situation where he cannot imagine a rhetorical defense. He is silenced as he bears witness to both racial profiling and his own invisibility in state-sponsored violence against Black bodies.

KEREN: "I WASN'T SURE IF I SHOULD BE PRIDEFUL OR SHAMEFUL OF THE WAY I SPOKE"—COSMOPOLITAN CODE-SWITCHING AND INTERSECTIONAL POSSIBILITIES

I was born in India; however, I came to the United States when I was one year old. I first learned English from my parents, who went to school in India. As a result, I learned the "Indian form" of English. . . . By the time I was in first grade, I had been speaking just like the other children. However, I was still learning from the way my parents were speaking. Even though I mostly spoke like the others, I often

*pronounced words and organized sentences like my parents. The teachers decided
to put me in a class that teaches English as a second language. I wasn't sure if
I should be prideful or shameful of the way I spoke. There really wasn't anything
wrong in the way I spoke and the teachers quickly realized that I didn't really need
to be in that class. I now realize that my experience was the school's way of trying
to force me into conforming to a "standard form" of English.*

Keren addresses this anecdote in a letter to Canagarajah, whose
views on language diversity she had read in an excerpt from "The Place
of World Englishes in Composition." She agrees with his point that
people like her teachers, who are unprepared to understand a variety
of Englishes, will be marginalized themselves in a global economy. She
writes, "I agree with your point about a 'standard form' of English lim-
iting the amount of international business with multilingual people.
These people have learned their own form of English and conforming
to a 'standard form' can hinder communication."

Her idea of linguistic competence in World Englishes that engages
varieties of English quietly places responsibility on her teachers for
failing to be "cognizant of other cultures." She thus constructs their
misrecognition of her Indian English as *their* deficit, rather than hers.
She does not shout down her teachers for mislabeling her as "ESL"; she
simply observes their error and the fact that they ultimately recognized
it themselves. She affiliates with World Englishes and World English
speakers, agreeing with Canagarajah that ignoring this group will sideline the United States in the global economy.

Keren then goes beyond pointing out the provincialism of her monolingual teachers. She models how she moves among different Englishes
to demonstrate how US teachers could become more culturally com-
petent with language differences, unlike many students who actually
expressed terror at what seemed to them the cultural relativism and
logistical complexity of translanguaging, Keren described her languaging interactions with her cousins as an alternative cosmopolitan ethos
for US schools to emulate. On a trip to India with her father, Keren
speaks both English and Malayalam. She tracks her own response to her
cousins' English, implicitly comparing it to her teachers' response to her
childhood English.

> I noticed that my cousins in India spoke English in a slightly different
> manner than I did. I'm not talking about the Indian accent, which is often
> mocked in TV shows and movies. I'm talking about the way they orga-
> nized their sentences and the amount of formality in the way they spoke.
> They said phrases like "What is your good name?" and "God promise!" At
> first, I thought they were speaking incorrectly and I wondered whether I

should correct them. However, once I took a moment to think about it all, I realized that they are not necessarily wrong and that I am not necessarily right. We are both correct. We live on opposite sides of the world; therefore, we speak different forms of English. There is no single "correct" form of English.

Keren's cousins reciprocate this stance of openness and curiosity about the features of Keren's more "American" English. After seeing how their language initially looks "marked" to her by peculiarities, she then sees how her own language has similar peculiarities, when seen through others' eyes.

> I mostly spoke Malayalam, while I was in India, but my cousins did urge me to speak my "American" English. They didn't judge me or state that my English was wrong. They accepted it and tried to understand it. One of my cousins even found my use of the word "yeah" interesting. Over there, the use of the word "yeah" isn't very common. They mostly use the word "yes" instead. Most of the time when I spoke English, I would speak my usual form of English. Sometimes, however, I would speak in a slightly different form. I tried to speak their form of English. I wanted to incorporate their form of English to show them that I accepted their form and that I was trying to understand it.

Casually mentioning that these subtle gradations in varieties of English were taking place on top of code-switching from English to Malayalam in the rich linguistic backdrop of her global family life, Keren makes clear the nontotalizing nature of the differences among World Englishes, and makes ridiculous the idea they need to be "translated" or remediated, as her misplacement in ESL might suggest. For Keren, experiences of fluid movement among languages give her a sense of agency.

After critiquing her US teachers for misperceiving her language differences as language deficits, Keren concludes her letter to Canagarajah with a twist, suggesting more openness to language diversity would actually be more "American":

> Our society constantly stresses the idea of individuality. Then why is it that this sense of individuality gets lost when it comes to language? People around the world have their own experiences and their own stories to share in their own way. The world around us is very diverse so why can't our language be diverse? There should be no need for any individual to have to stick to one form of English. Preserving language and culture is vital in society. The English language should involve all the aspects of diversity in our world. We should all take pride in our languages and, most importantly, ourselves.

Beneficial experiences of negotiating her way through multiple versions of English, as well as multiple languages, authorize Keren to assert translingual practices as more in line with "American" values than monolingual practices. Her message of strategic, beneficial toler-ance among diverse World Englishes feels potentially intersectional, like Sarah's. However, it is unclear how this translates into issues of interracial alliance. This point of transfer is especially important to my questions about the connections between studying language diversity and building interracial solidarity, so I will explore one more of Keren's essays to flesh out the connections between her ideas and experiences with language and with race.

In her next narrative essay for the class, Keren wrote about being the only girl of color in an elementary school recess game of "High School Musical." She revised this piece into a Spoken Word she performed for the class. Keren explains that while all the white girls want to play Gabriella Montez, the Latinx lead, someone says Keren should play the part of "the black girl because she has dark skin." Keren is floored by this comment, and she walks away from the game. She recalls her train of thought in her Spoken Word performance.

> Why don't they remember that this character's name is Taylor?
> Is this role insignificant?
> Why can't an Indian girl play the role of a hispanic girl?
> Why can a white girl do it?
> Why isn't there a role for an Indian girl in the first place?

Her questions hold up her racial interpellation in the "game" of mak-ing mainstream movies "multicultural" and how her white classmates interpret Disney's casting decisions into their own racial role-playing. She attempts to read the racial map of both the Disney movie, in which Gabriela gets the lead and dates the white male lead, two Black charac-ters get secondary roles and date each other, and no Indian characters appear at all. She finds herself peripheral to the racial vision of her classmates, her position as a South Asian American inscrutable in the Black-white racial paradigm of the United States.

Keren's rejection of being labeled "the black girl" may convey a fear of being labeled as "Black" in the US racial hierarchy that pressures immigrants to ally themselves with whiteness, in order to reap the ben-efits of white privilege. However, she never voices that rejection. Instead, she rejects the erasure of Indian diasporic people and other non-Black people of color in the United States. She asks why her friends can't remember the Black character's name and whether that role is "insig-nificant." Her storm of subsequent questions—why the "Brown" part of Gabriela can't go to her as another "Brown" girl (and casting across

Indian and Latinx roles certainly happens), and, perhaps, why Latinx identity can be considered "white," as well as why there isn't a part for her to play in the first place—all lead her to sit out the High School Musical game she had been looking forward to for days.

In a cover letter to this essay, she writes that she deliberately avoided a "happy ending" so that her audience will "understand that I am not okay with being erased." Keren finds that she is consistently miscast, whether it's in ESL or the twenty-first-century American "multicultural" drama.

Having offered a new vision of moving among different Englishes as uniquely "American"—if we could only grasp it—she then shows how a linguistic perspective like hers, which could be uniquely healing to this country, is erased in the racial politics she sees around her. This monolingual landscape appears one where differences of language and race become illegible, and people who deviate from central casting are sidelined and misapprehended.

One of my central goals for language study such as this is to create opportunities for intersectional alliance among communities in New York. Shared experiences of language marginalization in school appear to create that possibility. Sarah expresses an explicit fellow feeling with all Black and Brown students at her majority-white school, Keren feels allied with the global Indian diaspora but misaligned with the Black-white racial paradigm she sees around her, and Rashad is outraged on behalf of Black peers who are routinely frisked in front of him.

RACIOLINGUISTIC IDEOLOGY AND BLACK LANGUAGE IN MULTILINGUAL STUDENT WRITING

While I have cited productive instances of intersectional racial literacy sponsorship that allows multilingual writers a broader, more intersectional view of their own language situation, I certainly do not wish to assert that all marginalized World English writers turn universally to Black language for racial literacy sponsorship. In fact, some of the evidence I have collected from student writers points in the opposite direction.

Some multilingual student writers actively adapted raciolinguistic stances toward language after reading scholarship on language rights and resources. Their stances formed despite—or perhaps because of—their own experiences being sidelined in language. What is curious is that these student writers are equally preoccupied with Black language in contemplating the prospect of pedagogies that encourage translingualism's stance of openness to difference. Black language, instead of being the sponsor of new literacy, becomes the specter they invoke to point out the dangers of linguistic openness itself. I will sketch out two instances along these lines to suggest that the "special case" of Black language can be wielded to promote, as well as contest, raciolinguistic ideology. Further, I speculate that the anti-Blackness that erupts in these two students' writing correlates directly with their stances against translingual approaches in the classroom, or against SRTOL itself. I postulate that these students' lack of racial literacy may differ from Sarah's due to a lack of support for translanguaging in their own lives, across language varieties and conventions. They are multilingual, but they don't describe opportunities to practice translanguaging across their language communities, using the resources at their disposal.

Maja, who entered US schools at age seven after growing up in Poland, describes her own success in school as a result of speaking and writing "standard English." She accepts that she has a "right" to speak Polish, but she dismisses any need for support of that right. Further, she marks the dangers of supporting other novice speakers of English, both in public and in school.

She offers her own story of learning English in the United States not merely to argue against SRTOL but to imply that an English Only approach might be better. Describing her arrival in US schools as a young child who did not understand English—"No, seriously like teachers would say 'Hi' and I would just stare at them with a blank expression"— she became "Student of the Month" in her third month of school in the United States.

> Why? Because I worked my butt off to learn English as fast as I could because I knew that I wouldn't be able to live in New York, anywhere in America for that matter, if I didn't know the language. I knew (with the help of my teachers and parents) I had to accept the responsibility to learn English in order to survive in a country where the most prevalent language is English.

"I have the right to speak Polish," she clarifies, "[but] I don't expect everyone to understand Polish or cater to my needs when it comes to speaking that language." There appears to be a note of resentment in her formulation "cater to my needs" here, and she explains in the next sentence, "if I was of Hispanic descent, I wouldn't expect people who live in America to have everything translated to Spanish (which a majority of it is now anyway, but that's a separate discussion that I have a strong position on)."

Maja moves toward an English Only approach as the linguistic moral to her experience of immigration and assimilation, ending with an explicit monolingual stance much more extreme than the academic code-switcher she addresses, Stanley Fish, who critiques SRTOL's impact on teaching writing but renounces the English Only movement she begins to endorse:

> I speak the "official" (I put that in quotes because the United States doesn't have an official language) language of the United States; English because that is the most prevalent language in which all documents are written. They are not written in slang from the hood using "n****" after every sentence, they do not use contractions such as a "ya'll" from the southern states. They are written in proper grammatical sentences, such as "clean English sentences."

Maja's uses of a racial epithet, imagined as part of "slang from the hood," to warn her audience about the dangers of abandoning "clean English sentences" is alarming and explosive. She invokes both a "hood" version of English and a southern version to introduce terms that are anomalous to "clean" English sentences, making these racially coded geographic terms sound "dirty." Choosing two words with long linguistic histories both associated with Black people and/or Black speech, she uses Black language to signal what lies outside of acceptable language. Maja's rhetorical positioning reads as "nonattuned." Her pugilistic style cordons off non-White Mainstream English English, keeps Polish entirely up her sleeve, sends up flares around Black language, flames Spanish without explanation, and dead-ends with an unexplained imperative to use "clean" English. The topic of language diversity seems to have short-circuited her thinking, which is elsewhere fairly flexible and creative. In both cases—her rejection of Spanish and of Black language—the raciolinguistic logic of her embrace of monolingualism is pronounced.

In fact, it seems to me that Maja has learned the mostly implicit racial hierarchy of language pedagogy in the United States. As a new immigrant with the "epidermic capital" to read as "white"—which she ties directly to her investment in "good, clean" English—she compulsively contrasts herself with people who "won't" or "can't" perform English—people she very clearly identifies as Black and Latinx. Her directness in absorbing and embracing monolingualism's affiliation with whiteness is alarming, as she lays bare raciolinguistic hierarchies implicit in more subtle articulations of the benefits of "learning Standard English."

Anika's trajectory in analyzing her experiences learning English in US schools follows a similar trajectory to Maja's. First, she embraces the liberatory potential of exposing "ESL" as an unproductive description of the language abilities of multilingual Americans. She begins by using Canagarajah's designation "simultaneous bilingual" to situate her own experience as a Queens-born speaker, from birth, of English, Hindi, and Punjabi. Excited by the idea that English really isn't a second language for her, after having been placed for several years in ESL classes, she described feeling haunted by "this concept of English as a second language [which has] followed me around even after I had passed the [ESL] exam." Canagarajah's idea that one can be at home, a "native speaker," of more than one language, appears important to her as she has felt stigmatized by the label "ESL." She writes, "I knew [my] errors had nothing to do with English being a second language, but that's what others claimed the cause was." This experience leaves her feeling underconfident and "non-native" to English, symbolized by the freighted label "ESL."

Anika seems ready to launch a critique of raciolinguicism, as Canagarajah does when he writes: "Only the color of my skin would influence someone to call me a nonnative speaker of English—not my level of competence, process of acquisition, or time of learning" (586). She is on the verge of a move like Aja Martinez's, who reflects on why her college English professor referred to Martinez's "background in ESL," which grossly mislabeled and misunderstood her linguistic marginalization in English *and* Spanish, which she describes as "two broken languages" ("Personal" 213). Martinez identifies the raciolinguism in her lifelong exclusion from "native speaker" status in both English and Spanish. "Even though US imperialism denied me Spanish, society will never permit me to be the person who can truly claim Standard American English. I'll never be white. I am not middle-class white. I am not the standard; American standards do not apply to me." (213). After describing her inability to "claim" either "proper" Spanish or "Standard American English," Martinez instead claims a "Chican@ identity and a *mestiza* consciousness," affiliating with all her language and racial genealogies. In doing so, she offers a map for students such as Anika, raised in Queens' linguistic richness, working many linguistic and cultural codes.

But Anika goes in the opposite direction. Instead of critiquing the raciolinguistic profiling of her form of English, she turns against the inclusive embrace of linguistic difference advocated by writers such as Martinez and Canagarajah. In Anika's letter to Canagarajah, she discourages him from pursuing translingual pedagogies. Like Maja, she uses Black language as a marker of the racially coded chaos that she imagines will ensue: "As a code-switcher and multilinguist yourself, I ask, will you be able to learn all the possible vernaculars of English and keep up with the changes that each new generation brings? Will you accept code-switching in your classrooms especially if it's a 'ghetto' version of English?"

Anika's foreclosure of multilingual writing in school—a foreclosure that was forced on her in school, and that she has enforced on herself as well to survive and succeed—is echoed in her other writing about race. She forecloses empathy toward differences. Her intermittent moments of interracial solidarity—at one point she writes favorably about the Black Lives Matter movement and expresses agreement with the struggle against colorblindness—go up against her invocation of "ghetto" language as a danger to effective teaching and her allegation in a reflection journal that Black and Latinx activism on campus is "very selfish" and not "relevant" to her.

I argue that as a result of the curtailing of their linguistic *and* racial empathies—as well as their perceived access to white or pseudowhite privilege through loyalty to White Mainstream English—Maja and Anika imagine a raciolinguistic threat unleashed by a more open stance toward language differences. Unbidden by the assignment or texts they are responding to, both of these multilingual writers summon up Black language, racial epithets, and racially coded language to condemn pedagogy geared toward language rights or translingualism. Further, their skepticism toward translingual pedagogy and linguistically inclusive notions of English has direct parallels in their racial attitudes. Maja advocates English Only policies in public discourse, while Anika finds that "ghetto" language and Civil Rights lack "relevance" in her education. While both of them have multilingual experiences and resources, they both cast their lot with an implicitly white or white-adjacent monolingualism.

One way of reading Maja and Anika's affiliation with a "white" form of language uniformity is to observe that it lacks empathy. That lack of a "connecting quality" is consistent across linguistic and racial lines. I have already established my belief that Sarah's refusal of raciolinguistic attitudes by her classmates stemmed from a network of linguistic and racial allegiances. And I believe that something like Lorimer Leonard's notion of "empathy" may be an effective term for the ways in which she formed allegiances to other people marginalized through language *and* race. Sarah certainly does not describe these empathetic connections as linguistic or literate resources per se, but rather as a function of sharing community with marginalized and racialized people.

I contend that some combination of factors foreclosing their own translanguaging skills and opportunities—the trauma of monolingual education for a multilingual student, family and community racism unmitigated by integrated schools or neighborhoods, fetishization of Black language, access to white privilege (in Maya's case) and pseudowhite privilege (in Anika's case)—may have caused these multilingual writers to support monolingual education, and to use anti-Blackness to mark the need for it. They are prey to what Guinier calls "the distinctive, racialized asymmetries [in] the DNA of the American dream" (116). Because they have not been able to contradict the lies, and the racism, of that "dream," Maja and Anika lack intersectional empathy and instead voice pervasive raciolingual ideologies. This includes the linguistic corollary to anti-Blackness: a fear of Black language as a polluter of "proper English." Their adoption of the connection between linguistic and racial discrimination divides them from their natural allies, and isolates them.

TENUOUS EMPATHY AND THE "SHARED HARDSHIP" OF IMMIGRATING INTO ENGLISH

The writing of a final student, Hyun, foregrounds struggles and resources in forming cross-cultural alliances that are both more explicitly linguistic and also more tenuous than those Sarah forms. Since I am interested in the possible connections between language and racial attitudes of my students in a landscape saturated with raciolinguistic ideologies, Hyun's experience demonstrates the particular instability of linking linguistic dispositions and interracial empathies, especially when questions of citizenship arise.

Arriving in the United States as a middle-school-age speaker of four Korean dialects, Hyun experienced his first year in the United States to be "like walking in an invisible storm." Struggling profoundly to understand or make himself understood, he describes developing an extreme sensitivity to "body language and face expression," growing "shy at the sight of a frown," while his "nerve system began to develop to catch every detail of physical expressions." This physiological image helps convey a sense of high alert brought on by living outside of the dominant language: "While there are some people who try to understand what I am trying to say with patience, others throw frowns at me and disregard me as soon as they realized my inability." Hyun's phrase—"walking in an invisible storm"—became a class touchstone phrase to describe the struggle of language learning. His propensity for unexpected metaphor and intriguing juxtapositions meant his writing commanded attention from his peers, despite the devastating reception his Englishes had received throughout his schooling in the United States.

Hyun described that as he grew more accustomed to the US language scene, he gained a sense of linguistic multiplicity, of easy movement among the language communities he inhabited:

As I gained confidence, I could switch from one dialect to the other. I try to speak "Standard English" in front of teachers or professors because that is what they want students to learn in school or college. I speak Konglish (Korean + English) with my friends because, sometimes, mixing them can convey my meaning more clearly. And I let myself free of sticking to grammars at home by speaking my own version of Korean. Even in Korean, I speak "broken" language. I do not care orders of verbs and subjects. I switch them as I want and still people understand.

Hyun sounds much more confident than Sarah, who claims she "sucks" at English *and* Malayalam. However, despite having acquired languaging skills, Hyun expressed leeriness of the course's investment in accepting multiple versions of English. He was both intrigued by and skeptical of widely anthologized texts we read by multilingual writers supporting the value of multilingualism and nonstandard English, such as Amy Tan's "Mother Tongue" and Gloria Anzaldúa's "How to Tame a Wild Tongue." Although he says they "easily arouse my empathy and interest" and agrees "there is no such thing as 'Standard English,' and it is fine as long as you convey your idea clearly," he is not sure how useful this insight is, since "some people are not that liberal as I think to accept that idea."

He finds these texts unrealistic about the "liberal" acceptance of multiple forms of English and other languages in schools, where he finds himself "afraid to make a statement in class because I felt everyone was eager to check my grammar and make fun of me." The lack of empathy he experiences in his attempts at mastery of standard, school-based forms of English contrast with moments outside of school, when relaxed language rules actually increase connection:

There is also advantage in speaking different dialects of the language. For example, there are a lot of Spanish workers at my job. People who stick to "Standard English" would not understand them because their English is not in complete sentences and mixes English with Spanish. But we can communicate and be friendly because we go through same hardship. Speaking "broken" English can be a way to be friendly to those who speak "broken" English as well. Similarly, I could easily be friend with someone who came from same part of Korea because we spoke same dialect.

In Hyun's description, language differences create opportunities for very different kinds of connection. First, in cross-language encounters, native speakers of other languages can build connections through their shared "breaking" of English into a form they can mutually understand, and additionally through their shared "hardship"—he does not clarify whether that's exclusively linguistic hardship or other hardships immigrants experience. Second, in almost the same breath, he equates friendships forged through sharing "broken English"—a term he adopts from Amy Tan—to friendship he would share with anyone from his region of South Korea, who would speak the same dialect he does. He equates these two very different forms of kinship, defining both as "advantages of speaking different dialects." His fluidity in describing translanguaging appears linked to his hard-fought confidence in translanguaging.

Hyun's description of empathy for other immigrants marginalized by language is highly tenuous. In the course of end-of-semester research he did into the DREAM Act, which was being implemented during the semester he was my student, Hyun struggled with whether or not to endorse the policy and support other students in his generation in obtaining a path to citizenship. He reversed his position several times over the course of his research. On the one hand, he was swayed by anti-immigrant arguments in his school that the DREAM Act would make college, financial aid, and the workplace more competitive for current US citizens. On the other, he heard the painful stories of his friends who were unable to go to college because they were undocumented. The final factor in developing his opinion was his anger at the great expense and stress he and his family had endured fighting for his green card, which he had recently obtained. This factor perhaps unexpectedly interfered with his solidarity with undocumented immigrants, since he thought it was unfair for people to have an "easier time" than he did going through legal channels to get papers.

Eventually endorsing the DREAM Act, he described being swayed by his friends' stories, rather than his own. I believe these stories, shared in "broken English" outside of formal spaces, created a thin but vital thread of empathy running between himself and even more vulnerable immigrants. His attunement with their experiences of "shared hardship" in language and citizenship appears to offer a linguistic roadmap to highly idiosyncratic, tenuous, interracial and intercultural allegiances.

Like Sarah, and unlike Maja and Anika, Hyun's descriptions of translanguaging with other marginalized English speakers tip the balance of his empathetic response. He and Sarah both interacted with linguistically and racially marginalized people who weren't from their group, and whose language resources were also nonstandard but different from theirs. Positive translanguaging experiences seemed to produce greater racial literacy in my students' writing. Such out-of-school translanguaging opportunities are especially critical due to the challenges of implementing language rights and resources pedagogies.

SARAH FOSTERS CONNECTION: "I NEED YOU TO TELL ME WHAT THIS LOVELY FAMILY IS TRYING TO TELL ME."

I conclude by returning to Sarah, whose story began this chapter. When she was attacked for "talking ghetto," Sarah accused her "irrelevant" interlocutor of not understanding bilingualism. Conflating her multiple fluencies in English and Malayalam, Sarah suggested that understanding these languages was an asset. To be clear, she is not talking about a linguistic asset. Sarah avoids claiming linguistic pleasure or skill when she describes speaking three languages—Malayalam; the English she learned in ESL classes in New York City, which she calls "ghetto English"; and the language spoken in her suburban school, which she calls "proper English." However, she does ultimately identify strategic uses of her multilingualism in her senior year at a majority-white suburban high school.

> During my senior year of high school, there was a foreign exchange student from India who didn't know any English and neither did her parents. This family just happened to be from the state my parents were born and raised, so I knew their language. My guidance counselor called me down to her office so I can interpret things to them as best as I can. My guidance counselor knew I spoke Malayalam because it was in my records that I was an ESL student.
>
> I walked into the office, expecting to be in trouble (not that I was a troublemaker, but if you think so. . . . Let it be), and I heard my guidance counselor call my name. This doesn't happen often. So many thoughts were racing in my mind. What could this be? I didn't get into Saint John's University? Baruch? Binghamton? My ACT scores were declined? Basically, I thought about everything that can screw up a senior in high school. Then when I saw these Indian parents waiting in her office, I wondered to myself if she thought these people were my parents.
>
> "Sarah, I need you to do me a HUGE favor!" My guidance counselor exclaimed.
>
> I mumbled, ". . . What is it?"
>
> She gave me a look and then looked back at the family and then looked back at me. "I need you to tell me what this lovely family is trying to tell me."
>
> So, I translated what they said, which was they wanted to enroll their child to the school and needed to know where to fill out the paperwork. Simple as that, they went off to the registration office and my guidance counselor nodded and thanked me.

Sarah wraps up this anecdote by saying, "Knowing all these 'types' of English and another language shaped who I am now." It also demonstrates an investment in the same values that my students articulated for multilingualism—intercultural connections, devoid of linguistic benefit. In this case, Sarah was singled out for the ESL classification in her record and brought into the office, a potentially marginalizing moment of being interpellated as "foreign." But as in elementary school, being identified as "ESL" gave her a chance to connect with other marginalized English speakers, to their advantage and her own. Suspecting at first a microaggression on her guidance counselor's part—"When I saw these Indian parents waiting in her office, I wondered to myself if she thought these people were my parents"—she then realizes her guidance counselor needs help with basic communication with an international South Asian family.

Sarah identifies multiple benefits to this moment of translation. First, she feels "a connection with this Indian family." In addition, "ever since I did that favor for my guidance counselor, we became good friends and I know for a fact she wrote me a kick-ass recommendation for college." She benefited concretely from the network of relationships involved in helping families like, but also unlike, hers navigate her school. She makes very clear that she is not setting another immigrant family on a road to assimilation. Instead, she is brokering language for an Indian family who needs temporary access to US education as part of their own global movement. Their daughter, who she now sees in the halls, will add English to her arsenal of linguistic resources.

Sarah thus sketches out a complex network of relationships through translanguaging. The language she learned at home as a child connects her to the global Indian diaspora. Even though she believes she "sucks at English and Malayalam," she has a connection to home that she would not give up and it pays off in unexpected ways when other Indians enter the apparently monolingual space of US schools and she is the only person able to translate. Further, the "ghetto English" she learns in New York City ESL classrooms inoculates her against critique by monolingual English speakers who put down her languaging skills in ways she might have internalized as a learner of English at school.

Sarah's narrative, and some of the others I have discussed in this chapter, voice a form of tentative, idiosyncratic interracial allegiance developed through shared language marginalization and afforded through spaces such as ESL programs, integrated classrooms, and quiet moments of language allegiance in cafeterias and guidance offices.

CONCLUSION

My analysis of these First Year Writing student texts has two implications that have changed my teaching of this material and may be applicable in other classrooms. First, it suggests that the more students are ruled by fear, by accepting their own linguistic devaluing and marginalization, and by monolingual and raciolinguistic ideologies, the more vulnerable they are to anti-Blackness and anti-immigrant beliefs. Second, it suggests that the more they risk miscommunication, discomfort, looking stupid and being novices, the more likely they are to push back against raciolinguistic and straight-up racist beliefs. In short, language segregation correlates with racial segregation.

Observing these parallels between language and racial segregation in my students' writing over many semesters has inspired me to change some of the ways I ask students to write about their languaging practices. The assignment has evolved in its audience, topic, and purpose. In the student work included in this chapter, I required that they identify and describe a "language" of their own and make an argument about its potential use in formal educational spaces. I wanted them to articulate the value of their variety of languages, and that was one way of doing it. Here is the original charge in the assignment:

Your letter needs to accomplish the following tasks:
1. Tell a compelling story about your experience with language(s).
2. Use your story to make an argument (or a point).
3. Pick a specific audience who needs to hear your story, and understand your point. Have a clear reason for addressing this particular audience.
4. Strategically appeal to this audience, increasing their chances of hearing your story and understanding your point.

After years of reading their writing, that set of questions came to feel like a narrow approach to defining "value," and also a little stiff as a "for or against" formulation. Because of the value students such as Sarah, Rashad, Keren, and Hyun articulated in both (1) struggling across languages and (2) the relationships they formed in the course of those struggles, I've expanded the assignment to include relationships formed around language learning, as well as analyzing and celebrating the insights born from language struggles. Here are the questions I now ask students to write about:

- Under what conditions did your family start speaking English? How does it impact your relationship with language in academic, home, and public life?
- Who has helped you learn language? How did this person impact your relationship with language? How did language impact your relationship with this person?
- When have you faced a language challenge? Where have you struggled, faced confusion, misunderstanding? What came of this challenge?
- What language(s) do you speak?

This reorientation of the assignment has made space for students to articulate a set of translanguaging practices that have—perhaps unsurprisingly at this point—substantial racial corollaries as well. In particular, it has made room for students to push back against the ways in which linguistic geographies reinforce and participate in racial geographies, foreclosing empathy and fostering disconnection. Stigmatized languages are often labeled by racially coded, anti-Black place markers, for example, "ghetto" or "hood," and given racially coded value descriptors: "good," "bad," "proper," "broken." Students willing to move past perceived boundaries among languages have countered those racialized divisions and hierarchies. Crossing linguistic boundaries seems to offer a freedom of perspective and a greater empathy and openness. Breaking rules or experimenting with them seems to create communities. Students who have contended with language shaming and loss often describe it as part of a developmental process of maturation, self-love, and rejection of internalized raciolinguism.

Thus, this student writing strongly suggests that historical and ongoing assaults against both language *and* Civil Rights can be countered by building translingual competencies likely to support building racial literacies. Teachers can counter both linguistic and racial segregation by supporting intersectional experiences and histories, responding to Guinier's call to "extirpate the distinctive, racialized asymmetries from the DNA of the American dream" (116). When students have opportunities for language celebration, reclamation, and experimentation to build language awareness, appreciation, and risk-taking, to dig into the paradoxes and multiple meanings unearthed during miscommunications, they exhibit greater linguistic openness with strong corollaries in greater racial openness. By providing translanguaging opportunities and spaces for reflection on translanguaging into our writing instruction, we can increase students' chances of imagining and building multilingual alliances, in particular in the face of raciolinguistic pressure to assimilate to an implicitly white monolingualism. If we provide opportunities to do these things, translanguaging can support racial literacy.

SECTION 3

Mapping Futures

4

"SAYING HONEST THINGS WE WISH WEREN'T TRUE"
Racial Literacy Sponsorship and Challenges to White Hypersegregation

The field of English in the United States fails to confront de facto segregation in all of its forms (racial, ethnic, cultural, economic, geographic, generational, etc.) as a drag on the literacy of everyone. The illiteracy that segregation breeds—especially as it spreads into teaching, policing, hiring, law, policy, politics, you name it—poses an existential threat to people's lives and to the promises of democracy. Spreading communicative competence—the skills and knowledge necessary to engage intelligently with the sounds and signs of fellow human beings—must be the most urgent goal in language education.

Deborah Brandt, "Awakening to Literacy circa 1983"

Institutional racism is much harder to see than day-to-day racism, such as microaggressions. Like those forms of racism, it comes from historical and present-day causes. Unlike those forms of racism, it is deeply rooted in the social institutions that govern our lives. We will use this project to analyze and make visible these roots, so that we can begin to see them more clearly, understand their impact on us all, and think about ways to eradicate them.

"Institutional Racism Think Tank Digital Essay," First Year Writing 1000c: Writing across Difference: Race, Language, and Digital Composition

Throughout case studies of their writing, I have shown a range of ways in which students use cross-racial opportunities to acknowledge and counter the harms of racism—and segregation in particular—on psychological and personal levels. In general, though, students' understandings of segregation as a tool for enforcing massive inequality is deferred in these collaborations. In particular, I have documented work done regularly by students of color, especially Black students, to act as racial literacy sponsors. Ultimately, several chapters illustrate the process through which non-Black students come up to the edge of structural thinking and teeter there, describing vertiginous problems with racial vision.

DOI: 10.7330/9781646421107.c004

This leads to an important question: Is it worth it to ask students of color to tell their stories and listen to those of white students? To explore this question, I look in-depth at one white student's engagement with the charge to write, read, and talk about the role of race in her personal life and in the structures governing her society throughout the semester. Like many of her classmates, this student—Rose—struggled to articulate racial dynamics in her highly segregated white community and, once she began doing so, to perceive the roots of those racial dynamics. Using the concept of racial literacy sponsorship, which I introduced in chapter 3, I will interrogate the ways in which Rose responded to a wide range of racial literacy sponsorship in the course—from me, from her peers, from authors and researchers. I need to know whether this is a two-way street. Does Rose in turn contribute in meaningful ways, or is this a one-way street? Does the work done by her racial literacy sponsors result in her growth? My speculative answer is yes. Her racial literacy grew in unexpected and idiosyncratic ways as she struggled to assimilate input from a wide range of racial literacy sponsors. Ultimately, she made some highly unexpected contributions to the class's conversations about race.

Rose's racial literacy sponsors challenge her to be more direct in talking about race, to identify racist messages in her head and speak back to them, and to think in more elastic ways. These mental exercises all have inherent value but obtain particular value when she applies them to race. Rose begins the semester coming up against cognitive and rhetorical difficulties with speaking about race and against racism. Her early life makes this understandable, and her future career as a teacher makes it potentially very harmful.

I follow Rose's work through assignments that will be familiar to readers of earlier book chapters and that are available in the appendix. I also describe her work on a new assignment, also available in the appendix. This culminating project, the "Institutional Racism Think Tank Digital Essay," focuses on difference as a resource in solving social problems, rather than a liability or stumbling block. Inspired by Linda Flower's call to begin with "a constituency of people willing to engage with a problem of which they were probably not yet fully aware" (308), this model aims to use the disparate beliefs among students to build consensus around naming, condemning, and combatting racism.[1]

INTRODUCTIONS: "INSTITUTIONAL RACISM 101" AND ROSE

Here is a map of the assignment sequence Rose and other students undertook in this new part of the course. I begin by introducing the concept of a "social institution" as a network of relationships that control social order and brainstorming with them how many institutions govern their own lives. I then introduce films that offer narratives of institutional racism—films in particular on housing discrimination, citizenship discrimination, and the racial caste system of mass incarceration. They respond in reflection journals, summarizing and reacting to these historical narratives of institutional racism, either venting about the films themselves or the narratives the films tell, connecting with their own experiences, or rigorously questioning what they hear.

I define "institutional racism" in class as "the unequal distribution of a society's resources along racial lines."[2] When I introduce this topic for study, I offer three benefits for studying it:

1. If you don't look institutionally, you're not really understanding race. Studying race on an interpersonal level is important. It can add to your self-awareness and cultural competence. But the ways race works in our society are deeper and wider than that. It is important to see beyond individual, psychological racial dynamics to understand how race works in our society.

2. Institutional racism is an excellent topic for conducting academic research that matters. These are urgent social problems we have not yet solved. You have an opportunity to contribute to understanding that could help solve these problems.

3. Studying social phenomena, finding excellent—often new—information about them, and sharing that information with a group of peers doing similar research is a crucial skill of academic research. You will all benefit from the research done by others here. That's why I'm calling this class a "think tank."

Students next identify which social institutions they are most interested in exploring further. Almost every semester, most students identify education, the justice system, and the media as social institutions impacting them most immediately, though some choose to look at other institutions. I ask students to look at what's going on with race in the social institution they have chosen, inventorying the narratives they have shared and the texts we have read and viewed. Generally, there is a thread they begin to follow about race and the ways it is woven through the institution they have selected. I show several texts that I consider introductions to Institutional Racism, texts I call "Institutional Racism 101," in the spirit of learning racial literacy.

Students do some research exercises to collect information on the role of race in their social institution. They collect this information in a "Digital Annotated Bibliography," inspired by the projects Carmen

Kynard assigned her students at John Jay College, on a password-protected WordPress page, which they then use to share information with each other on their topics.[3]

Once the Digital Annotated Bibliography is complete, students can opt to join with other students. They compare research findings and find other students whose interests overlap with theirs, and, either alone or in groups, they undertake the final project of the semester—an "Institutional Racism Think Tank Digital Essay." (This digital assignment in full is in the appendix.)

I organize the digital essays into panels by social institution, and we spend the final days of the semester presenting and discussing them. Students take notes on one thing they will remember from each presentation, one thing that disturbed them or they need to fact-check, and a question for the presenter. After the series of presentations, they write a final reflection on their learning from creating and witnessing these presentations.

"IS EVERYTHING YOUR FAMILY SAYS TRUE?": RACIAL LITERACY SPONSORSHIP IN ONE STUDENT'S TRANSFORMATIVE UNDERSTANDING OF RACISM

I could select any student at random to apply the model of racial literacy sponsorship to one student's learning, but I chose Rose for a few reasons:

1. Because of my own experience of trying to better understand my racial identity development as a white person. Concern that any effort by a white person to acknowledge racism gets "credit," as opposed to building substantial understanding. Throughout the analysis of Rose's work I ask: "What was the discernible result of the work she did? What were the discernible results of the work others did to sponsor her racial literacy?"

2. She struggled with the understanding goals of the class, and with many assignments, but she persevered. Watching how she did that promised important insights into the course. Her work demonstrates a blend of what looks like "remedial" racial understanding, and some crucial, uncanny insights.

3. She reinterpreted many of the assignments to serve her own needs throughout the semester. She negotiated with the assignments and interesting new understandings emerged.

4. She made varied use of a range of racial literacy sponsors, in the class and in her research. I was curious to understand how she did that.

Ultimately, I believe Rose's particular sequence of assignments offers a tentative model for strengthening students' racial literacies through collaborative knowledge production and racial literacy sponsorship. As with Danielle's peer review group, Rose's work—and my investigation into it—have led me to revise the course and altered my understanding of the meanings my students make of the opportunities it affords them.

Rose is a middle-class white woman from a small Long Island town that is over 90 percent white. Her father is a retired police officer. She took my class in 2017 during her second semester of college, where she was an elementary education major. Her racial identity essay—titled "Is Everything Your Family Says True?"—begins by describing her racial isolation without any hedging. Unlike many white students raised in majority-white communities, she never wrote that there "was no race" in her community. Instead, she clarifies that despite her community's ethnic diversity (she mentions neighbors of Hungarian, Polish, and German descent), "the majority of kids I went to school with were like me, white." She further clarifies that she had not understood herself as white until coming to St. John's in the fall, four months earlier. "I think once I started college is when this has come to light for me. Since starting St. John's I feel like I have been thrown into a melting pot of people who have different cultural backgrounds and come from other places from within the United States and around the world."

At least within the "melting pot" of our classroom, (quadruple scare quotes), Rose sets herself the difficult task of naming racial messages she has heard growing up in a majority-white community and explaining her struggle to respond to these comments. These stories are difficult for her to tell for several reasons. First, they are painful and embarrassing. "It is hard for me to say this but I have heard people in my own family say things that are stereotypes about different races." Second, she either cannot remember these instances clearly, does not feel comfortable fully revealing them, or both. "I do not remember exact instances when they were said but I remember what was said and how it made me feel." Third, the majority of the comments she quotes actually refer to white people. She describes family members saying, "Asians are really bad drivers"; then, in a dispute with a Polish neighbor, a relative said, "Polish people are stupid"; finally, people in her family referred to television characters as "white trash." Of these moments, which she describes as articulating "racist stereotypes," only one is directed at a racially marginalized group—Asian Americans. The second is an "white ethnic" slur, aimed at a group that is racially "white," in the current US racial lexicon. The third is a class-based insult. It is notable that Black people are entirely absent from this list of comments, since the whiteness of her community on Long Island is certainly founded in anti-Black housing policies. In her first attempt to look at racism in the setting of this class, she appears to select "safe" comments.

In the extended quotation below, I see Rose's syntax wind itself into circuitous collapse as she attempts to narrate the casual racism in her majority-white life without betraying herself or her family. In addition to shielding the direct words of her family, I believe her rhetorical indirection signals Rose's sense of futility and confusion about engaging these comments, which she has tried to do without feeling she's made an impact:

> I felt whatever I did say did not make a difference in changing their minds or getting him or her to not say it ever again. That is why at times I did not say anything because I did not think anything I said would make a difference. Looking back I understand why I did it but it does not make it ok for the person to make a generalization about a whole race and for me at times to not say anything about it. For me, I think it was hard to try and explain that using the stereotype is not good and we should try and think about others before we say something that could be racist.

This passage studiously avoids concrete moments of speech and clearly identified speakers. She hopscotches between gender binaries, suggesting either multiple speakers or curious abstraction. Her verb tenses lean toward the habitual present, expressing repeated experiences rather than describing one incident in detail. Rose's own choice to speak or not speak in this long string of conversational moments makes no discernible difference. Her difficulty in making sense both *during* these moments—and *in telling about them*—drains the energy and direction from her prose.

In contrast to the futility of her attempts to describe and speak back to racist views at home, Rose describes a sense of agency over her own views on race, developed since arriving at college. "As race has become a more prevalent issue in politics and society today, I think it is opening my eyes to how I have experienced race in my life. I am starting to think where I live has an impact on how I view race along with how I interpret and react to what others say towards different races. I believe that I am realizing that race is everywhere." However confusing her heavily qualified syntax, Rose nevertheless tentatively articulates appreciation for the opportunity to examine race at college. Her first attempt at public writing about race (she knew this essay would be read by a few of her peers, as well as by me) is much more convoluted than her other writing early in the semester. However, while she struggles to write about race, she shoulders on.

Rose shared her "Racial Identity Narrative Essay" (see appendix for full assignment)—with three other students, in a randomly formed group: Chelsea, a Haitian American student from another suburb of New York City; Khalil, a Black student from Prince George's County, Maryland; and John, a white student from another majority-white town in Long Island. These students commented on Rose's draft while she commented on theirs. They all met briefly to discuss their comments in class. Their feedback to Rose boiled down to three central points: (1) Everyone hears, and to some extent believes, stereotypes; (2) it is important to speak up against them, even if the attempt is a failure; (3) keep writing.

Chelsea responded:

> Honestly this is courageous of you to admit that in your family you have heard them say stereotypes about other races. I think that in a sense EVERYONE no matter race, gender, culture etc., has at least said something stereotypical or even racist about one another, I know that I may have. Admitting is honestly the first step to fixing a problem and I appreciate that you realize that some of the things that people in your family have said are stereotypes and not true.

Adding that she has herself remained silent when hearing stereotypes articulated, Chelsea identifies silence as the real problem: "I think the problem is that instead of correcting one another on why this is seen as racist or demeaning we stay silent, which perpetuates the cycle of these stereotypes being used." Khalil agrees, writing, "I believe that all people use stereotypes at one point or another but that people should not allow that to be the lens in which someone is viewed." Both Chelsea and Khalil then emphasize that the most important thing is to attempt to intervene. Being heard or making a difference is less important, since those things are out of one's control. In addition, Khalil writes, "While I enjoyed this inclusion of stereotypes I got kind of confused when you began talking about them." He suggests,

> adding in some more descriptive language to really put the reader in your shoes as you heard the stereotypes being said or better yet make the reader feel as though they were the ones the stereotypes were being directed to. This type of language could allow the reader to be more empathetic and better understand how hurtful these half thought judgements really are. I enjoyed hearing that you are an advocate for a true vision of people and hope you try to be the change you want to see in the world!

His encouragement to write more vividly and to speak up challenges Rose to keep going. Further, her comments in his margins suggest she appreciates his ability to name and combat racism, and explicitly asks about it. When he wrote about working with a white friend to expose retail racism, she writes: "This was such a brave thing for you to do and

I could never imagine having to do that after you figured out what happened. What were you thinking —— as you were confronting the man?" Khalil used this question to experiment with some revision. He did not ultimately use that material in his final piece, however, opting instead to look more directly at white gentrification.

John wrote the following in Rose's margins: "I'm also glad that you decided to come here because this campus is a melting pot of all sorts of ethnicities and I think these next four years will be the most amazing of your life if you get the chance to become friends with people from all sorts of different backgrounds especially for a person like yourself who never was exposed to diversity growing up." John offered himself throughout the semester as a white person from suburban Long Island who has been less racially isolated than most other white people in his situation. He supports the value of white people being around people of color.

Immediately following this exchange of feedback, all students did a brief revision exercise in class. They selected a place in their racial identity narrative where they wanted to make their experience more clear for readers, and they spent time writing new material. Rose's in-class revision begins more concretely: "My family is sitting at the dinner table talking about their days." However, her prose grows murky again almost immediately: "Something in the conversation comes up, something that triggers someone to say a comment about race." Passive voice allows the comment to hang over her family. "The racial comment is said and for a second there is silence. I think we all knew that a stereotype was just made."

While the speaker remains shrouded in gender-neutral language, the listeners become a collective first-person entity who share a "second of silence" as an important moment of decision-making. Her final sentence below, while still spectacularly indirect in constructing herself as a speaking subject, is written to herself and others in her family in the imperative: "It was however, in that second of silence where *someone including me* had to decide if we will say anything back. Call that person out on that stereotype and try and convince them to not say that" (italics mine).

Following this drawn-out moment of suspense, the scene immediately splits into two outcomes, neither of which changes the speaker's behavior. The subject becomes "nobody," rather than "us," and verbs go from imperative to conditional, littered with "woulds": "It is bad to say this but nobody, not even me would say anything and brush off the comment. Other times I would say something, nobody else would, but I feel like what I said was not fully heard and the stereotype would be used again."

Despite encouragement from her peer review group, Rose appears to be rhetorically paralyzed by several factors: the difficulty of outing members of her family for their racist views; an overwhelming sense of the futility of her own speech, which appears to thwart her efforts to speak and write about race; and also potentially the fact that she is writing for a majority-Black-identified audience in her peer review group.

"THOSE WHO STAND OUT": FACING ANTI-BLACKNESS IN A HYPERSEGREGATED COMMUNITY

Rose shared her second narrative, her "Race and Space Essay" (see appendix for full assignment), with the same group. I believe three factors—(1) the charge to look at racial geography, (2) feedback from her peers, and (3) an intervention from me—helped her revise toward greater racial literacy in this piece than her first.

She begins concretely: "When you turn on to [my street] it is an unsuspecting hill you don't realize until you are driving too fast down it." Further, she begins to talk about Black people and white people. She represents them very differently—Black people are hypervisible and create a crisis of interpretation, whereas white people remain disembodied, ubiquitous, afraid, and hyperisolated. The essay, titled "Those Who Stand Out," describes her majority-white neighborhood as "a revolving door of white people leaving and coming in." She describes a peculiar racial vision problem, perhaps akin to Grace's vision problem in chapter 2. There is one Black family that lives in her neighborhood, and she has "never seen this family." "It is like they live there but you never see anyone leave or come home and I wonder why. Do they like to keep to themselves? Are they just very busy? Does race play any role in this situation? I have no idea."

Questioning her Black neighbors' apparent invisibility without trying to answer her own question, she exhibits an openness in this piece. She also uses some straightforward description of her town and less syntactical complexity early on. I'm tempted to speculate that she is encouraged by her initial peer feedback to let down her guard a bit and be more observant and descriptive.

After warming up by talking about the invisibility of her only Black neighbors, she introduces the main point of her essay, and the inspiration for her title, "Those Who Stand Out."

> I remember a few years back hearing about guys who would get off at the train station here in [her town] who were coming in from towns close by. It was said that these guys were coming here in attempt to sell drugs. They

would walk around near the middle or high school or by the after school hang out near the pizza and Italian ice shops. These guys who were coming were black.

Rose finally names Blackness here. One can feel the effort it took; she puts it off as long as possible, using the word "Black" at the tail end of a long sentence. Immediately after using the word "Black," Rose's prose introduces an apology and a qualification: "Now it's terrible that stereotypes got put on these guys but because these guys were coming to a predominantly white area, they would be noticed very easily." She returns to this point repeatedly, that judging people for looking different is wrong but that the sheer visual contrast between their skin (and later, she adds, their style of dress) from the white people in her town, makes them "stand out." She brings readers into her own perspective here:

> I remember seeing at different times black guys walking down [X] Road, one of the main roads in [my town]. I had no clue where these guys were going or coming from but they dressed a little different then the people around here and they were deemed as being out of place. Parents, mine included, were telling their kids just to be aware of these guys and to not get involved with them.

This is the closest she comes all semester to naming the source of the racist comments she is troubled by in her family, and she embeds it in a description of many parental comments about Black people. She wants to separate herself from the stereotyping mindset, but it has a disembodied force, seeming to arise naturally from the situation of segregation, rather from individual minds themselves. Her use of the passive voice and vague, disembodied subjects reinforces the sense that white people's prejudices are a result of segregation itself, rather than segregation being a result of white people's prejudice. In this passage, Rose is simultaneously analyzing the ideological operation of colorblind racism and dismissing that ideology as "natural." I read her as rubbing up against what Eduardo Bonilla-Silva calls the "elastic wall of colorblind racism" here.

In naming the harm white hypersegregation does, Rose also displaces agency onto it. She writes, "The fact that these guys were coming to a town that was not racially diverse in a way was setting them up for stereotypes and judgements to be made." The subject of this sentence is "the fact" of Black men coming to a white town. She blames segregation but also the crossing of lines under segregation. Instead of people saying racist things about these men, the "guys" were "set up for stereotypes and judgments to be made." As in her first essay, Rose's syntax hobbles her thinking about racism by evacuating white people from the subject position of sentences about racism. No one occupies her subjectless sentences. Thus, they lack a compass. In the following paragraph alone, she reverses course at least three times in evaluating her white community's response to Black men in their town. I quote her at length to demonstrate her circularity in confronting segregation.

> If a community is used to most everyone being white in their town people are going to notice someone who looks different. This leads to stereotypes, judgements and assumptions being made because since we do not know for sure why any of these guys were coming into town, we were going to assume the worst and think negatively towards them. This should not be the case but people still made or thought these kind of remarks towards those guys who come into town. Instead, we should embrace and welcome anyone of any race who comes here. However, with the threat of drugs being brought with these guys it is hard for those guys to be welcomed. I do think we should not as a community assume anything about these men. What if these guys were not here for any drug related reason? What if one of them was here visiting a friend or had to run an errand. We do not know their circumstances but at the same time we do not know the exact reason why they were here in the first place. It's hard to not be cautious and assume anything when there is a possible threat of drugs being distributed into the community.
>
> The one question I have is, how can we as a community not be judgmental towards others especially if they pose a possible threat while still thinking about the wellbeing of the people who live here? How can we become more diverse if we make assumptions about others of different races who we don't even know?

I believe Rose's attempt to describe the collective prejudice in which she was raised, and how it impacts her own thinking, is weighed down by many factors: her loyalty to her community, her rational rejection of prejudice, her inability to determine a rational attitude toward Black men, and her awareness that two of her readers identify as Black. I believe the pressure of all these factors cause her prose to repeatedly lose its sense of direction. In fact, this pressure cooker of discomfort and confusion leaves Rose's prose ready to burst. I have seen many white students give up at this critical level of discomfort and write about safer topics or write entirely euphemistically about race. Several white students over the years have proven entirely unable to bring themselves to write about race at all, in which case my strategy is to simply name that phenomenon when I see it.

Part of why I think Rose is able to move forward—despite her deeply constricted ability to articulate what it's like to hear racist talk and to form and articulate her own counterviews to it—are her peer reviewers, who act as racial literacy sponsors. Chelsea and Khalil respond by pointing out how uncomfortable Rose's town would be for them, her college classmates. Chelsea begins by revealing that she had been to Rose's town: "I've actually been to [your town] and I do agree with you that the town isn't too racially diverse. Actually my cousin who lives in Long Island had told me about it but I didn't think it was true until I actually was there. It was weird for me because when we had walked into a pizza shop everyone was staring at us." She validates Rose's assertion of the harm of racial isolation, using her own first-person account of how "weird" it was to be stared at by the people in Rose's community.

Khalil's feedback takes a twist on the charge I give peer reviewers to let writers know whether they felt "like you were there," based on a writer's description. He writes: "It really painted the picture thanks to the descriptive language you used. I felt like I could imagine walking in your neighborhood, even if I would be out of place lol." He uses his position as a Black man to show how uncomfortable he would be if subjected to the white anxiety and scrutiny she writes about. (More could be written about the use of "lol" to signal humor in serious situations, but I will simply mark it as a light touch here.) Next, he makes an interesting comparison to his own essay, in which he writes critically about white gentrifiers in his traditionally Black community in Maryland—"The way you describe it seems like it is a similar community to mine where someone of the majority would stand out." Khalil lightly invokes the mutual hostilities between their two communities, affirming he would not want to go to her town, and alluding to his own position against the incursion of white gentrifiers in his. While this created limited common ground, he used it to affirm that one shouldn't "judge a book by its over," as well as affirming that the topic is worth thinking about more: "The idea that stereotypes can really affect your view on a person is something that I think about a lot." He invites her to "think more" about stereotypes as well.

Finally, John compared the rumored "drug dealers" in Rose's town to his own: "I had a similar experience in my neighborhood where these teenagers would do drug deals all throughout the neighborhood but it went against the stereotype because these kids were all white kids selling the drugs." He encouraged Rose to consider how things would have been different if the "drug dealers" had been white.

Rose's peer reviewers all offer perspective flips, jarring but with a light touch. Chelsea and Khalil place themselves in the racial landscape of her all-white community and expose how they had been or would be targeted by her family and community. All three peer reviewers ask her to consider if she would feel differently if the "drug dealers" were white. Finally, Khalil writes about the frustration of white gentrification in his majority-Black community, and Rose writes sympathetically about that dilemma: "I also really like how you take pride in where you live and how it is ok that there was only one race living there. That is what made your community special and you definitely show that in your writing. It must have been quite a change when white people started moving in and changing things."

"HEAD GAMES": INTERROGATING ANTI-BLACK MESSAGES THROUGH REVISION

After these two peer exchanges, I met with students to help plan their Spoken Word performances based on their experiences with race. In Rose's conference, we discussed her two pieces and the responses she had received. I considered her to be at an interesting point, since her apparent desire to discuss the impact of hypersegregation on herself, her family, and her community kept getting swamped by her rhetorical indirection when she tried to do so in writing. She had gotten relaxed, supportive feedback from her peer reviewers, two of whom were Black, and integrated their perspectives as people of color, and specifically Black people, into their feedback on her tentative early writing. They pushed her to say more. I wondered if this invitation would help her become more direct.

Relying on the idea that Rose was struggling with multiple perspectives, I read back to her some of the writing I've mentioned above and commented that I heard multiple voices going through her head and that she could consider writing her performance as a dialogue between these voices, rather than needing to come up with her own answers. This idea was driven by the early work we had done in the semester, when I asked students to write dialogues animating contemporary debates on academic code-switching to capture multiple points of view and locate themselves in the conversation.

Most students turn down ideas like this, in which I ask them to dig deeper into contradictions in their writing and thinking. However, rather than switch to a "safer" topic, Rose took this idea and ran with it. She externalized the circular thinking that appears to have paralyzed her in earlier writing on race—in which she described herself as unable to speak effectively when she hears racist talk and also susceptible to racist messages herself when she sees people of color in her majority-white community. She used internal dialogue to narrate her own struggle with seeing Black people in her town without panicking. By identifying the voices floating around her, and placing them inside her own head in this piece, she seemed to increase her capacity to articulate them.

She set out to dramatize the psychological impact of white hyper-segregation, constructing a dialogue between two voices in her head as she drives down the main street in her town and sees a Black man walking down the street. One voice believes the rumors about Black drug dealers in her town and also buys into media representations that criminalize Black men. The other voice questions those beliefs and advocates a more neutral stance toward the man she sees. Here is the piece she performed.

Head Games

I'm driving up [a street in my town] when I turn and look over.
I see a Black man.
This Black man is walking with this swagger that looks like he belongs here.
He's dressed in a jacket, baggy jeans, and sneakers.
My head takes over.
What's that Black man doing here? He doesn't belong, he's dangerous, a drug dealer! He will hurt the kids of this town. Kids, watch out!
Wait, what? Why are you saying that, do you know him?
I don't know him but his kind is no good.
THAT'S RACIST!
Yeah but it may not be wrong with hearing those rumors about guys coming into town who are drug dealers.
It may not be true either. What does that Black man look like to you?
I see a Black man walking some place where he shouldn't. I see a man that looks nothing like the rest of us who are white.
Fine but all those things you just said you were seeing and not looking. You can miss a lot when you are only seeing.
Like what?
You see only the physical but when you look you go deeper. When you look you wonder, is the Black man visiting someone here? Is he running an errand that doesn't involve drugs?
Well, I don't know any of those things for sure.
That's my point, you don't know anything so how do you know for certain that the Black man is selling drugs?
He's Black. Black men deal drugs.
Not all Black men! You can't assume all Black men are dealing. You can't assume this Black man sells them.
Why not?
You don't know him, I don't know him but I know our assumptions are not always right.
There are guys just like him all over the news who get caught with illegal substances. You'll probably see his head shot on tv eventually.

The news can hide the full picture. The news doesn't talk about the guys
   behind the drug charges. You believe all that you watch and hear on tv?
No, but I can't disregard it either.
My head hurts.
I don't know what to believe.
That Black man is walking down the street.
He's only walking down the street but I'm used to seeing only white along
   these streets.
Seeing Black mixes everything up in my head, it plays head games.

Unlike her earlier writing about race, in which she uses passive voice
and repetitive indirection, Rose's shorter sentences here offer more direct
description and clarity about warring ideas inspired by the simple sight of
a Black man in a white town. To some extent, she seems more rhetorically empowered here, better able to write about the conflicted racial
beliefs inside her own head. She is able to let her family and community
off the hook as she herself becomes the filter for racist messages, whose
exact origins are now somewhat beyond the point. Self-implicating as it
is to name racist views as her own, she does not betray anyone else here.
She can name the values behind each side—the voice for suspicion, the
voice for open-mindedness—and look at those values more clearly. In
short, she creates the only conversation she is currently able to have on
this topic—with herself. And she performs this internal dialogue for our
class in an effort to get out of her head.

What is the impact of this rhetorical decision for other members of
the class? Rose's reflection on her Spoken Word voices this fear about
that: "While writing my piece, I experienced feelings of anxiousness.
Not just for the fact of presenting but also to not offend anyone. Race
is a hard topic to discuss and I feel at some point in discussing it some
people may get offended and that is one hurdle we have to overcome."

She was right. . . . At least one student—an West African student who
identified as Black—was upset by Rose's initial naming of her racial fear,
writing the following in his reflection journal:

I understood that [Rose] tried to be as honest as possible in recounting
her thoughts but some things that came up were rather discomforting to
me. I wished she had held back some of her thoughts. I guess what I didn't
know couldn't hurt me. She eventually admitted her wrong and used the
story to drive towards her message of the importance of looking and not
just seeing. . . . No one can travel back to the past to prevent Rose's experience from playing out as it did, but now, even Rose, along with the rest of
us, has a different opinion towards the experience. We can only be understanding enough to realize that we can't change people's experiences (as
in Rose's case) but we can change our thinking so that no one gets hurt.

Rose has opted, with my encouragement, to air her white racism in a mixed-race class, and—as she and I both feared—this has placed a burden on at least one student of color put in the position of listening to her. She did offend this listener. He subsequently works through his "discomfort" and his desire that she had "held back some of her thoughts," offering the generous interpretation that Rose was attempting to "change her thinking . . . so no one gets hurt." However, it is not hard to imagine that this generosity is a part of his navigation of the course, and my expectations.

In another strike against her piece, Rose's own reflection on her Spoken Word piece concludes that her circularity signals failure:

> Both inside and outside yourself you may be trying to compare what the news and your experience tell you about race with your morals on how people should be treated. From this comparison, you then try and make sense of everything. In my poem, as hard as I try to make sense of these things, I keep on going in circles and can't make sense of all my thoughts and feelings.

If the goal of her piece, as she and I had imagined it in her conference, was to get out of the endless loop of tolerance versus racism, then it certainly fails. She remains stuck. She is unable to see Black people in a way she finds socially or morally acceptable. As she concludes: "Seeing Black mixes everything up in my head, it plays head games."

I read this conclusion two ways. First, Rose's insights are highly limited. Syntactically, she moves into a new space as she works out this mental struggle—the second person. Displacing her dilemma onto a "you," she appears unable to face her racist feelings. Further, she leaves open the possibility that the arrival of a Black man on her white landscape is at fault, not the racist ideas aimed at him.

However, a second reading sees more potential. Her admission of failure identifies an alternative strength of the poem as a performance. She has found a purpose for speaking—to show people this battle in her head and to invite them to look at the battles in their own heads. Perhaps the "you" she creates in her reflection invites other people to share her dilemma:

> I want to tell people that you are not alone in struggling with the idea of race. People have this battle with race internally and it can almost be like a cycle because you are constantly going back and forth with how you feel and how your experiences and society have taught you about race. This battle of thoughts can affect your emotions and make you question what you believe in. This battle is not always easy but it can help you determine where your beliefs and values lie when it comes to race.

Rose's racial literacy at this point is highly tenuous. She is clear on the damage she has incurred by living in a segregated community and is absorbing harmful racial messages about Black people. However, it is not yet clear what this struggle will yield. Will she simply blame these bad feelings themselves for her discomfort and retreat back into white fragility and colorblindness? Further, is it worth the effort of the class, especially students of color, to endure offenses, microaggressions, or worse while she works through this? I believe Rose is occupying a crucial tipping point for white racial identity development as theorized by Janet Helms and adapted by Tatum ("Talking about Race") and others. Rose is attempting to assimilate new ideas into her worldview, navigating the guilt and shame that threaten to pull her back into colorblind modes of thinking. She sees the harm of living in this way, but will she come to understand how she came to be in this position, and fight against it? What will happen if she "tips"?

"WE LIKE TO THINK THAT COPS ARE NICE PEOPLE": RACIAL LITERACY SPONSORS GIVE TESTIMONY

While Rose struggled to write herself past internalized anti-Black messages, a Black male classmate from a Long Island town near hers described the impact of such anti-Blackness in his own Spoken Word. Jordan described being harassed by a police officer who stopped his car and accosted Jordan when he was walking home from middle school. The officer asked him many questions and made Jordan open his saxophone case to make sure it didn't hold a "bomb." When Jordan asked, "Is this racial profiling?" the officer got back in his car and drove away. Jordan's experience is such a clear inversion of Rose's—his harassment by a white police officer in a town like hers was blatantly absurd and also frightening. His piece was cited by other students in their reflection journals as one of the most impactful in the class.

In listening to Jordan, Rose is confronted with the harmful effect of an officer's gross misreading of twelve-year-old Jordan as a threat—the logical outcome of the messages in her head. The judging of Black male bodies in white spaces presents Rose with a "head game," but has much higher stakes for Jordan. Rose wrote: "I feel like it is one thing to hear about someone being racially profiled. It is another when someone is right in front of you telling you that it happened to him personally. I could not believe how the cop was talking to Jordan."

After listening to Jordan, Rose is no longer able to imagine her "head game" as a victimless event, an issue that takes place primarily in her head. Her hyperdistance from people of color is contracted by hearing from Jordan. However, her thinking remains convoluted and circular:

> We like to think that cops are nice people and would not try and target you if you are just minding your own business while walking home from school like Jordan said he was. It seems like though, cops can also have preconceived ideas about people depending on your race and that is what offended me. . . . It is hard to imagine that cops, those who are supposed to keep us safe without judgments, would in fact judge you based on the color of your skin. I think that many people would not think that cops would do this. We do though have to keep in mind that race is everywhere even in places and in people who we think we can trust.

"PRETTY MUCH EVERYONE KNOWS THERE IS RACISM IN LAW ENFORCEMENT": TRANSFORMATIVE UNDERSTANDING IN ROSE'S INSTITUTIONAL RACISM RESEARCH

At some point during Rose's research, or while listening to other students' research presentations, she experienced a dramatic turn in her sense of how people view the police. By the time she finished presenting her work and listening to other presentations, she voiced a down-to-earth acceptance—"pretty much everyone knows there is racism in law enforcement." Her changed understanding appears to coincide with a simpler, more straightforward syntax.

As Rose responded to my charge to think "institutionally" about the questions she has raised about harmful racial messages that surrounded her growing up, she had many opportunities to receive "racial literacy sponsorship" in this effort. Ultimately, I find that she negotiated with the expectations of the assignment, bending them into a shape she can use to advance and articulate her own thinking. To do this, she had to fail at many of the course goals and subvert many of the research requirements I laid out.

When I introduce the research project on institutional racism, I tell students that the more perspectives one can bring to bear on a social problem, the better. Until Rose was my student in 2017, I used police violence against Black people as an example of a topic that no student had been able to successfully research from both police and Black Lives Matter perspectives. I cited two students who had tried. One was my student in 2014, the daughter of a police officer of color who couldn't find robust enough sources from police voices that attended to systemic racism within the police force. The other student was a white student who tried to put Black Lives Matter and Blue Lives Matter perspectives in dialogue, but found the divide between them too wide. In Rose's class, I mentioned these projects as usual. Rose decided to take it on.

The digital essay Rose then produced on "Racism in Law Enforcement" could easily be deemed a failure as a presentation on institutional racism aiming to promote "transformative understanding." It has the following significant problems:

- In an assignment based on looking at systematic patterns in the ways racial injustice is carried out by social institutions, she expresses distrust in numbers and also avoids using them for the most part. In execution, she has some of her facts wrong; her presentation of numbers is confusing, and the class was not heavily impacted by her findings—instead they coached her on more effective presentation of statistics when she presented a draft.

- The central story that grounds her digital poster—the 2015 shooting of Jamar Clark by Minneapolis police officers—is unfamiliar to her audience. Her digital essay neither explains his story, nor does she use it to generate any kind of statistics or data.

- Her interpretation of what constitutes "institutional"-level analysis is limited: The academic source she cites is itself largely a first-person story, and much of the evidence she presents is not quantifiable. The historical narrative she creates in her digital poster is unwieldy—it isn't entirely accurate or based on sources.

- Other students in class did not mention her digital essay as particularly impactful in their reflection journals.

- Rose was less informed than other presenters on criminal justice. They were mostly Black students whose presentations were very much in step with a critique of mass incarceration along the lines Michelle Alexander has laid out, and which were familiar to most of these students through their own research, including Ava Duvernay's film *13th*, which many of them had seen. Most of the other five projects on criminal justice took on an aspect of mass incarceration, such as the war on drugs (2), women's incarceration (2), or the school-to-prison pipeline (1). In contrast, even after her research, Rose seemed unfamiliar with the basic concepts behind mass incarceration, commenting after the other presentations, "I never realized the large number of people being incarcerated especially in the United States. All these different facts just makes me think that we have to do something to reduce the different kinds of racism out there in order to make the world a better place."

However, through her highly unusual uses of the basic elements of this assignment (academic sources, visual elements, data), she was able to create some powerful connections that remain difficult to spot on a cursory view:

- Her essay describes policing as inherent to creating an ongoing "separate but equal" racial reality for Black people in the United States. Framing the police as enforcers of the suppression of public protest by Black people, whom they have been trained to mistrust, she toggles back and forth between police violence against criminal activity and Civil Rights actions, showing how both are falsely constructed as "threats" for the police to attack.

- She takes on segregation both textually and visually. She places Black men and white police officers together in multiple visual frames, countering the ubiquitous segregation that she argues contributes to inhumane policing practices.

- Her project adapts unexpected aspects of Black-authored Critical Race Theory scholarship into a collagelike, uncannily radical critique of the ways that police officers have been positioned to repress Black life and Black activism as criminal activities.

The introduction of Rose's digital poster struggles with the nature of "institutional racism." Her first panel bears the subtitle "Negative Stereotypes . . . Common Culture for Police Officers?" along with a short blurb summarizing the work of anthropologist Robin Oakley, who "believes that police work can be an opportunity for officers to gain skewed views on society. Negative stereotypes can form and become part of the common culture within the police occupation due to white officers having experiences with minority groups" (Oakley). This social psychological explanation of a "culture" of "skewed" social views resulting from police work itself is what I might deem "quasi-institutional," a common response from students when I ask them to see things "institutionally." The problems they describe occur in institutions, but they are not rooted in the work the institution does. I have come to see such quasi-institutional thinking as a way that students can scaffold themselves toward institutional thinking. In general, I don't reject it when they offer it, but I ask students who present such psychological dynamics to look at economic factors as well. I believe Rose is trying out some "quasi-institutional" analysis here.

From this tentative, race-muted take on police violence as a psychological problem, Rose then catapults herself into visual iconography that far exceeds the analytic reach of her opening text. First, she sets about the visual task of "reseeing" Black men. She uses several images that emphasize the vulnerability of Black men and the violence of white police officers: a young Black man being handcuffed; a young Black man being attacked by a police dog; a young Black man's smiling face in a news story about his shooting death at the hands of the police; and finally, supplicating hands at the bottom of a visual frame, with a police officer, baton raised, suspended above him. The young Black men in these images are depicted as objects of white violence. None of them is threatening. Instead, the threats come from the police.

Second, she demonstrates how white police officers have been placed on the front lines of state repression of Black people since the establishment of Jim Crow laws. She places a screenshot of a tweet about a memorial for Jamar Clark, killed by police officers in Minneapolis in 2015, beside an iconic black-and-white photo of a middle-aged white police officer whose dog attacks a young Black man during the 1963 Birmingham antisegregation protests in 1963 (Hudson).[4] Rose places this image directly under the word "THEN," and the Jamar Clark tweet under the word "NOW," firmly connecting the two events.[5] Her blurb reads "'Separate but equal' treatment among blacks and whites was established by the Jim Crow laws in the 1890s. Pictures of the police force were captured at this time." This is an awkward and inaccurate historical gloss, but placing Birmingham 1963 and Minneapolis 2015 side-by-side links two moments when police were called in as agents of state control of Black Civil Rights protesters. Visually, this juxtaposition demonstrates how white police officers have been set in the path of Civil Rights throughout US history. It connects the Black Lives Matter protesters demanding police accountability for taking Black lives to Civil Rights protesters demanding integration in daily public life.

In juxtaposing these images and text in this captioned collage, I believe Rose is engaged in the work she laid out for herself in her Spoken Word—to be better able to see Black men's humanity, which has been obscured for her due to white isolation, media distortion, and the filter of her father's experiences as a police officer, making men like him—she implies in this digital essay—into foot soldiers in the repression of Black people. With this inaccurate but visually compelling set of images and claims, she places the history of white police officers as violent repressors of Black Civil Rights in the explanatory frame of current police violence against Black men.

"COURAGE UNDER FIRE": ACADEMIC RESEARCH AND RACIAL LITERACY SPONSORSHIP

How did Rose come to this unwieldy but powerful historical narrative? What forms of racial literacy sponsorship helped her produce this particular visual text? In the course of research in the university library databases, she located an article titled "Courage under Fire: Handcuffed and Gagged by the Streets," by Yvette LaShone Pye, a Black professor of education at St. Mary's University. Pye's article appears to be Rose's chief racial literacy sponsor in creating this project. Pye is the author of the tweet that appears in Rose's digital essay, as well as the article Rose cites. Her scholarship and activism offer Rose two crucial ingredients: (1) a model for speaking to hostile white audiences about racism in law enforcement, and (2) an introduction to the history of police violence against Black Americans as a Civil Rights issue. Pye's article describes her vulnerability while articulating a Black Lives Matter perspective on policing to two hostile white audiences. First, as an invited speaker on a panel at her university titled "#Black Lives Matter and the Unfinished Business of the Civil Rights Movement," she felt vulnerable and uncertain about whether her largely white audience had the capacity to hear her perspective or that of the students of color at their university. Second, in a twitter exchange, she criticized the Minneapolis police. They erected barriers around their precinct during a 2015 Black Lives Matter protest against the failure to prosecute two white police officers who killed Jamar Clark. She received a negative response calling the protestors "trash" from someone who appeared to be an anonymous police officer. Days afterward, white supremacists fired on the protestors (Baumhardt et al.).

The very thing that made Pye's article an unusual choice for this assignment on institutional racism—its focus on a narrative of Pye's own experience of fear and silencing while voicing a Black Lives Matter perspective in academic and public digital spaces—made it useful for Rose. Pye's article filters information on police violence against Black people through her own personal struggle to render the "traumatic" (Pye's word) nature of being Black in the United States visible to a white audience. Pye thus wrote from a position Rose could not inhabit but modeled for Rose the ethical value of speaking about white racism even when it is dangerous to do so.

In adapting points from Pye's article to her digital essay, Rose took visual elements that do not appear in the article itself—an iconic photo of a police dog attacking a Black man in Birmingham 1963 and one of Pye's tweets about Jamar Clark, which Rose appears to have found on twitter—to create an historical collage that exceeds her knowledge of the situation but does adapt the spirit of Pye's purpose—to educate herself (a white college student, part of Pye's target audience) about the history of the Black community's targeting by the police and the ways that targeting is aimed at curtailing their basic Civil Rights.

I see no evidence that Rose's classmates were able to perceive the deeper work her digital essay performed, since she presented it in such confusing ways, and since the larger insights of the project appear some-what unconscious or at least intuitive. Their in-class comments after her presentation all focused on improving her presentation of data. No one chose to write about her piece in their reflection journals afterward. In contrast, Rose was highly influenced by the projects of other students. Responding to a project that demonstrated media representations of Black men as "criminals," she reflected on new institutional aspects of her troubles seeing Black men humanely: "I never realized that the media did this type of distortion between races." Her comment on another media presentation suggests new institutional vision. Responding to a student's description of racial and gender disparities in the demograph-ics of the Academy of Motion Pictures' voting members, she wrote: "I'm almost getting the vibe that we are going back in time when white men were really considered superior when they were allowed to vote and buy property. . . . I think this is crazy how we are supposed to be in an age of diversity but this looks to be a prime example of white superiority." She looks institutional racism in the face here, a new ability that may result from multiple experiences of racial literacy sponsorship.

ROSE AS RACIAL LITERACY SPONSOR

Rose may have learned over the course of the semester, but the ques-tion remains whether this is a two-way street. Is a student like her able to contribute to the class's knowledge, as well as to benefit from it? This study of her work so far has not suggested a meaningful contribution from Rose in return for the valuable and generous input she received from others.

Rose's research and presentation offered two surprising impacts. First, she revealed in an end-of-semester reflection that the form of insti-tutional racism she learned most about was not law enforcement—the topic she researched and presented on—but "the family." Although students change topics all the time, it is very unusual for a student to complete, present, and revise a piece of work, and *then* observe that their topic was different than everyone thought. However, as I read her reflec-tion, I had to agree. Rose wrote:

> I now have a better understanding of different types of institutional racism and how they can be seen in society. I was also able to reflect on the racial institutions that have impacted me. My family as one of the biggest racial institutions in my life has said things that can be racist. This has made me feel uncomfortable and I realized it wouldn't make me uncomfort-able if it was not an important issue that I should try more to address and

discuss my thoughts and feelings on it rather than saying nothing. I have also come to realize that race is prevalent in everyone's lives whether we realize it or not.

Rose locates her most profound learning about institutional racism within her own family. She is no longer weighed down by the question of whether it makes sense for her to speak up. She takes her discomfort as a sign that she must speak. I speculate that the histories and experiences she learned about during the semester gave her some tools to analyze the factors influencing racist discourse in her family: the hypersegregation of her community, her father's experiences in the police force. However, she leaves the curtain down over her family's views, as she has done all semester. She focuses instead on her own need to speak.

The second surprise Rose's work yielded occurred after she was my student. While her digital essay made almost no impression on her own class, it ended up having a significant impact on future students. She inspired white students, and non-Black students of color, to research police relations with communities of color in much larger numbers than they had in the past. While Black students had been choosing the topic of police racial profiling since I initiated a final research project on race in 2014, few non-Black students had done so.

The semester following the one in which Rose was my student was the fall of 2017. When I introduced the institutional racism research project, I gave the same warning that I had given to Rose's class the semester before. Students who want to research police treatment of Black people from a pro-police perspective should beware that some great students have foundered on this topic, especially in looking for sources that meaningfully engage steps against racial profiling. However, there was one difference this time. I showed Rose's infographic essay briefly in my presentation, mentioning that she was the daughter of a police officer who had made some progress in looking at the psychology of officers' roles, the ways that they are positioned to criminalize Black people, and the harm that can result.

That semester, several non-Black students independently elected to research policing practices, more than they ever had before. A white-appearing mixed-race daughter of a Latinx police officer, herself a criminal justice major, investigated practices for improving police relations with communities of color, concluding that community policing practices are more successful than recruitment of officers of color. A Chinese American student who attended a majority-black New York City high school discovered "Broken Windows" policing and presented a scathing indictment of its racial targeting of poor Black and Latinx

New Yorkers, agreeing with the adoption of community policing. These students' research was much more deeply engaged with police reform efforts, in part because one of them was a junior and a criminal justice major, so very comfortable mentoring her classmate through navigating sources. Rose's only impact on them was her positionality, but that impact led to some effective research and important insight.

Another Latinx student from the Bronx presented some very hard-hitting numbers that supported the idea that current policing practices in New York City target and criminalize Black and Latinx New Yorkers and also yield little good policing. Finally, a white male student who appeared new to thinking about race chose racial profiling by police as his topic. His project was less sophisticated but demonstrated an ability to grasp some of the basics of the issues and get up in front of a mixed-race class and lay out some of his thinking and findings on race and policing. All of their work kept Rose's project alive enough for me to choose to interrogate it further here, coming to a deeper understanding of the ways she engaged or adapted the charge to research institutional racism.

In each class in which I have introduced Rose's work as a model when students are choosing their institutional racism research topics, some number of non-Black students have opted to research the policing of Black people. Before this, only two non-Black students had ever done so. Many of these students describe their motivation as that of a close relative on the police force whose perspective on race and policing they are trying to understand. In taking on this challenge, Rose appears to have inspired other students to do so as well.

How did this inspiration work? It wasn't the digital essay itself, which remains challenging to decipher. I have worked hard—including reading all Rose's original sources—to come up with my reading of the work she did there. In her case, the digital poster—for me the centerpiece of the community think tank—did not itself transform other students' understanding. Instead, it appears that her decision to research police racism as the daughter of a police officer is what motivates other students to try the same thing.

What does Rose's work tell me about racial literacy and racial literacy sponsorship? She was multiply sponsored by her classmates while she worked out her problems seeing race and racism in her family, in her community, and in her own mind. She is not done with that work by a long shot. However, she has now made a contribution, serving as a racial literacy sponsor without even knowing she has done so. Rose struggled to deepen her racial literacy, combatting her previous isolation and discouragement in an explicitly racist white hypersegregated community. She is more ready than before to participate in a movement such as the ones called for by Lani Guinier and Eduardo Bonilla-Silva, who maintain that interracial, cross-class alliances of antiracist activists are essential to overcoming racism in its current form. Anyone who wants to launch a deeper attack on racial inequality must look at the dynamic interplay among race, class, and geography in order to make change. In other words, a broad coalition of people, using racially literate analysis, could bring about deep social change that a narrow coalition, united to preserve class interests and narrowly define the problem they addressed, never could. That coalition will need everyone, including Rose. Her work reenvisioning and untangling racism in the police force, in her family, in her community, and in education is important to her future contributions to mitigating racism where she finds it in her life ahead.

I don't know if the racial literacy sponsorship she received in my class will give her strong enough tools to learn to effectively counteract racism. However, my final sighting of Rose gave me cause for hope. Recently, having already written an earlier draft of this chapter, I attended a workshop led by Yolanda Sealey-Ruiz, who shared her activist practices in building communities around racial literacy with our faculty. At Dr. Sealey-Ruiz's workshop, several students in an undergraduate education class joined the audience. Rose was there, sitting in a group of future teachers, listening to the nation's preeminent leader in building educational communities that foster racial literacy. Dr. Sealey-Ruiz offered a compassionate, incisive vision for how to create classroom communities where race can be seen, racism can be combatted, and teachers can themselves serve as racial literacy sponsors. She invited us to take on the personal, pedagogical, and political work required to promote racial literacy for ourselves and our students. She offered us opportunities for "critical reflection," "critical humility," and "critical love." I don't know what Rose took from the workshop, but when she and I spoke briefly afterward, she mentioned bringing Dr. Sealey-Ruiz's work into her own future classrooms. While a single workshop is a drop in the bucket, I was encouraged to see that our education school is offering her—and other future teachers—ongoing opportunities to develop racial literacies. Her path forward is likely to be as bumpy and unpredictable as her work in my class. But she is getting support as she prepares herself for a role in the broad social coalition that Guinier and Bonilla-Silva call for and Sealey-Ruiz is enacting.

Epilogue
MAPPING COUNTERGEOGRAPHIES
IN "HOW RACISM TAKES PLACE"

This epilogue has two very different jobs to do. First, I will briefly return to affordances and pitfalls of teaching about race as a white woman with which I began the book, offering strategies that sustain me in that work to others interested in the same project. Second, and at greater length, I will map the ways my curriculum itself is evolving in response to student writing and chart some potential ways forward for the work captured in this book.

In assessing the potential of this work, as well as its limits, it is important to account for the ways in which my own racial position impacts my role in my classes and in my university. Ironically, introducing race explicitly into my classroom assignments and discussion has actually been made easier for me because I am white. Many of my colleagues of color have described being challenged and targeted by students—in class, in one-on-one conversations, and in class evaluations—when they implicitly or explicitly address race in their classes. This has rarely happened to me. I believe my whiteness is a shield around me when I stand up to start these conversations in class, one I have to make an effort to see.

Although I've thought about it quite a lot, I am not certain why I've received relatively little pushback from students in teaching about race and racism. Perhaps because of my real and perceived forms of power as a white professor, students of color might decide not to challenge me when I make mistakes in addressing race or might respond ineffectively to events in class as they unfold. Perhaps they hold justifiably low expectations of my class's ability to achieve its ambitions in the first place; perhaps they decide to give me a pass; or opt not to challenge me as their safest route forward; or their own internalization of racism or white language supremacy prevents them from calling me out. In my experience, white students are no more likely to call me out. Even the white students most resistant to acknowledging the role of race in their own lives—students whose writing and conversation about race remains stuck

DOI: 10.7330/9781646421107.c005

in euphemism, avoidance, incoherence, colorblind, and even explicitly racist stances—don't tend to take out their struggle on me.

This is not to say students of all races have never taken the brave step of correcting me, resisting the challenges I offer and the ways I offer them, or helped me improve the course. They do that work every day. I invite it and expect such resistance and feedback. As this book has illustrated, every aspect of the course has been shaped by student responses. Sometimes I can name a particular student whose writing, insight, failure, resistance, or direct suggestion inspired a new assignment or a change in how I teach something. Other times, dozens—or even hundreds—of students respond to an assignment and move it in a particular direction through trends and patterns in their responses. But they approach me, almost to a person, in a spirit of something such as "Let's help this nice white lady with what she's trying to do." When they challenge me, it is generally done with a gentle, polite encouragement. I know this is not true for my colleagues of color who introduce race into their classrooms. This is also not entirely about my race—it is also a complex function of age, class, and experience.

I have tried to take advantage of the space afforded me—to leverage my whiteness in service of my goals that students see and name race and segregation. I contribute to denorming whiteness, referring to myself as "white" often, and talking about my choice to use that word. I encourage my students to make deliberate choices about racial naming, as Glenn Singleton does in *Courageous Conversations about Race*. I tell stories about my segregated childhood, and my lack of awareness of having a racial identity until my twenties (see introduction for more on this). I solicit feedback throughout the semester, including anonymous feedback, attempting to keep open channels of communication and correction.

However, it is not my students' job to address my conscious or unconscious investment in white privilege while I do this work. Nor is it the job of my colleagues of color. That's my job. To do so, I need trusted white colleagues, friends, and family who will critically debrief with me, work through inevitable but tiring and unproductive white guilt and other forms of white fragility, and generate productive ideas for repairing and renewing my efforts. And I need to do that for them as well. In addition to historians of whiteness such as Lipsitz, Roediger, and Ruth Frankenberg, we need to read and discuss scholars such as Eduardo Bonilla-Silva, Ibram X. Kendi, Carol Anderson, and Robin DiAngelo, who are mapping ways to practice this work personally, interpersonally, and institutionally. We need to study our own whiteness—not to recenter it as a field of study but to undo its harmful effects and to counteract both the ways it silently shields us and the ways we bring it into our interactions with other people. I hope that this book contributes to that effort. In that spirit, I offer a final reflection on the work itself and how it continues to evolve.

* * *

> *When I say that racism "takes place" I mean it figuratively, in the way that historians do, to describe things that happen in history. But I also use the term as cultural geographers do, to describe how social relations take on their full force and meaning when they are enacted physically in actual places.*
>
> Lipsitz, *How Racism*, 6

As I designed, assigned, responded to, and reflected on the assignments and student texts in this book, this work developed a focus on geographical understandings of race. This focus was somewhat unexpected. First, in archiving and coding student work, I came to see geography as a major route through which students experience and articulate how race operates in their lives, through what Lipsitz calls "overt and covert understandings of race." Second, my own two primary racial literacy sponsors, Tatum and Guinier, imagine racial literacy itself as a function of, and a response to, geographies of racial segregation. Developing racial literacies in my teaching, and in my research about that teaching, has meant grappling with the geographic dimensions of how racism "takes place," as Lipsitz puts it.

Lipsitz describes segregated neighborhoods and schools as "nodes in a network of practices that skew opportunities and life chances along racial lines . . . Racialized space gives whites privileged access to opportunities for social inclusion and upward mobility. At the same time, it imposes unfair and unjust forms of exploitation and exclusion on aggrieved communities of color" (6). He describes racialized space as an ideological problem—a "crucible" for cultivating a "white social imaginary" characterized by "hostile privatism and defensive localism as suburban structures of feeling"—as well as making "racial segregation seem desirable, natural, necessary, and inevitable" (13–15). Further, he argues, "these sites serve to produce and sustain racial meanings; they enact a public pedagogy about who belongs where and about what makes certain spaces desirable" (15). These accounts of my exchanges with students, and their exchanges with each other, chart attempts to create an alternative crucible, one with a very different "public pedagogy."

Two specific countergeographies are currently emerging in my teaching of race and space. While the work of critiquing institutional racism through a spatial lens continues to require more sustained analytic work than we can reliably produce in the span of this course, the affirmative work of calling for and imagining countergeographies based on different principles has gained momentum in recent semesters. I conclude with it because of its role in building my—and my students'—capacities to combat racially divided and unequal geographies through imagining and/or experiencing more equitable, less divided ones. Imagining and creating countergeographies together map future priorities and strategies for my course and for others interested in asking students to grapple with their racially segregated personal and collective geographies. The first countergeography involves looking back and understanding the divided racial geographies of the majority of our home spaces as a paradoxical common ground, while the second involves looking forward at the racial landscapes of new educational and professional spaces students are entering and creating.

COUNTERGEOGRAPHY #1: HOME. THE COMMON GROUND OF NO COMMON GROUND

Racial division and separation make an ironic, often bitter, shared experience for most of my students, providing them a kind of paradoxical common ground. I am currently looking for ways to take better advantage of this paradoxical common ground to authorize and inspire students to critically rethink the historical forces and current policies that drive people of different races apart and inequitably allocate resources across race. Currently, I am working on three fronts to improve my practice.

(1) Naming and Describing (Re)Segregation and Racial Inequality

As students have grappled with and pushed back against my call to articulate what they see in the racial geographies that they have inhabited prior to college, I've been moving away from trying to spark something as simple as "empathy" in each other's racial geographies. Focusing on empathy seems to flatten and erase our own implications in these histories. Instead, my approach going forward is more direct: (1) to simply keep trying to name and describe the (re)segregation of our communities—including the structural ways such resegregation privileges white people and disadvantages people of color—to make (re)segregation itself the premise of our study.

My goal here is something like philosopher George Yancy's edited essay collection in which he asked white writers this question—productively inverting W.E.B. DuBois—"How does it feel to be a white problem?" In his introduction to that volume, Yancy wrote that his goal for white people—"[c]oming to recognize themselves as white problems"—was not a process that would ever reach completion. Instead, he described this as ongoing—"a form of work, self-work, a socio-ontological project that will not conclude in the form of a *fait accompli*" (xxv). Seen through Yancy's vision, the work of divesting from racism—especially for white people but also anyone invested in the racial status quo—is lifelong. Yancy writes, "[A] single action or intention does not 'undo' whiteness. The concept of *deciding* denotes a life of commitment to 'undo,' to 'trouble,' over and over again, the complex psychic and socio-ontological ways in which one is embedded in whiteness. The decision is one that is made over and over again for the rest of one's life" (xiv).

This class presents opportunities recommended by Yancy to *decide* to see the white supremacist history and policies surrounding us. Yancy's goal is less to succeed and more to "linger" or "tarry" over the "truth about one's white self and the truth about how whiteness has structured and continues to structure forms of relationality that are oppressive to people of color" (xiv). Above all, he urges white people to avoid "suturing" over this truth, cordoning themselves off from a continued embrace of its pain. Such suturing resembles Bonilla-Silva's concern that colorblind racism may have infinite elasticity to sustain itself against attempts to pierce it. This unit of study asks students to practice this kind of work and challenges my own ability to both practice and teach it. Confronting the harm done by segregation is not a one-time mental and emotional operation. My students and I will need to continually recommit to *deciding* to look at these divisions in our life and to use all the tools at our disposal to do so.

(2) Students as Co-researchers Rather than Research Subjects

The strength and dilemma of my class lie in being what Linda Flower calls "a constituency of people willing to engage with a problem of which they were probably not yet fully aware" (308). Treating the writing and conversations we do together as collaborative research requires me to continue to engage multiple robust models for students to conceive of themselves in this way. Models for this kind of research include Flower's "community literacy think tank" at Carnegie Mellon's Community Literacy Center and Michelle Fine et al.'s "Youth Critical Participatory

Action Research" at CUNY's Public Science Project. Elements from both of these groups have filtered into my teaching for years. These collaborative research methods allow groups to map the social problems surrounding them and to share their findings with their communities. We can potentially unite around the collective effort to conceive of our communities as spaces where hypersegregation and racial inequality have determined the conditions of our lives and the messages we believe about each other. And we can try to stop accepting those conditions and believing those messages.

As I move in this direction, I have begun framing an overarching question we can only answer together, something like "How does (re)segregation impact multiple racial and economic groups?" I have started asking students to do rounds of "rapid research" about their own neighborhoods, building on brief introductions to the historical and institutional roots of segregation, such as redlining and racial covenants—and their own questions about their own neighborhoods and others, developed in their peer review groups. I am finding that it is not difficult to find local research online, as researchers in most of my students' home communities appear to have begun this work. The search "[my town] and redlining" almost always yields interesting results. In particular, a Freirean "problem tree" could make a productive conclusion to this unit of study.

Engaging with the real physical spaces students are from will not lead to mutual agreement on the histories that brought us here and the meanings we draw from those histories. Instead, it invites a stance of mutual engagement through telling one's life story with a racial lens and listening to the stories of others. It asks students to "tarry" collectively over the effort to see the racial inequities surrounding us and to consider that work both research and art.

(3) Going Public / Amplifying Student Voices

The student writers whose work I have celebrated and critiqued in this book all gave consent for me to study and write about their work pseudonymously. This model of me as researcher and them as consensual subjects of my research is practical. It protects them, allowing them to explore their own prejudices and received beliefs in contained, relatively private settings. It also protects me from being judged for their mistakes, and hopefully, protects them from being judged for mine. However, such protection limits the impact of their own insights to featuring in my curation and analysis. Going forward, I hope to find ways for them to share and confront their ideas more directly and with more ownership.

I am currently developing ways to amplify the voices of students who risk self-disclosure and historical, institutional vision. I am working with my current and former students to determine the terms and modes of sharing this work with a larger audience. The ideas my former students and I are exploring include former students returning to class and addressing my new students, creating publications of former student writing available only to current students, and campuswide or online publications and presentations, or submitting work to external journals or other venues. I hope to enlarge the platform for sharing the most critical and important visions that students articulate about the racial landscapes where they have grown up.

Sharing artistic efforts aimed at seeing race counters what Lipsitz describes as the white spatial imaginary's "racially propelled logic of hostile privatism and defensive localism" (*How Racism* 13). Instead, it aspires toward something along the lines of Lipsitz's proposal of a "black spatial imaginary" characterized by a "democratic and egalitarian ethos," in which artistic reckonings imagine "diverse efforts to turn segregation into congregation, to transform divisiveness into solidarity, to change dehumanization into rehumanization" (19). While I do intend to counter the implicit anti-Blackness that has surfaced in every aspect of this work by affiliating with the "black spatial imaginary," I do not intend this to focus exclusively on Black students but rather, as Lipsitz suggests, to appreciate and learn from the legacy of US Black cultural production that aspires toward democratic, humanizing, communal values and practices. Public sharing of these acts of witness, moments of insight, historical research, and imagined solutions will not result in unitary or complete analysis, but it will potentially constitute multiple incursions into the "white spatial imaginary."

COUNTERGEOGRAPHY #2: BUILDING NEW GROUND, ENTERING EDUCATIONAL AND PROFESSIONAL SPACES

Since Danielle's call to her peer reviewers to see the reality of present-day racism in their communities contended with elastic, colorblind resistance from her peer review group described in chapter 2, I have spent a few years developing a follow-up project that asks students to research institutional racism itself. To do so, I have charged them with identifying a crucial "social institution" in their lives and analyzing institutional racism there. I discuss Rose's response to this project in chapter 4. Despite this mandate to analyze institutional racism, I have continued to feel that students' potential to move from personal to institutional analysis at this juncture in the course remains largely untapped. While every once in a while, a student breaks down a chunk of institutional racism and racial geography directly, more often they struggle. I also noticed very few students opted to study their neighborhoods and communities in this research project, though we had explored many tools for doing so. Very recently, I stumbled on a way to bring this new final project into better alignment with the geographic metaphor developed in the student exchanges described here.

This past semester, I began asking students to consider investigating forms of institutional racism in their majors or future careers. This development emerged fairly organically, in one-on-one conversations with students about their studies and the topics we were discussing in class. As the students who chose to research institutional racism in their future professions began to discuss their research with their classes, it caught on quickly. A future obstetrician studied disparate infant and maternal mortality rates, a future filmmaker studied Maryann Erigha's concept of the "Hollywood Jim Crow," a public health major studied health insurance rates among different races, future teachers studied the evisceration of *Brown v. Board*, a pharmacy student studied the lack of Black pharmacists. The quality of research among students investigating their own future fields of work and study was generally higher than students looking at other areas. New patterns emerged in these students' findings, with discernible connections within and across the professions, as well as among strategies to combat institutional racism in many fields.

This precedent may set a course for the future of my sequence of assignments. Whereas early in the course, I ask them to analyze their origins, I may have to say something like "That's as far as we will try to take this together. Keep going." And when we transition to in-depth research, I may say something like

> Now we are looking forward for each of you. Not because you are done looking at your home communities, but because looking back at one's early years is difficult, lifelong work. It is time to take the skills you use to look at race in your pre-college life and your home communities, and apply it to your studies and careers. In your education and profession, your own race will impact you, and your ability to see race in your chosen areas of study and work will impact the extent to which you can make a difference in those fields. So let's take a look. What is going on with race in education, homeland security, pharmacy, criminal justice, environmental studies, sociology, education, healthcare, hospitality, government, biology, economics, finance, insurance, marketing, public relations, sports management, accounting, literature, film and television, legal studies, chemistry, radiology, graphic design? What is the history behind it? What is being

taught about that here? What else needs to be taught? Who is doing work to make your chosen field more racially inclusive among its practitioners and less racist in its practice? How can you be part of building antiracist work in your chosen field?

I still attempt to use this course to make a map of twenty-first-century racism with my students. However, instead of a more general map, in which they begin at the center and then fade to the background as we look at institutional issues—which has been accompanied by a fading in the clarity of their vision—the maps they made last semester when they investigated their future careers kept them at the center of the map. I hypothesize that student research appears stronger when they investigate their future careers because they can see themselves at the center of the maps they are making without feeling implicated.

Educational and professional maps center college as a space between their pasts and their futures. This keeps the students in the picture I'm asking them to look at, unlike a focus on something more abstract like institutional racism, which is visceral for some and nearly invisible for others. I now think the hinge in the course—from personal experiences with race to larger social patterns—allows them to set a course forward in looking at, critiquing, and imagining ways past daily and systemic forms of racism. They look into the terrain they are poised to enter, or are entering, in order to set an intention about changing the profession before they enter it. I hope their maps of the future can create strategic hopefulness about their capacities to make their fields less racist. As I continue to ask my students to map out racism in the spaces around them, I will make sure that (1) they remain at the center of those maps; (2) they draw the map themselves; and (3) the maps are useful to them.

My course's new emphasis on embracing local institutional challenges to systemic racism coincides with similar developments on my campus and may help this conclusion function for this book in something of the way this new project does in my classes. The introduction lays out my university's twentieth-century racial geography, aimed at evading and marginalizing students of color. During this period, the university exhibited little to no institutional capacity to acknowledge or address racism on campus, in the classroom, or in hiring and treatment of faculty. However, led by student activism beginning in 2016, the university has begun to form new structures—both institutional and extrainstitutional—to face and address intersecting forms of inequity. My university's approach to race looks very different than it did when I began assigning this work and writing this book.

It is an exciting and uncertain time for my university, and the need for affirmative visions of a possibly emergent antiracist university are acute. It thus appears that we all need to map our place in the university and the world at large, to sharpen our compasses and chart countergeographies.

APPENDIX

RACIAL IDENTITY NARRATIVE ESSAY

The purpose of this essay is to ask you to write a narrative of one very specific moment in your life that demonstrates something important about the impact of race in your life—in order to share and understand each of our stories better. One point of this assignment is to just get to work telling stories about race. If we keep chipping away at the ways in which the different forms of racism haunt all of our experiences, we have a better shot at getting as free of it as we can. A second point of this assignment is to reflect on what Beverly Daniel Tatum would call your "racial identity development," your lifelong process of incorporating messages about race out in our world into your sense of yourself and how you fit into that world.

This assignment will help you write about a difficult topic, and help other people do the same. The strategy is to blow up one moment for all its significance, rather than trying to cover a lot of experiences all at once.

Before You Write: Brainstorm a list of memories about a time when you noticed something going on with race in your life. (You may have noticed it then, or you may have noticed it later. Even now.) What happened? Bring it to life so other people reading your narrative can walk in your shoes through that experience.

Here are some possible places where you could start your narrative (But when you start actually writing, CHOOSE ONE! Don't try writing about them all!):

1. When were you first aware of yourself as a member of a particular racial group?

2. When were you first aware of people from other races? Which races?

3. When did you first witness or experience someone being treated differently because of his or her racial group?

4. When was a time that you were proud of your racial identity?

5. When was a time you realized you would be treated differently because of your race?

DOI: 10.7330/9781646421107.c006

6. What are some times when you had (have) friends from different racial groups?

7. What is one significant event in your life related to race or racism?*

* *These questions are taken from Adams, Bell, and Griffin's Teaching for Diversity and Social Justice (132).*

Writing the Narrative: In 800 words or more, tell the story of this moment *as vividly as you can.*

- The idea is to capture one memory as vividly as possible, so that a reader can follow your mind through the moment, and understand what you were thinking and feeling.
- Use language that appeals to the five senses and put your readers in your shoes.
- Use dialogue so readers can hear the voices in your narrative.
- Frame the moment you describe so that readers know what you want us to take away from it. Use your beginning and ending to impact your reader. Your audience for this piece is the community of St. John's University. More specifically, this class.

  * *This assignment is based on one I wrote collaboratively with Amanda Moulder and Octavia Davis when we first assigned a version of this assignment in 2011. At that time, it was more broadly focused on a range of social identities, rather than race in particular. It is no longer possible for me to remember which of us wrote which parts of this collaboratively-invented assignment.*

RACE AND SPACE ESSAY: WRITE ABOUT YOUR NEIGHBORHOOD WITH ATTENTION TO RACE

Before you write: Brainstorm a list of who lives, works, and spends time in your neighborhood. Then brainstorm a list of possible moments you could narrate that involve race in your neighborhood in some way. You have been writing about coming from places where everyone is the same race, where your family is in a radical minority compared with your neighbors, and everything in between. Many of you noticed race for the first time after moving somewhere new. Jot down everyone you can think of who comes through your neighborhood, and the stories (small moments!) you could tell about their interactions there.

When you write your essay, please include two sections. You can blend them together, or separate them from each other—when you are done writing, give it a shape that you think works.

Section 1: Description. Write an overall description of the racial groups who live in your neighborhood—get really really local (like just your block) and then, if you want, zoom out a bit to include the surroundings. Describe your neighborhood in such detail that if one of your peer reviewers woke up there, they would know exactly where they were. Is the racial make-up of your neighborhood uniform/ diverse? Consistent/changing? How so? What do you think of what you notice?

Section 2: Narrative. Tell a story about a time when you noticed race in your neighborhood in some way. Or when, looking back, you see that race was a factor in something going on that you didn't notice at the time. Bring this moment to life so other people reading your narrative can walk in your shoes through that experience.

SPOKEN WORD PERFORMANCE

The final version of your chosen identity narrative will be a Spoken Word performance. This assignment serves multiple purposes:

- It employs the power of speech to improve writing.
- It taps into the tradition of speaking truths about race through Spoken Word.
- It provides an opportunity to share crucial moments from your longer narratives to a larger audience.
- It gives you an opportunity to take a risk in front of an audience, which can catapult learning.

PEER REVIEW

Focus on helping your peers understand how they can tell their stories so that you can step inside their experiences. Your perspective is important because writers can't often step outside their experiences and see what they're making clear and what they aren't making clear.

Questions to Think about as You Read

1. Did the writing ever—even momentarily—transform you from an outsider into an insider? If so, where?
2. And, where did you still feel like an outsider, but understood something about the writer's experience in a new way?
3. You got confused. Where did the writer lose you?
4. Were you ever drawn into the narrative by a piece of imagery or language? What did you see in your mind at this spot?
5. Were you reminded of a connection? What did it remind you of? How did that impact you as you read?

6. You noticed something about the way the writer is using language. What was cool about it to you?

7. You thought of something in a new way. How did the writing inspire new thinking?

8. You drew a blank. What new information—visual, sound, smell, etc.—do you need to see and hear the action?

9. You felt like the writing lost focus. Where did the writing feel disconnected/unrelated? You wanted to know more about what the writer was thinking. What did you want to know? You wished a topic would come up, but it didn't. Explain.

Comfort Zone and Learning Edge. Move out of your comfort zone in your feedback, and approach the learning edge where you and the writer can learn. That is, offer constructive criticism as well as supportive feedback. Everyone will be revising their narratives into Spoken Word pieces, and they need help seeing them in fresh ways. Show them how they can take their writing to another level.

*   *This assignment is also based on one I wrote collaboratively with Amanda Moulder and Octavia Davis when we first assigned a version of this narrative in 2011. As with our other assignments, it is no longer possible for me to remember which of us wrote which parts of this collaboratively-invented assignment.*

   For each of these three assignments, I ask students to post their narrative drafts in a Google Drive folder shared by a randomly-selected group of three or four students. These groups respond to each other's narratives in two ways. First, they respond in margin comments and endnotes that are visible to the whole group on a Google Doc. They have the option to respond to each other's comments as part of their feedback. Second, the group meets in class, reads aloud their endnotes, and gives each writer time to ask questions about the feedback they received and make a revision plan. After going through this review process with both narrative essays, each student then selects one of their essays to revise and perform for the whole class as a Spoken Word. They record their performances and post them to the class website, where they are used for reflection and research within the class for the rest of the semester. During this process, I participate in feedback in two ways. First, I generally write a short comment to the writer once the peer reviewers' work is done, but before the writer selects their piece to revise. Second, I meet individually with each writer to discuss their ideas for revision and performance of their narratives. I emphasize to students that each of these stories is an artefact, and also a gift, that each member of the class contributes to the collective project of understanding the impact of race on the lives of the people in the room. Each contribution deepens that collective understanding and equips us as a whole and as individuals to think and act around race in more informed and compassionate ways. This series of assignments creates highly contested narratives and interactions. Students' processes of making racial meaning from their lived experiences is negotiated and re-negotiated in composing, responding to, revising, and performing narratives with peers and with me.

INSTITUTIONAL RACISM THINK TANK DIGITAL ESSAY

Institutional racism is much harder to see than day-to-day racism, such as microaggressions. Like those forms of racism, it comes from historical and present-day causes. Unlike those forms of racism, it is deeply rooted in the social institutions that govern our lives. We will use this project to analyze and make visible these roots, so that we can begin to see them more clearly, understand their impact on us all, and think about ways to eradicate them.

You will produce your own piece of activism. Your action is to inform the rest of us in this class about the aspect of institutionalized racism that you have studied this semester. Because we have short attention spans, you must design a short text and a 2–3 minute presentation to impart this information to us memorably and accurately.

To do this tricky job, you will create a photo, video or sound-based digital text that shares the most crucial data you learned in your research on an aspect of institutional racism with this class. Your text will share this information in a way that will appeal to the particular audience of our class. Your audience will gain a basic understanding of your topic, including

- the history of this form of institutional racism
- whom this form of institutional racism harms, and how
- who benefits from this form of institutional racism, and how
- why it matters that people in our class understand this issue
- who is fighting against this form of institutional racism

You have researched your topic in depth, so you will likely have a lot of material to sort through. Only share the most essential information. Your job is to give the rest of us a clear, succinct picture of what is going on, and why it matters.

DIGITAL ESSAY REFLECTION JOURNAL ENTRY

Your own presentation: Reflect on your own Digital Essay. Consider the following: What did you learn from creating and presenting it? What did you hope to convey to others in class? Why did you think this information was important for them to understand? What do you think was most/least successful about your presentation? Why? What revisions could improve this project?

Most powerful learning: Choose one presentation that was particularly interesting or powerful to you and describe what you learned from it. What new information did you hear? What is important to you about this information?

Most troubling information: Choose one presentation that troubled you. Did someone present information or analysis that was disturbing, or seems like it can't possibly be true? *Find information to refute what someone said that sounded wrong to you.* Are you right? Are they? *Describe your source.*

Connections and disconnections: Write about any patterns or themes that emerged. In addition, consider any contradictions and disconnections that emerged as you were listening. What new insight did you gain into how race plays out in social institutions? What new (or old) questions do you have about this topic?

NOTES

INTRODUCTION: GROUNDINGS

1. I am grateful to Sonya Manes, who copyedited this manuscript, for her helpful feedback about the ableism embedded in critiquing "colorblindness." Because this book relies on visual metaphors for students' efforts to perceive race and racism in their lives, it thus inevitably participates in such ableist rhetoric. I have attempted to mute the visual metaphors where possible, and focus on the literal target in my classes: student insight and understanding, rather than vision per se. However, the visual metaphors remain.

    Annamma, Jackson, and Morrison argue that the insights made possible by the frame of "colorblind racial ideology" retain their value in the face of this disability critique, but scholars should consider a move to reframing it as "color-evasiveness." This strikes me as productive.

2. Seventy-seven percent of public school teachers were women in 2015–16, according to the National Teacher and Principal Survey (see Loewus). "In the 2011–12 school year, 82 percent of public school teachers were white. In comparison, 51 percent of all 2012 elementary and secondary public students were white," according to "The State of Racial Diversity in the Educator Workforce," a report from the Department of Education. See bibliography for citations.

3. The expansion of composition programs since the Civil Rights Era has created jobs for white women, as the American professoriate has simultaneously been casualized and feminized. By and large, these jobs do not offer the same status and security as tenure track positions, but the resources they impart go largely to white women (Flaherty).

4. The UCLA Civil Rights Project (Orfield and Kucsera) identifies Sheff as a bulwark against extreme racial segregation in Connecticut schools. In 2019, *The Nation* reported on a case moving through the courts to undermine it (Cohen).

5. Robin DiAngelo's vision of racial literacy also draws heavily from her teaching of preservice teachers. For her, "racial literacy" is the opposite, not of "racial liberalism" but of "racial illiteracy," specifically but not exclusively "white racial illiteracy" (*What Does It Mean to Be White?* 8). She wants to move white people from articulating "the most predictable, superficial, and distorted understandings of race" to "a framework for understanding racism as a system of unequal social, cultural, and institutional power, rather than as individual acts of prejudice" (16). In order to obtain racial literacy, according to DiAngelo, one must grapple with the fact of segregation, gaining the ability "to critically analyze the fundamental question . . . how the vast majority of whites can live in racial segregation even as we insist that race has no meaning in our lives" (17).

    France Winndance Twine and Howard Stevenson use the concept of racial literacy to analyze ways in which individuals develop skills to combat racism as they encounter it. Twine, who studies white women parenting multiracial children with partners of color, often in communities of color, writes that "racial literacy includes discursive, material, and cultural practices in which parents train themselves and their children to recognize, name, challenge, and manage various forms of every-day racism" (8). Stevenson has developed an approach to train community leaders, parents, children, and schools to support (primarily) Black children in responding resiliently against the psychological, academic, and health stresses of daily racial encounters. He asserts that "the teaching of racial literacy skills protects students from the threat of internalizing negative stereotypes that undermine academic critical thinking, engagement, identity, and achievement" (2).

Mara Grayson's work on incorporating racial literacy curriculum and orientation, particularly into teaching first year composition, offers a panorama of factors for teachers of many backgrounds to consider when adopting a racial literacy approach.

Most recently, Carmen Kynard has proposed "race-radical literacies" to name the activist rhetorics of "young black vernacular intellectuals/activists," pushing universities to name and address the "structural violence of our institutions (our local settings, colleges, nation, and our field)" ("Stayin Woke" 523).

Many thanks to Collin Craig for pointing me to this group of scholars of racial literacy.

6.   *U.S. News and World Reports* ranks it among the top 40 "national universities" for "campus ethnic diversity" (https://www.usnews.com/best-colleges/rankings/national-universities/campus-ethnic-diversity).

7.   Much more thorough research into the history of St. John's "diversity" is now being conducted by Susie Pak, a member of the St. John's University History Department. Her research is being presented in a 2020-2021 lecture series titled "Who Was St. John's?: A Historical Audit."

8.   One area studies program on campus yields further insights into the university's particular racial investments in "multicultural curriculum." The Institute for Asian Studies was founded in 1959 and directed until 1978 by Dr. Paul K. T. Sih. Born in Shanghai, Sih was a professor of history and translator of Chinese classics. He worked for the Taiwanese government in Rome, Italy, where he converted to Catholicism. Under Sih's leadership at St. John's, a distinctive pagoda-style building, Sun Yat Sen Hall, was erected to house the Asian Studies program, and the St. John's University Press, briefly in operation, published books on Taiwan, China, and Christianity.

Sih's vision of Asian Studies was firmly enmeshed in a Cold War geopolitical view in which anticommunism could unite East and West. Specifically, he advocated Christianity as a tool for building East-West unity against communism. His spiritual autobiography, *From Confucius to Christ*, published in 1952 by Sheed and Ward, Inc. and then republished by St. John's University Press in 1975, articulated two related goals. The first was to reveal Confucian principles as precursors to Christian ones. He described his work as part of "the immense task of re-evaluating Oriental culture in light of Christianity" (225). His second goal was to use this specifically Christian understanding of "Oriental culture" to fight mainland Chinese communism. This passage lays out his position: "Marxist Communism, which has plunged humanity into the limestone lake of materialism in which rationalism and positivism alike are drowned, aims only at making man less than a man by reducing him to a tool, while Christianity is destined to make man more than a man by making him a child of God" (69).

Sih's impassioned work on behalf of the Taiwanese government, the Catholic Church's missionary work, and St. John's University left a legacy at St. John's in which academic study of China was directed toward very particular spiritual and political goals. Attracting periodic censure for its partisan stance on Taiwan and its financial relations with the Taiwanese government, as well as its lack of transparency and tight control by upper administration rather than faculty (see Maeroff; Fishman), the currently named Institute for Asian Studies prioritizes globalizing higher education and the study of Asian countries and cultures, operating without any course offerings or attention to Asian American issues or students.

9. One model for this is Sara Ahmed's "ethnography of texts" in her interviews with university diversity workers and, in particular, her insights into their relationships to the documents involved in their work (12).

10. I do not plan to share this project with my former students, unless they ask to read it. This is because I take a critical approach to many of their texts that I did not lay the groundwork for in discussions with them. I was very clear that I would consider their work for inclusion in my scholarship and stated so on the consent forms. A more powerful version of this kind of research would include students as researchers. I did not have the capacity, while teaching and researching for this project, to create a collaborative model of research with them. I hope to build such collaboration and transparency into my next research project.

11. Until recently, I used the term "African American Vernacular English" (AAVE) to refer to traditions of speech and writing in US Black communities to be able to name and link disparate moments in which this set of traditions is referenced by my students. To refer to the set of linguistic norms often misperceived as "standard," I used "Standard English," employing scare-quotes on "Standard" most—but not all—of the time and on the whole phrase "Standard English" at times as well. You can see from my students' writing that this is the term we used in class.

   However, more recently, I have been influenced by April Baker-Bell's use of "Black language" and "White Mainstream English" to refer to these same sets of linguistic practices. Baker-Bell writes: "By linking the racial classifications Black and white to language, I am challenging you, the reader, to see how linguistic hierarchies and racial hierarchies are interconnected. That is, people's language experiences are not separate from their racial experiences" (2). Her purposes resonate deeply for me, given the connections between language and race that I attempt to make in my classroom. Further, her political purpose of using Black language "to align with the mission of Black Liberation movements like Black Lives Matter" is highly strategic and worth emulating (3).

CHAPTER 1: MAPPING WHITENESS

1. I have used the introduction to Tim Wise's talk based on his book *Colorblind: The Rise of Post-racial Politics and the Retreat from Racial Equity*. More recently, I have used Jay Smooth's TedxHampshire College Talk "How I Learned to Stop Worrying and Love Discussing Race," to make the point.

2. See these and other matrixes for racial identity development (e.g., "Summary of Stages of Racial Identity Development").

3. Three white students wrote about living in "diverse" neighborhoods, but when I Googled their neighborhood demographics, they were over 80 percent white, so I've counted them in that group.

CHAPTER 2: "IT'S REAL"

1. Amy Traub et al. cite the 2013 Survey of Consumer Finances as finding "the median white household possessed $13 in net wealth for every dollar held by the median Black household in 2013. That same year, median white households possessed $10 for each dollar held by the median Latino/a household."

CHAPTER 3: "YOUR GRAMMAR IS ALL OVER THE PLACE"

1. Trimbur's essay, "Translingualism and Close Reading," appears in the same special issue of *College English*—"The Translingual Work of Composition"—as Gilyard's "The Rhetoric of Translingualism," and Horner and Lu's "Translingual Work in Composition Studies."

2. I accept Horner, Lu, Royster, and Trimbur's assertion that there are no "monolingual" English speakers and writers, since "virtually all students who are monolingual in the sense that they speak only English are nonetheless multilingual in the varieties of English they use and in their ability to adapt English to their needs and desires" (311–12). Despite the importance of this insight, Otheguy et al. describe a key difference in the experience of monolinguals and bilinguals: "[A]ll speakers, even monolinguals, monitor their speech to some extent in order to adapt to the interlocutor and social situation at hand. Our point has been that since bilinguals have idiolects with larger sets of lexical and structural features than monolinguals, and since they are often of necessity in situations where they must communicate with monolinguals, more of the language features of their idiolects are often of necessity suppressed, that is, their monitoring is more intense than is usually found in monolinguals. For most monolinguals, to deploy all, or nearly all, of their linguistic resources, that is, to translanguage, is closer to normal everyday behavior, because monolinguals are usually granted license to operate at full or nearly full idiolect. But for bilinguals, the deployment of full linguistic resources can run up against strong norms articulating the sharpness of linguistic boundaries" (297).

3. What Sarah does with language certainly represents cultural appropriation of Black language as well. As a white teacher, the limits on my ability to perceive such dynamics is palpable. I do not wish to discount the ways in which Sarah is appropriating Black language to signal shifts in her tone, but to emphasize that she is appropriating it in service of multiracial translingual solidarity. I believe Sarah adopts features of Black language to signal resistance to raciolinguistic attitudes and to fortify her defense of Black and South Asian multilinguals and their communities. However, the appropriative move in her assumption of Black-inflected speech is real.

4. Shondel Nero explains that in a Caribbean context, most Creoles, which have their origin in the encounter of English with the languages of people enslaved by English speakers, have been labeled as English. She writes that New York City educators who teach Caribbean Creole speakers "encounter speakers and writers of English who see themselves as very much part of the family of World Englishes, and feel a legitimate claim to, and identification with, English, however different their variety of English is from the standardized variety privileged in school" (503).

CHAPTER 4: "SAYING HONEST THINGS WE WISH WEREN'T TRUE"

1. My end-of-semester research project is loosely based on Flower's model but has several key differences. While Flower uses community think tanks exclusively in "local publics" in which students engage community arenas outside their classrooms, I am interested in learning to what extent collaborative inquiry across difference can be put to work within the confines of a required core course in which the "local public" is the students themselves, confronting institutional forms of racism that impact them all differentially.

2. I have chosen the term "institutional racism" from among available terms such as "systemic racism" and "structural racism." All of these terms get at the crucial insight necessary for racial literacy—that racism is woven among historical and ongoing forces in our society, rather than being located exclusively in the past or in everyday

interactions with the few remaining "racists" among us. I choose "institutional" not because it is the best description of what I see in my country but instead because of its developmental usefulness for the traditional college-age students I teach. The concrete nature of a focus on "institutions," which is a new concept for the large majority of the students I have taught, allows then to follow specific threads of interaction among government, private, individual, and collective forces to weave a web of relationships, almost always following a trail of money, to understand the way racism is built into many of the networks governing social life.

3. This assignment was once available on Carmen Kynard's teaching and research website, "Education, Liberation & Black Radical Traditions for the 21st Century." The assignment is no longer accessible.

4. The photo, made into a statue in a park there and readily available online, is actually the subject of an investigation by Malcolm Gladwell that I did not encounter until after Rose was my student. According to Gladwell, the photo actually depicts—it turns out—a Black passerby accidentally stumbling onto a police officer with a dog, who is trying to fend him off in the photo. Gladwell's "Revisionist History" podcast lays out this perspective.

5. This photo, while I have been unable to find the original for it, appears in several online reports about Jamar Clark's shooting and subsequent events, including the following: https://www.cnn.com/2016/10/21/us/jamar-clark-shooting/index .html; https://minnesota.cbslocal.com/2019/05/21/advocates-for-jamar-clark-call -for-20m-death-settlement/.

WORKS CITED

Adams, Maurianne, Lee Anne Bell, and Patti Griffin, eds. *Teaching for Diversity and Social Justice.* 2nd ed., Routledge, 2007.

Ahmad, Dohra, and Shondel Nero. *Vernaculars in the Classroom: Paradoxes, Pedagogy, Possibilities.* Routledge, 2014.

Ahmed, Sarah. *On Being Included: Racism and Diversity in Institutional Life.* Duke UP, 2012.

Alexander, Michelle. *The New Jim Crow: Mass Incarceration in the Age of Colorblindness.* New Press, 2010.

Ancheta, Angelo. *Race, Rights, and the Asian American Experience.* 2nd ed., Rutgers UP, 2006.

Anderson, Carol. *White Rage: The Unspoken Truth of Our Racial Divide.* Bloomsbury, 2016.

Annamma, Subini Ancy, Darrell D. Jackson, and Deb Morrison. "Conceptualizing Color-Evasiveness: Using Dis/ability Critical Race Theory to Expand a Color-Blind Racial Ideology in Education and Society." *Race Ethnicity and Education* special issue: "Racialising Rural Education." Vol. 20, no. 2, 2017, pp. 147–162.

Anyon, Jean. "What Counts as Educational Policy? Notes toward a New Paradigm." *Harvard Educational Review,* vol. 75, no. 1, April 2005, pp. 65–88.

Anzaldúa, Gloria. *Borderlands/La Frontera: The New Mestiza.* Aunt Lute Books, 1987.

Baker-Bell, April. *Linguistic Justice: Black Language, Literacy, Identity, and Pedagogy.* Routledge, 2020.

Baumhardt, Alex, Lindsey Bever, and Michael E. Miller. "Two Men Arrested in Shooting of Black Lives Matter Protesters in Minneapolis." *Washington Post,* November 24, 2015. https://www.washingtonpost.com/news/morning-mix/wp/2015/11/24/five-people-shot-near-minneapolis-protest-cops-searching-for-3-white-male-suspects/.

Bell, Derrick. *Silent Covenants: Brown versus Board of Education and the Unfulfilled Hopes for Racial Reform.* Oxford UP, 2004.

Bell, Sophie. "Whiteboys': Contact Zone Pedagogy, Internalized Racism, and Composition at the University's Gateway." *Performing Antiracist Pedagogy in Rhetoric, Writing, and Communication.* WAC Clearinghouse, UP of Colorado, 2017.

Blum, Lawrence. *High Schools, Race, and America's Future: What Students Can Teach Us about Morality, Diversity, and Community.* Harvard UP, 2012.

Bonilla-Silva, Eduardo. *Racism without Racists: Color-Blind Racism and Racial Inequality in Contemporary America.* 3rd ed, Rowman and Littlefield, 2010.

Brandt, Deborah. "Awakening to Literacy circa 1983." Symposium: What Will We Have Made of Literacy? *College Composition and Communication,* vol. 69, no. 3, February 2018, pp. 503–9.

Brandt, Deborah. *Literacy in American Lives.* Cambridge UP, 2001.

Bryant, A., and Charmaz, K., eds. *The SAGE Handbook of Grounded Theory.* Sage, 2007.

"Campus Ethnic Diversity: National Universities." *U.S. News and World Report,* https://www.usnews.com/best-colleges/rankings/national-universities/campus-ethnic-diversity. Accessed December 9, 2020.

Canagarajah, Suresh. "The Place of World Englishes in Composition: Pluralization Continued." *College Composition and Communication,* vol. 57, no. 4, Jun 2006, pp. 586–619. Rpt. *Students' Right to Their Own Language: A Critical Sourcebook,* edited by Staci Perryman-Clark, David E. Kirkland, and Austin Jackson, Bedford/St. Martin's, 2015, pp. 279–304.

DOI: 10.7330/9781646421107.c007

Chang, Mitchell J., et al. *Beyond Myths: The Growth and Diversity of Asian American College Freshman, 1971–2005*. Higher Education Research Institute, UCLA, 2007.

Clark, Kenneth. "Moral Schizophrenia of America." Address, 1972. Duke University, Durham, NC.

Clotfelter, Charles. *After Brown: The Rise and Retreat of School Desegregation*. Princeton UP, 2004.

Cobb, Jelani. "The Matter of Black Lives." *New Yorker*. March 17, 2016. https://www.newyorker.com/magazine/2016/03/14/where-is-black-lives-matter-headed.

Cohen, Rachel M., "A Lawsuit Threatens a Groundbreaking School-Desegregation Case," *Nation*, February 11, 2019. https://www.thenation.com/article/archive/connecticut-segregation-schools-sheff/.

Danielowicz, Jane, and Peter Elbow. "A Unilateral Grading Contract to Improve Learning and Teaching." *College Composition and Communication*, vol. 61, no. 2, December 2009, pp. 244–68.

Demby, Gene. "How Code-Switching Explains the World." *NPR*, April 8, 2013. https://www.npr.org/sections/codeswitch/2013/04/08/176064688/how-code-switching-explains-the-world.

DiAngelo, Robin. *What Does It Mean to Be White? Developing White Racial Literacy*. Peter Lang, 2016.

DiAngelo, Robin. *White Fragility: Why It's So Hard for White People to Talk about Racism*. Beacon Press, 2018.

Duvernay, Ava. *13th*. Kandoo Films, 2016.

Eaton, Susan, and Gina Chirichigno. "METCO Merits More: A Pioneer Institute White Paper in Collaboration with the Houston Institute for Race and Justice at Harvard Law School." Pioneer Institute for Race and Justice, No. 74, June 2011.

Erigha, Maryann. *The Hollywood Jim Crow: The Racial Politics of the Movie Industry*. NYU press, 2019.

Fish, Stanley. "What Should College Teach? Part 3" *New York Times Opinionator*, September 7, 2009. https://opinionator.blogs.nytimes.com/2009/09/07/what-should-colleges-teach-part-3/.

Fishman, Steve. "The Dean of Corruption." *New York Magazine*, February 24, 2013.

Flaherty, Colleen. "More Faculty Diversity: Not on Tenure Track." *Inside Higher Ed*, August 8, 2016. https://www.insidehighered.com/news/2016/08/22/study-finds-gains-faculty-diversity-not-tenure-track.

Flores, Nelson, and Jonathan Rosa. "Undoing Appropriateness: Raciolinguistic Ideologies and Language Diversity in Education." *Harvard Educational Review*, vol. 85, no. 2, Summer 2015, pp. 149–71.

Flower, Linda. "Difference-Driven Inquiry: A Working Theory of Local Public Deliberation." *Rhetoric Society Quarterly*, vol. 46, no. 4, 2016, pp. 308–30.

Frankenberg, Erica, et al. "Harming Our Common Future: 65 Years after Brown." *UCLA: The Civil Rights Project/Proyecto Derechos Civiles*, 2014.

Frankenberg, Erica, and Gary Orfield, eds. *The Resegregation of Suburban Schools: A Hidden Crisis in American Education*. Harvard Education Press, 2012.

Frankenburg, Ruth. *White Women, Race Matters: The Social Construction of Whiteness*. U of Minnesota P, 1993.

Gershenson, Seth et al. *The Long-Run Impacts of Same-Race Teachers*. IZA Institute of Labor Economics, March 2017. http://ftp.iza.org/dp10630.pdf.

Gilyard, Keith. "The Rhetoric of Translingualism." *College English* special issue: "Translingual Work in Composition," vol. 78. no. 3, January 2016, pp. 284–89.

Gladwell, Malcolm. "The Foot Soldier of Birmingham." *Revisionist History* (podcast), season 2, episode 4, 2017.

Goodwin, Christine, and Blythe Roseland-Brenton. "Ethnicity in 1950, 1964, 1974, 1987," St. John's University Office of Institutional Research, 1991–2004.

Grayson, Mara. *Teaching Racial Literacy: Reflective Practices for Critical Writing.* Rowman and Littlefield, 2018.

Guerra, Juan. *Language, Culture, Identity and Citizenship in College Classrooms and Communities.* Routledge, 2016.

Guinier, Lani. "From Racial Liberalism to Racial Literacy: *Brown v. Board of Education* and the Interest-Divergence Dilemma." *Journal of American History,* vol. 91, no. 1, June 2004, pp. 92–118.

Haney-Lopez, Ian. *White by Law: The Legal Construction of Race.* NYU Press, 1996.

Hannah-Jones, Nikole. "School Segregation: The Continuing Tragedy of Ferguson." ProPublica, December 19, 2014. https://www.propublica.org/article/ferguson-school -segregation.

Harris, Cheryl. "Whiteness as Property." *Harvard Law Review,* vol. 106, no. 8, 1993, pp. 1707–91.

Helms, Janet E. *Black and White Racial Identity: Theory, Research and Practice.* Greenwood Press, 1990.

Horner, Bruce, Min-Zhan Lu, Jacqueline Jones Royster, and John Trimbur. "OPINION: Language Difference in Writing: Toward a Translingual Approach." *College English,* vol. 73, no. 3, January 2011, pp. 303–21.

Hudson, Bill. "Police Dog Lunges at Demonstrator during the Protest against Segregation in Birmingham." *New York Times,* Version 112, no. 38,451, The New York Times Company, May 4, 1963, https://timesmachine.nytimes.com/timesmachine/1963/05/04 /issue.html.

Inoue, Asao, and Mya Poe, eds. *Race and Writing Assessment.* Peter Lang, 2012.

Jacobson, Matthew Frye. *Whiteness of a Different Color: European Immigrants and the Alchemy of Race.* Harvard UP, 1998.

Johnson, Rucker J. "Long-Run Impacts of School Desegregation and School Quality on Adult Attainments." National Bureau of Economic Research Working Paper Series, Working Paper 16664, July 2011. https://www.nber.org/papers/w16664.pdf.

Kendi, Ibram X. *How to Be an Antiracist.* One World, 2019.

Kerschbaum, Stephanie. *Towards a New Rhetoric of Difference.* National Council of Teachers of English, 2014.

Kozol, Jonathan. *Savage Inequalities.* Harper Perennial, 1991.

Kucsera, J., and Orfield, G. New York State's Extreme School Segregation: Inequality, Inaction and a Damaged Future. *UCLA: The Civil Rights Project/Proyecto Derechos Civiles,* 2014. https://escholarship.org/uc/item/5cx4b8pf.

Kynard, Carmen. *Education, Liberation, and Black Radical Traditions for the 21st Century: Carmen Kynard's Teaching and Research Site on Race, Writing, and the Classroom.* http:// carmenkynard.org.

Kynard, Carmen. "Stayin Woke: Race-Radical Literacies in the Makings of a Higher Education." Symposium: What Will We Have Made of Literacy? *College Composition and Communication,* vol. 69, no. 3, February 2018, pp. 519–29.

Kynard, Carmen. *Vernacular Insurrections: Race, Black Protest, and the New Century in Composition-Literacies Studies.* SUNY Press, 2013.

Ladson-Billings, Gloria. "Landing on the Wrong Note: The Price We Paid for *Brown.*" *Educational Researcher,* vol. 33, no. 7, 2004, pp. 3–13.

Landor, Lee. "Malverne School District Racial Discrimination Suit Causes Rift." *Long Island Herald,* December 21, 2011. https://www.liherald.com/stories/Malverne-school -district-racial-discrimination-suit-causes-rift,37810.

Leonard, Rebecca Lorimer. "Multilingual Writing as Rhetorical Attunement." *College English,* vol. 76, no. 3, January 2014, pp. 227–47.

Lipsitz, George. *How Racism Takes Place.* Temple UP, 2011.

Lipsitz, George. *The Possessive Investment in Whiteness: How White People Profit from Identity Politics.* Temple UP, 2006.

Loewus, Liana. "The Nation's Teaching Force Is Still Mostly White and Female," *Education Week*, August 15, 2017. https://www.edweek.org/ew/articles/2017/08/15/the-nations -teaching-force-is-still-mostly.html.

Lu, Min-Zhan, and Bruce Horner, "Translingual Work." *College English* special issue: "Translingual Work in Composition," vol. 78, no. 3, January 2016, pp. 207–18.

Maeroff, Gene I. "St. John's Faculty Rebukes President." *New York Times*, March 23, 1983.

Martinez, Aja. "'The American Way': Resisting the Empire of Force and Color-Blind Racism." *College English*, July 2009, 584–95.

Martinez, Aja. "Critical Race Theory: Its Origins, History, and Importance to the Discourses and Rhetorics of Race." *Frame*, vol. 27, no. 2, November 2014, pp. 9–27.

Martinez, Aja. "A Personal Reflection on Chican@ Language and Identity in the US-Mexico Borderlands: The English Language Hydra as Past and Present Imperialism." *English Language as Hydra: Its Impacts on Non-English Language Cultures*, edited by Vaughan Rapatahana and Pauline Bunce, Bristol, Multilingual Matters, 2012, pp. 211–219.

Martinez, Aja. "A Plea for Critical Race Theory Counterstory: Dialogues Concerning Alejandra's 'Fit' in the Academy." *Composition Studies*, vol. 42, no. 2, 2014, pp. 33–55.

Mills, C. W. *The Sociological Imagination*. Oxford UP, 1959.

Miyares, Ines M. "From Exclusionary Covenant to Ethnic Hyperdiversity in Jackson Heights, Queens." *Geographical Review*, vol. 94, no. 4, October 2004, pp. 462–83. https://www .jstor.org/stable/30034291.

Morris, Barbara. *To Define a Catholic University: The 1965 Crisis at St. John's*. Columbia University Teacher College, EdD, 1977.

Nero, Shondel. "Language, Identity, and Education of Caribbean English Speakers." *World Englishes*, vol. 25, no. 3/4, 2006, pp. 501–511.

Noguera, Pedro. "Why School Integration Matters." *Educational Leadership. Special Issue: Separate and Still Unequal. Race in America's Schools*, vol. 6, no. 7, April 20–28, 2019, pp. 20–28.

Oakley, Robin. Quoted in "The Concept of Institutional Racism" (Extracts from the Report of the Stephen Lawrence Inquiry, 1999). *Race, Racism, and the Law since 1995*. https://racism.org/articles/defining-racism/325-racism08c.

Oktay, J. S. *Grounded Theory*. Oxford UP, 2012.

Omi, Michael, and Howard Winant. *Racial Formation in the United States*. Routledge, 1986.

Orfield, G., and J. Kucsera. "Connecticut School Integration: Moving Forward as the Northeast Retreats." *UCLA: The Civil Rights Project / Proyecto Derechos Civiles*, 2015. https://escholarship.org/uc/item/99n1f39x.

Otheguy, Ricardo, Ofelia García, and Wallis Reid. "Clarifying Translanguaging and Deconstructing Named Languages: A Perspective from Linguistics." *Applied Linguistics Review*, vol. 6. no. 3, 2015, pp. 281–307.

Pak, Susie. "Who Was St. John's? A Historical Audit." Public lecture, St. John's University, October 19. 2020.

Perryman-Clark, Staci, David E. Kirkland, and Austin Jackson, eds. *Students' Right to Their Own Language: A Critical Sourcebook*. Bedford / St. Martin's, 2015.

Prendergast, Catherine. *Literacy and Racial Justice: The Politics of Learning after Brown v. Board of Education*. Southern Illinois UP, 2003.

Pye, Yvette LaShone. "Courage under Fire: Handcuffed and Gagged by the Streets," *Reflections: Narratives of Professional Helping*, Special Issue on Dismantling Social and Racial Injustice, vol. 21, no. 3, Summer 2015, pp. 38–49.

Race: The Power of an Illusion. California Newsreel, 2003.

Rampell, Catherine. "SAT Scores and Family Income." *New York Times*, August 27, 2009. https://economix.blogs.nytimes.com/2009/08/27/sat-scores-and-family-income/.

Ransby, Barbara. *Making All Black Lives Matter: Reimagining Freedom in the 21st Century*. U of California P, 2018.

Ratcliffe, Krista. *Rhetorical Listening: Identification, Gender, Whiteness.* Southern Illinois UP, 2005.

Reed, Conor Tomás. "'Treasures That Prevail': Adrienne Rich, The SEEK Program, and Social Movements at the City College of New York, 1968–1972." *"What We Are Part Of" Teaching at CUNY: 1968–1974. Lost and Found: The CUNY Poetics Document Initiative,* series 4, no. 3, part 2, Fall 2013, pp. 36–71.

Roediger, David. *The Wages of Whiteness: Race and the Making of the American Working Class.* Verso Press, 1991.

"School History." *St. John's Prep,* https://www.stjohnsprepschool.org/apps/pages/index .jsp?uREC_ID=445932&type=d&pREC_ID=961666.

Scimecca, Joseph, and Roland Damiano. *Crisis at St. John's: Strike and Revolution on the Catholic Campus.* Random House, 1967.

Sealey-Ruiz, Yolanda. "Talking Race, Delving Deeper: The Racial Literacy Roundtable Series at Teachers College, Columbia University." *Confronting Racism in Teacher Education: Counternarratives of Critical Practice,* edited by Bree Picower and Rita Kohli, Routledge, 2017, pp. 127–132.

Sealey-Ruiz, Yolanda. "Towards Racial Literacy and a Culturally Sustaining Pedagogy." Lecture, St. John's University Writing Across Communities and Academic Center for Equity and Inclusion, May 16, 2019.

Sheff v. O'Neill. Connecticut Law Journal. July 1996.

Sih, Paul K. *From Confucius to Christ.* Sheed and Ward, Inc. NY 1952. Copyright transferred to and reprinted by St. John's UP, 1975.

Singer, Alan. *The Civil Rights Movement on Long Island: A Local History Curriculum Guide for Middle and High School.* Hofstra University Social Studies Education Department. https://studylib.net/doc/14226989/the-civil-rights-movement-on-long-island–table-of -contents.

Singleton, Glenn. *Courageous Conversations about Race: A Field Guide for Achieving Racial Equity in Schools.* 2nd ed., Corwin, a Sage Company, 2014.

Smitherman, Geneva. "Foreword." *Students' Right to Their Own Language: A Critical Sourcebook,* edited by Staci Perryman-Clark, David E. Kirkland, and Austin Jackson, Bedford / St. Martin's, 2015, pp. v–ix.

Smitherman, Geneva. "'Students' Right to Their Own Language': A Retrospective." *The English Journal,* vol. 84, no. 1 (January 1995), pp. 21–27. Rpt. in *Students' Right to Their Own Language: A Critical Sourcebook,* edited by Staci Perryman-Clark, David E. Kirkland, and Austin Jackson, Bedford / St. Martin's, 2015, pp. 140–149.

Smooth, Jay. "How I Learned to Stop Worrying and Love Discussing Race." *YouTube,* uploaded by TedxHampshire College Talk, November 15, 2011, https://www.youtube .com/watch?v=MbdxeFcQtaU.

Solorzano, Daniel, and Arnida Ornelas. "A Critical Race Analysis of Latina/o and African American Advanced Placement Enrollment in Public High Schools." *High School Journal,* vol. 87, February/March 2004, pp. 15–26.

Stevenson, Howard. *Promoting Racial Literacy in Schools: Differences That Make a Difference.* Teachers College, Columbia University.

"Students' Right to Their Own Language." Special Issue: *College Composition and Communication,* Fall 1974, 25.

"Summary of Stages of Racial Identity Development." https://www.racialequitytools.org /resourcefiles/Compilation_of_Racial_Identity_Models_7_15_11.pdf. n.d.

Tan, Amy. "Mother Tongue," *The Threepenny Review,* vol. 43, Fall 1990, pp. 7–8.

Tatum, Beverly Daniel. *Can We Talk about Race? And Other Conversations in an Era of School Resegregation.* Beacon Press, 2007.

Tatum, Beverly Daniel. "Talking about Race, Learning about Racism: The Application of Racial Identity Development Theory in the Classroom." *Harvard Educational Review,* vol. 62, no. 1, Spring 1992, pp. 1–24.

Traub, Amy, et al. "The Asset Value of Whiteness: Understanding the Racial Wealth Gap."
    Dēmos, February 6, 2017. https://www.demos.org/research/asset-value-whiteness-under
    standing-racial-wealth-gap.

Trimbur, John. "Translingualism and Close Reading." *College English* special issue: "Trans-
    lingual Work in Composition," vol. 78. no. 3, January 2016, pp. 219–227.

Twine, France Winndance. *A White Side of Black Britain: Interracial Intimacy and Racial Lit-
    eracy*. Duke UP, 2010.

"University Factbook," St. John's University Office of Institutional Research, https://www
    .stjohns.edu/fact-book. Accessed January 1, 2021.

US Census, "Table 33. New York: Race and Hispanic Origin for Selected Large Cities
    and Other Places: Earliest Census to 1990." https://www.census.gov/content/dam
    /Census/library/working-papers/2005/demo/POP-twps0076.pdf, December 10,
    2020.

US Department of Education, Office of Planning, Evaluation and Policy Development,
    Policy and Program Studies Service, the State of Racial Diversity in the Educator Work-
    force, Washington, DC, 2016. http://www2.ed.gov/rschstat/eval/highered/racial-di
    versity/state-racial-diversity-workforce.pdf.

Vasquez, Miguel. "WE Care: The Truth behind the St. John's Demonstration." *Odyssey
    Online*, February 16, 2016. https://www.theodysseyonline.com/we-care?fbclid=IwAR1f
    Ij6EEToVdajEwwBAEeMwfWsdZc50lTpKixI9zzhNOmJacVuje_cev-o.

Villanueva, Victor. *Bootstraps: From an American Academic of Color*. National Council of Teach-
    ers of English, Urbana, 1993.

Wells, Amy Stuart, et al. *Both Sides Now: The Story of School Segregation's Graduates*. U of Cali-
    fornia P, 2009.

Wexler, Laura. *Tender Violence: Domestic Visions in an Age of U.S. Imperialism*. U of North
    Carolina P, 2000.

Wise, Tim. "Colorblind: The Rise of Post-racial Politics and the Retreat from Racial
    Equity." University of San Francisco talk. *timwise.org*, February 26, 2013. http://www.tim
    wise.org/2013/03/tim-wise-at-the-university-of-san-francisco-february-26-2013/.

Woodsworth, Michael. *Battle for Bed-Stuy: The Long War on Poverty in New York City*. Harvard
    UP, 2016.

Yancy, George, ed. *White Self-Criticality beyond Anti-racism: How Does It Feel to Be a White Prob-
    lem?* Introduction by George Yancy. Lexington Books, 2015.

ABOUT THE AUTHOR

Sophie Bell is Professor in the Institute for Core Studies at St. John's University in Queens, New York. She studies and teaches in the following areas: rhetoric and composition; culturally sustaining pedagogies; literacy and education; race, ethnicity, and culture; and American literatures. In all of these areas, she is committed to tenacious close reading. Her First Year Writing classes focus on writing's potential to build connections across social differences. Prior to teaching First Year Writing, she taught in high schools and middle schools. In addition to her own classroom practice, she is deeply invested in creating and participating in faculty development to increase cultural capacity in the classroom. She is a member of the editorial board of the journal *Radical Teacher*.

INDEX